CREATIVE
HOMEOWNER®

TRELLISES & ARBORS

LANDSCAPE & DESIGN IDEAS, PLUS PROJECTS

Bill Hylton

CREATIVE HOMEOWNER®, Upper Saddle River, New Jersey

Editorial Director: Timothy O. Bakke
Production Manager: Kimberly H. Vivas

Project Editor: Therese Hoehlein Cerbie
Senior Editor: Fran J. Donegan
Assistant Editor/Photo Researcher: Sharon Ranftle
Editorial Assistant: Jennifer Ramcke
Consulting Editors: Miranda Smith, Neil Soderstrom
Copy Editor: Bruce Wetterau
Indexer: Schroeder Indexing Services

Designers: Scott Molenaro, David Geer
Cover, Back Cover, and Interior Photography (except where noted): Donna Chiarelli
Cover Design: Clarke Barre
Illustrations (except where noted): Frank Rohrbach

Manufactured in the United States of America

Current Printing (last digit)
10 9 8 7 6 5 4 3 2 1

Trellises & Arbors
Library of Congress Control Number: 2001090507
ISBN: 1-58011-086-X

CREATIVE HOMEOWNER®
A Division of Federal Marketing Corp.
24 Park Way, Upper Saddle River, NJ 07458
Web site: **www.creativehomeowner.com**

METRIC CONVERSION

Length

1 inch	25.4 mm
1 foot	0.3048 m
1 yard	0.9144 m
1 mile	1.61 km

Area

1 square inch	645 mm²
1 square foot	0.0926 m²
1 square yard	0.84 m²
1 acre	4046.86 m²
1 square mile	2.59 km²

Volume

1 cubic inch	16.39 cm³
1 cubic foot	0.03 m³
1 cubic yard	0.77 m³

Common Lumber Equivalents

Sizes: Metric cross sections are so close to their nearest U.S. sizes, as noted below, that for most purposes they may be considered equivalents.

Dimensional	1 x 2	19 x 38 mm
lumber	1 x 4	19 x 89 mm
	2 x 2	38 x 38 mm
	2 x 4	38 x 89 mm
	2 x 6	38 x 140 mm
	2 x 8	38 x 184 mm
	2 x 10	38 x 235 mm
	2 x 12	38 x 286 mm
Sheet	4 x 8 ft.	1200 x 2400 mm
sizes	4 x 10 ft.	1200 x 3000 mm
Sheet	¼ in.	6 mm
thicknesses	⅜ in.	9 mm
	½ in.	12 mm
	¾ in.	19 mm

Capacity

1 fluid ounce	29.57 mL
1 pint	473.18 mL
1 quart	1.14 liters
1 gallon	3.79 liters

Temperature

Celsius = (Fahrenheit − 32) x ⅝

°F	°C
0	−18
10	−12.22
20	−6.67
30	−1.11
32	0
40	4.44
50	10.00
60	15.56
70	21.11
80	26.67
90	32.22
100	37.78

SAFETY

Although all the designs and methods in this book have been reviewed for safety, it is not possible to overstate the importance of using the safest possible construction methods. What follows are reminders—some do's and don'ts of work procedures and tool safety that apply to construction projects in general. They are not substitutes for your own common sense.

- Always use caution, care, and good judgment when following the instructions and procedures described in this book.

- Always be sure that the electrical setup is safe, that no circuit is overloaded, and that all power tools and outlets are properly grounded. Do not use power tools in wet locations.

- Always read container labels on paints, solvents, and other products; provide ventilation; and observe all other warnings.

- Always read the manufacturer's instructions for using a tool, especially the warnings.

- Use hold-downs and push sticks whenever possible when working on a table saw. Avoid working short pieces if you can.

- Always remove the key from any drill chuck (portable or press) before starting the drill.

- Always pay deliberate attention to how a tool works so that you can avoid being injured.

- Always know the limitations of your tools. Do not try to force them to do what they were not designed to do.

- Always make sure that any adjustment is locked before proceeding. For example, always check the rip fence on a table saw or the bevel adjustment on a portable saw before starting to work.

- Always clamp small pieces to a stable work surface when working on them with a power tool.

- Always wear the appropriate rubber or work gloves when handling chemicals, moving or stacking lumber, or doing heavy construction.

- Always wear a disposable face mask when you create dust by sawing or sanding. Use a special filtering respirator when working with toxic substances and solvents.

- Always wear eye protection, especially when using power tools or driving nails with a hammer. A mis-hit can cause a nail to fly at you.

- Never work while wearing loose clothing, hanging hair, open cuffs, or jewelry.

- Always be aware that there is seldom enough time for your body's reflexes to save you from injury from a power tool in a dangerous situation; everything happens too fast. Be alert!

- Always keep your hands away from the business ends of blades, cutters, and bits.

- Always hold a circular saw firmly, usually with one hand on the trigger handle and the other on the secondary support handle.

- Always use a drill with an auxiliary handle to control the torque when large-size bits are used.

- Always move a router across a workpiece so that the bit rotation pushes the tool toward the fence rather than away from it.

- Never work with power tools when you are tired or under the influence of alcohol or drugs.

- Never cut tiny pieces of wood using a power saw. Always cut small pieces off larger pieces that are securely clamped or fastened to a stable work surface.

- Never change a saw blade, drill bit, or router bit unless the tool's power cord is unplugged. Do not depend on the switch being off; you might accidentally hit it.

- Never work in insufficient lighting.

- Never work with dull tools. Have them sharpened, or learn how to sharpen them yourself.

- Never use a power tool on a workpiece—large or small—that is not firmly supported.

- Never saw a workpiece that spans a large distance between horses without close support on each side of the cut; the piece can bend, close on and jam the blade, and cause saw kickback.

- Never support a workpiece from underneath with your leg or other part of your body when sawing or drilling.

- Never carry sharp or pointed tools, such as utility knives, awls, or chisels, in your pocket. If you want to carry such tools, use a special-purpose tool belt with leather pockets and holders.

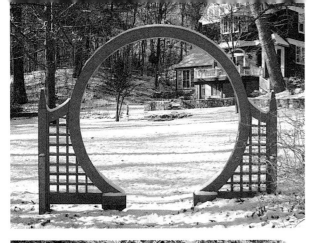

Contents

Design Guide

Trellises and arbors are among the most versatile architectural elements you can add to your yard or garden. They not only provide firm support for your climbing plants, their graceful, airy designs also add a touch of elegance to your landscape.

Make a landscape statement with the trellis or arbor you select. Arbors, far left, can divide spaces or serve as an entry to a small garden or shaded area. Trellises, left, screen unwanted views as they support climbing plants.

Adding a trellis or arbor to your yard provides instant vertical landscaping. Whether you attach the simplest lattice to the side of your house or spend time building a complex arbor or pergola, you will be able to grow climbing plants that otherwise would not survive without these structures. There are hundreds of climbing vines and dozens of types of climbing roses available. You can pick the species that best suits your existing garden, or use the trellis or arbor as a starting point for garden design. For more information on choosing plants for your trellis or arbor, see "Plants for Trellises and Arbors," page 30.

But there is more to these structures than the plants that they support. If you live in an area with cold winters, the trellis or arbor will become an architectural accent in the winter landscape. When selecting one, try to envision it with and without plants.

Use trellises and arbors to divide one section of the yard from another, or to signal a change in functions between areas in your yard. An arbor with built-in seating becomes a shady nook for spending an afternoon.

As you will see from the examples shown here, well-made trellises and arbors have graceful open designs. The structure often can be so attractive that it becomes a focal point in its own right, rather than a supporting player in the overall design of the yard.

Trellises

These structures are often attached to a house or garage wall to train climbing plants, but they can also stand alone to provide vertical landscaping in the middle of your yard. In either case, be sure to select a trellis that can adequately support the plants that you choose to grow.

Many homeowners use trellises to screen an unwanted view or as a divider. In designing your trellis, choose exactly how much privacy you want. Lattice pieces that are woven tightly together effectively block views even when plants are dormant during the winter months. They also serve as a windbreak. Open lattice patterns do not provide as much privacy, but they do give the structure a light, airy appearance. When used as a fence, a trellis is a more friendly way to separate your property from that of your neighbors.

Be sure to match the size of the trellis that you are installing with its location and use. A large trellis can overpower a small area, such as an herb garden, just as a small structure plopped in the middle of a large lawn will look out of place.

Stand alone trellises, below, provide a base for climbing plants such as clematis.

Wall-mounted trellises, above, offer the chance for creating dramatic plantings.

Stone walls, such as the one above, can anchor a trellis as well as a wood wall can.

Choose plants that are best suited for the size and type of trellis that you install.

Arbors

While trellises consist of a flat plane for supporting plants, arbors provide the added benefits of walls and a roof to create a sense of enclosure. They tend to make bolder design statements than most trellises do.

Many people use the words arbor and pergola interchangeably. Technically, an arbor is a sheltered area—even if it consists of bent twigs to support a vine; a pergola is a tunnel-like walkway supported by

Material choices for arbors range from solid wood to metal, right, to bent twigs.

columns. In either case, select the structure to match its location.

Arbors make great transition points. Place one on a path and you will lead people from one point in your yard to another. Install one at the entrance to a garden, and you've created a natural separation between the two areas.

Like trellises, arbors make attractive focal points, but they also serve as inviting destinations in the yard. Set up an arbor with seating

Frame a doorway with an arbor and flowering vine to create a sheltered entry.

Create a formal entry between your yard and the street or driveway.

in a shady spot and you will have a secluded area to get away from it all, and you will have expanded your outdoor living area.

As with any garden structure, be sure to select one that is in scale with your yard and home.

A casual arbor and gate form an informal entry to this garden.

Used as Dividers

Vertical landscaping adds a new dimension to your yard. The trellis shown left supports climbing roses and separates one yard from the next. The trellis below not only supports flowering plants but screens a porch from view as well.

Highlight a view by adding cutouts in the lattice of a trellis, top left, or by the careful placement of an arbor, above. Hide unwanted views, such as pool pumps, behind a trellis fence, left.

Used as Entries

Open wide. *Gateway arbors can make a definite design statement. The distinctive pergola-like top of the arbor at right is hard to miss. Garden entry arbors, below left and right, help define the gardens and yards that they are part of, and they invite passersby in at the same time.*

Careful placement of a trellis or arbor can create a mood or set a scene in your yard. The dramatic arbor above frames an attractive portion of this garden. The simple metal design at left adds height and directs anyone strolling in this yard directly to the garden.

Used as Focal Points

Even eye-catching arbors *should provide practical value. Simple arbor designs, top left, create an attractive setting for garden seats. Sturdy stone and metal, above, separate a formal garden from the wild. The imposing pergola, bottom left, signals the driveway opening in this fence.*

The gable-type roof and unusual scroll-work shown above contribute to the distinctive style of this secluded arbor. The large curving posts and oversize dimensions of the arbor below fit well with the large trees and rocks in the area.

Vertical Landscaping

What do you want to stand out? If you are more interested in the plants than the structure, choose arbor and trellis materials that fade into the background, top and below, when plants are in bloom. The alternative is a design where the structure always plays a prominent role, right.

Create a scene by combining structures with the right plants. The trellis and matching bench at top right hold their own among the plants in this garden. The clematis is the focal point in the photo at far right. Plants frame the latticework at right.

More Uses for Trellises & Arbors

The large pergola above divides a pool deck into shaded and sunny areas. Its large size and design make it the focal point of this yard. The trellis at right is also a focal point, but in this case, it is the colorful clematis that makes the structure stand out.

The swinging gate and high peaked arch at left give anyone entering this yard an open-armed welcome. Spacing out arbors along a path, below, breaks up the horizontal plane of the garden and adds an unusual visual feature. The pergola at bottom provides a real sense of entry.

More Uses for
Trellises & Arbors (continued)

Tower trellises *come in a variety of shapes and sizes, from the for-mal design shown above to branches loosely bound together.*

Ivy-covered arbors *and landscape tie steps soften the incline in this yard.*

Small white roses, top, fit the scale of simple wooden trellises. In a short time, the wall-mounted fan trellis above will support a decorative display. The bent-wood trellis at left has a unique style.

More Uses for Trellises & Arbors (continued)

A climbing rose on this gate arbor welcomes visitors to this garden.

Arbors make great get away-from-it-all spots, even if those places are confined to your backyard. Place a movable bench in an arbor, above, and you have a spot in your garden to read a book or enjoy the view. Note the potted plant and hanging baskets. Tucked along a garden path, right, an arbor provides a shady retreat from the afternoon sun.

Any vertical surface is a suitable base for a trellis. Thanks to the trellis and climbing roses, the garden shed above becomes the center of attention in this yard. Climbing plants atop the trellis at left complete the structure.

Ready-Made Trellises & Arbors

In addition to building one of the great trellises or arbors presented in this book, you can also purchase ready-made designs. Check at home and garden centers for structures that you can buy and take with you right away. There are also a number of mail-order catalogs and web sites that feature these types of structures. (See the Resource Guide, page 155.) Many fence companies will construct a custom trellis or arbor for you or build one based on its portfolio of designs.

Materials range from traditional wood to some you may not have thought of using, such as copper or aluminum. No matter which you choose, look for quality materials, such as cedar and redwood products and metals whose components are joined together securely. Finishes should be able to protect the structure from the elements.

Prices vary greatly, so it is best to shop around before making a final decision. Simple trellises can range from under $20 for a plastic model to several thousand for a large redwood arbor.

Large ready-made trellises and arbors are usually delivered in sections and assembled on site. The curved arbor at left is striking in its own right, or it can be used with a matching fence. The gate and fence shown above are from a design that was created by a fence manufacturer.

Custom designs, *such as the pergola roof over the porch at top, are offered by fence companies and garden centers. The elegant arbor shown top right contains concealed fasteners for a seamless appearance. Unusual metal tower trellises, right, can look like sculptures in the garden.*

Curves add distinction *to trellis and arbor designs. Some manufacturers match curves or other elements from their arbors with elements on fences, right. Metal trellises allow for unique designs, such as the sun motif shown bottom right. Simple designs, bottom left, combined with high-quality materials and workmanship lead to attractive and functional garden structures.*

Many manufacturers specialize in unusual designs and custom projects. A deck seating area can get a lift from a custom pergola roof, above. Metal allows for designs that just aren't possible when working with wood. The spiral trellis tower shown above right and the curved copper arbor shown at right will look great with or without climbing plants.

Plants for Trellises & Arbors

Whether you have an arbor, trellis, pergola, or archway, the right plant completes it and brings out the beauty of both the structure and the plant. To succeed, they must harmonize with each other in style as well as physical properties.

Vines and climbing roses are well suited to vertical structures, such as arbors and trellises. There are many from which to choose, and most are relatively easy to grow. All of them will reward you with an attractive focal point for your yard and garden.

SELECTING PLANTS

Typically, the plants used on trellises or arbors fall into one of two categories: vines and climbing or rambler roses. Within these groups there are many beautiful and interesting possibilities. But for success, choose a plant that is compatible with the style and physical characteristics of the structure, as well as the growing conditions that exist at the site of the structure.

Consider Style

Most plants have a style—that is, they evoke a certain atmosphere or feeling. A climbing nasturtium (*Tropaeolum majus*), for example, gives an informal, country feeling, while a well-trained and carefully pruned climbing rose (*Rosa* spp.) can look somewhat formal. English ivy (*Hedera helix*) speaks of tradition and culture; bright, heavy trumpet vines are cheerful and generous; and balloon vines (*Cardiospermum halicacabum*) are softly whimsical. When you set about choosing a vine, picture it in your mind and see what associations it brings.

Structures also have particular styles, thanks to their design and materials. A wrought-iron

arbor has a traditional feeling, while an arbor of the same shape but made from sleek, shiny tubing feels contemporary. A fan trellis made of wood lathing strips gives a decorative touch, while a rectangular latticework trellis made from the same material is a no-nonsense, practical structure.

The trick to developing a planting that will please you for years to come is matching the structure to the style of your home and the plant to the style of each. For example, if your house is a formal Federal design, a hyacinth bean (*Lablab purpureus*) growing on a vine arbor at the front gate is going to look out of place; a thornless rose on a simple wrought-iron arbor would be far more appropriate. But don't think that you can never grow that hyacinth bean—it could add a bright, cheerful touch to your more informal backyard.

Match Physical Properties

Structures must also suit the plant in strength and the way in which the plant "climbs." Imagine that you've built a wooden arbor out of 6- by 6-inch posts to complement your substantial-looking log home. This structure would completely dwarf a honeysuckle vine (*Lonicera* spp.) with its delicate foliage and small red blooms. But a wisteria (*Wisteria* spp.) would be right at home on it. After a few years, the thick, twining wisteria trunks and the sturdy posts will be in such good proportion that you'll barely notice the posts, but unlike most supports, this one will be strong enough to carry the weight of a full-grown wisteria vine.

Accommodate Climbing Style

Vines climb in particular ways. As illustrated and explained below, some stems twine around their supports; some vines grow tendrils that grasp and curl around any slender support that they touch; some grow grasping aerial roots from their stems; and a few are fitted with "holdfasts," small suction-cup like structures at the ends of short stems. Scandent vines aren't equipped for any of these climbing strategies. Instead, they lean on their supports. Climbing roses are an example of a scandent vine; even though they have thorns that catch on nearby shrubs, trees, and poles, you must tie them to a support to keep them upright. (See page 43 in this chapter.)

For success, the climbing style of the plant must be appropriate to the characteristics of the support on which you want it to grow. Information about climbing styles of vines is given in the Vine Directory, pages 36 to 41, but you can also figure it out just by looking at the plant.

Plants with tendrils, such as sweet peas and gourds, must have a network of thin supports to climb. Strings, nylon or woven netting, chicken wire, chain-link fences, and trellises that are made from slender lathing strips are all appropriate.

Vines with twining stems must be able to encircle their support; wisteria can easily twine around a 6-inch-square post, while morning glory vines thrive on anything from a piece of nylon cord to a 4-inch-wide post.

Ivies and other plants with holdfasts and aerial roots need a fairly continuous and rough surface to climb. Stone or brick walls are ideal for them. They also climb well on most wooden walls, but because they can sometimes damage them by growing under a board and prying it loose, this is rarely a good idea. Wrapping and tying these vines around their supports is another choice.

Meet Growing Conditions

Climbing plants, with the exception of some grapes, tend to be easy to grow. After all, they act in the wild as if they were weeds. They clamber over fences and walls, and weave through nearby shrubs and trees. They'll grow just as rampantly in a garden that meets their needs.

Soil and Environment. It's important to learn what kind of soil conditions the plant requires—fertile, moderately fertile, or even lean—and whether its water needs are high, moderate, or low. Most climbing plants require well-drained soil. Even if they use a great deal of water, their soil must drain quickly enough to allow some air into the soil's pore spaces.

Hardiness. Plants thrive in an environment that approximates their native habitat. For many years, plants have been labeled with their USDA (United States Department of Agriculture) hardiness zone rating, which indicates their tolerance to cold. When buying plants consider the rating it has been given. Although the USDA ratings are a good starting point, several factors can affect their accuracy. For exam-

Match the plant's climbing style to its support. *Delicate vines, like sweet peas and morning glories, can even climb on a simple arrangement of twine or wire.*

CLIMBING STYLE

Twining stems *simply wrap themselves around a support, even one as thin as twine or a metal wire.*

Tendrils wrap *tightly around their supports. Give them both vertical and horizontal structures to climb.*

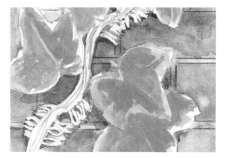

Aerial rootlets *grow into crevices in a wall. They are strong enough to pry boards loose but don't hurt bricks.*

Holdfasts *can attach themselves to smooth surfaces because they secrete an adhesive substance.*

Multiple types of support *are in place for this robust clematis. The fan trellis supported it when it was first planted, and now the lattice top of this board fence does, too.*

ple, city temperatures tend to be 5 to 10 degrees F warmer than those of the surrounding countryside, raising the hardiness rating of a city garden by a full zone. In addition, every garden has microclimates that may be warmer, cooler, drier, or more humid than another part of the property is. The longer you garden in one location, the more familiar you will be with its microclimates. If you choose a plant that is at the extremes of its stated zone rating, be prepared to give that plant more attention.

Light. You will also need to know what light conditions your climber requires—full sun, filtered shade, or shade. Full sun means that the plant needs a minimum of six hours of direct sunlight a day. Filtered shade means four hours of direct sunlight plus light filtered through a leaf canopy for the rest of the day. Shade means as little as two hours of direct sunlight or dappled shade for the entire day. Before you buy, observe the site where you plan to place the structure for a full day, noting how many hours of unobstructed sunlight, filtered light, dappled shade, and full shade that the area gets.

Wind. Few plants thrive in windy conditions. But a simple trick will allow you to grow climbing plants where winds are fairly constant. Grow them on a fence, screen, or trellis—not an arch, arbor, or pergola—placed with the long side parallel with the usual wind direction. When the wind blows, it will rush past the slender line of your plants rather than blowing against them and possibly pushing down their support.

Some sites are protected from cold winds by walls, trees, or hedges, and they maintain temperatures of up to 10 degrees F higher than surrounding areas. These spots are perfect for plants that may be marginally hardy in your area or those with fruit that you'll want to protect from the first fall frosts.

Other Siting Conditions. When you decide where to put your climbing plant, also think about your own comfort. For example, if you want plants to cover a trellis near an outdoor eating area, you'll be happier with nonflowering vines because they won't attract bees and other stinging insects. Or if you want to grow a rose up an arbor that covers a bench where people will be sitting, you'll be better off with a thornless cultivar.

Think about positive attributes, too. If you place a trumpet vine (*Campsis* spp.) on a pillar that you can see from the dining room windows, you can look forward to watching hummingbirds feed as you dine. Fragrant climbers trained to grow up the wall or a trellis near open bedroom windows adds a delightful touch all summer long. Eyesores such as service areas can become flowering walls with the right plants covering a fence around them.

PLANTING VINES

The first step in planting a climber is setting its supporting structure in place. Some supports, such as a tower trellis (pages 90–97), can be just placed where you want. Others, such as a fan trellis (pages 58–63), need to be staked into the ground and perhaps supported by a fence or tied into a wall. You might also want to add 10-inch-long spacers in between a trellis and a wall. This distance will allow air to circulate behind the plant, even a mature one, helping it to resist fungal diseases. Structures with

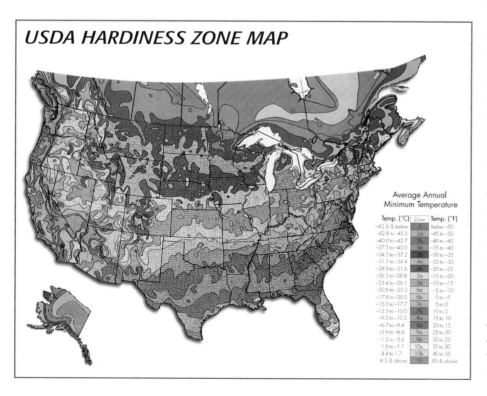

USDA HARDINESS ZONE MAP

Average Annual Minimum Temperature

Temp. (°C)	Zone	Temp. (°F)
−45.6 & below	1	below −50
−42.8 to −45.5	2a	−45 to −50
−40.0 to −42.7	2b	−40 to −45
−37.3 to −40.0	3a	−35 to −40
−34.5 to −37.2	3b	−30 to −35
−31.7 to −34.4	4a	−25 to −30
−28.9 to −31.6	4b	−20 to −25
−26.2 to −28.8	5a	−15 to −20
−23.4 to −26.1	5b	−10 to −15
−20.6 to −23.3	6a	−5 to −10
−17.8 to −20.5	6b	0 to −5
−15.0 to −17.7	7a	5 to 0
−12.3 to −15.0	7b	10 to 5
−9.5 to −12.2	8a	15 to 10
−6.7 to −9.4	8b	20 to 15
−3.9 to −6.6	9a	25 to 20
−1.2 to −3.6	9b	30 to 25
1.6 to −1.1	10a	35 to 30
4.4 to 1.7	10b	40 to 35
4.5 & above	11	40 & above

posts are often set into the ground. For information on setting posts into the ground, refer to instructions within the project "Grape Arbor," pages 142–149.

Annuals

Annuals last for a single growing season and are easy to plant. Although you can start them from seed in the garden, they will grow to cover their support more quickly if you start some plants indoors or buy healthy seedlings. Guarantee success by choosing plants with lush green leaves but no open flowers.

After all chance of frost has passed, transplant the seedlings just to one side of your support. If you are growing them on a trellis that is accessible from both sides, you can plant on each side of it, leaving a distance of 8 to 12 inches between the facing plant rows. Add compost to the area where you will be planting them, and dig it about 6 inches into the soil. If the fertility is low, add a fertilizer, too.

Perennials

Perennial plants live for three or more years and generally flower each year. You can buy perennial plants in containers or "bare root," that is, the plants have no soil around their roots. Container-grown plants can be planted at almost any time of year, as long as you keep them well watered while they are getting established. Bare root plants are more delicate; you must plant them in early spring so that they can

grow leaves and send roots into the surrounding soil before summer heat arrives.

To plant either type, start by digging a hole where you want the plant to grow. For a containerized plant, make the hole deep enough so that the soil in the container will be level with the ground around it. For bare root plants, soak its roots overnight in water; then spread the roots over a mound of soil that will bring the crown of the plant even with the surface of the hole. (Some plants are exceptions to this rule; follow directions that accompany the plant.) Keep plants moist for a few weeks.

Experts once advised that the soil around your plant be amended with fertilizers and other soil conditioners. But research has shown that plants grow better over the long term

Planting a vine or climbing rose in a pot and pairing it with a trellis can be the ideal solution if you have only a deck or patio. If you have a sunroom, use a portable trellis and the plant can go indoors to flourish during the winter.

if they are planted into unamended soil. Add organic mulches and slow-release, balanced fertilizers each year to provide the nutrition that your plant requires.

WINTER CARE

Most vines need only a little extra care to get them ready for winter. If they are herbaceous, meaning that their leaves and stems die back to the ground in fall, 6 inches of straw mulch or 2 to 3 inches of a dense material, such as bark chips, will protect the crown and roots during the winter.

Evergreen vines can require more care, particularly if they are planted in an unprotected spot where winter winds are fierce. The best protection is a winter wrapping of burlap. This material allows moisture to escape, so that it won't promote fungal diseases, but it still holds enough so that the plant won't become dehydrated. Mulch the crown of an evergreen vine in the same way as you would for a herbaceous one. Tie or secure the burlap in place if necessary.

PLANTING ANNUALS

Holding only the root ball, carefully lower the seedling into the planting hole. Fill in the hole, and press down gently to put the roots in contact with the soil. Water well.

PLANTING BARE-ROOT PERENNIALS

Mound the soil, and gently spread the roots out over the mound. Work soil around the roots, and when it's half filled with soil, water and let drain. Then fill the hole with soil.

TRAINING & PRUNING

Training and pruning requirements differ for various plants, even among species. For specific information, check with your supplier for pruning instructions for your particular plant. But no matter what plant you are growing, the following guidelines always hold true.

Training Techniques

Most climbing plants need at least a little training. If you are growing a morning glory on a chain-link fence, you won't have to do more than weave the stems through the bottom openings as soon as they can reach that far. However, if you are growing a vine, such as a clematis up and over an arbor, you'll probably have to tie it in place to direct its growth. A figure-eight tie, as shown on page 43, will give the plant some room in which to grow and move. If you tie branches for the first month or so, their habit will quickly take over and they'll climb by themselves. Check occasionally to see that all the branches are supported.

Time Your Pruning

The timing of major pruning is determined by the blooming style. If the plant blooms on "old wood," that is, growth that was formed the previous year, you must wait to prune until after the flowers have faded. But if the plant blooms on the current season's growth, you prune in the late winter or very early spring. In general, plants that bloom on old wood do so in spring and early summer, and those that bloom on current growth flower in midsummer, late summer, or early fall.

When a plant is damaged or diseased, it's important to break the timing rule. The minute you notice the damage, even if it is in the middle of the summer, it's best to cut out the affected branch right away. If the problem is a disease, cut well below the site of infection and disinfect your pruning tool before and after you make the cut.

Shape the Planting

You can affect the form that a plant takes by the way you prune it. The bud immediately below a cut will be the first to form a new branch. Because of this, it's usually best to cut above a bud that faces away from the center of the plant so that air can easily circulate through it. An alternative is to prune just above a bud that faces in the direction that you want the plant to grow.

Frequently, once you cut off the terminal growth, more than one of the remaining buds will develop into branches. Use this to your advantage: when you plant a new vine, cut the main stem back if you want it to become bushy. To encourage flowering plants to bloom more lavishly, always cut back the branches by about one-third when you prune.

Many vines bloom more vigorously on horizontal rather than vertical growth. When you are pruning, pay attention to this factor. Leave as many branches that are growing horizontally as possible, just cutting them back to stimulate lots of blooms in the coming season.

Branches cut in midsummer usually don't regrow as quickly as those that are pruned in late winter and early spring. If a plant is growing too quickly, slow it down by cutting it back when the temperature is warm and the days are long. If you are working to cover a screen with a great deal of horizontal growth, cut off the vertical shoots in summer to minimize the formation of new ones. But don't cut in the fall; you'll stimulate new growth that won't have time to harden up before winter comes.

SHAPE THE PLANTING

End Buds

Side (Lateral) Buds

Pruning Cut

***Pruning growing tips** stimulates lateral buds to develop. When cutting stems with alternate buds, prune at a 45-deg. angle just above the bud you want to stimulate. If buds are opposite, cut across the stem in a straight line.*

***A thick, lush grape vine** can provide welcome shade during a hot summer's day, as well as a tasty and rewarding snack. Flowering hanging plants add more color to the setting.*

VINE DIRECTORY

Explanation of Icons

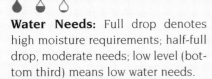

Light Requirements: Yellow sun means full sun; half-yellow/half-black sun means partial shade; black sun repesents shade.

Water Needs: Full drop denotes high moisture requirements; half-full drop, moderate needs; low level (bottom third) means low water needs.

Growth Rate: 12:15 represents slow growing; 12:30 means moderate rate of growth; 12:45 means fast growing.

F F **F**

Fragrance: F means fragrant; F denotes that only some species or cultivars in the species are fragrant; F means the plant is not fragrant.

Care Level: Green spade means easy-care; yellow represents moderate care; red means difficult.

Actinidia deliciosa, A. arguta, A. kolomikta
Kiwifruit, Hardy Kiwifruit
A. deliciosa ☀   A. arguta, A. kolomikta ◗

This perennial vine has cream-colored flowers that bloom in the spring. Both A. *deliciosa* and A. *arguta* have green leaves that are slightly reddish when young. Those of A. *kolomikta* are variegated in green, cream, and pink shades.
Climbing Style: Scandent; tie to supports
Soil Requirements: High fertility with high humus content.
Hardiness Zones: A. *deliciosa*, 7–10; A. *arguta*, A. *kolomikta*, 4–9

Ampelopsis brevipedunculata
Porcelain Berry

The leaves of this perennial vine are triangular and lobed or toothed, and bright red and yellow in autumn. Blooms mid- to late sum-

Actinidia deliciosa (Kiwifruit)

Ampelopsis brevipedunculata (Porcelain Berry)

mer. Its small, green flowers are followed by decorative berries.
Climbing Style: Tendrils
Soil Requirements: Fertile, well-drained
Hardiness Zones: 5–8

Campsis spp.
Trumpet Vine

◗ to ◗ ◆ ⊘ F ↓

This woody perennial punctuates late-summer gardens with vivid orange, yellow, or red flower clusters. It needs a strong support. The vines cling to their vertical supports, but blooming branches extend for several feet in all directions.
Climbing Style: Aerial roots

Campsis spp. (Trumpet Vine)

Cardiospermum halicacabum (Balloon Vine)

Soil Requirements: Moderately fertile and well-drained
Hardiness Zones: 5–9

Cardiospermum halicacabum
Balloon Vine, Love-in-a-Puff

☀   ◆ ⊘ F ↓

This tender perennial has delicate, deeply toothed leaves that can grow to about 8 inches long. It has small, white, summer-blooming flowers, but it's mostly grown for its balloonlike seedpods that start out a light green color, then turn brown as they age.
Climbing Style: Tendrils
Soil Requirements: Fertile, well-drained
Hardiness Zones: 10–11

Clematis 'Henryi'

Cobaea scandens (Cup and Saucer Vine)

Clematis 'Duchess of Albany'

Hedera helix (English Ivy)

Clematis
Clematis

The appearance of a clematis varies radically depending on group and cultivar. Flowers range from cross-shaped with only four petals to large double blossoms to bell-shaped, tulip-shaped, and tubular blooms. Colors range from deep purple to pink, white, and yellow, with orange being the only color not represented. Clematis is a perennial. Depending on its group, it blooms early spring to late summer and fall. Some species are deciduous; others are evergreen.

Climbing Style: Twining leaf stalks

Soil Requirements: Fertile, high humus

Hardiness Zones: 4–9

Cobaea scandens
Cup and Saucer Vine, Cathedral Bells

The common names for this fast-growing tender perennial refer to the shape of its flowers. It blooms summer into the fall. The flowers open as a creamy green color and age to purple, or in the case of C. *scandens* f. *alba*, white. It also makes a good sunroom plant.

Climbing Style: Tendrils, small hooks

Soil Requirements: Moderately fertile, or humus-rich potting soil

Hardiness Zones: 9–11

Hedera helix
English Ivy

Appearance varies depending on the cultivar, but ivies are grown for their leaves. In most species the leaves are triangular and lobed. Many species have variegated leaves, some have dark purplish leaves, and a few have leaves that are yellow. Ivies bloom late in the summer, and berries form on many cultivars. Because ivies do not twine, tie them to an openwork structure, or let the vine climb a tree or wall.

Climbing Style: Aerial roots

Soil Requirements: Moderately fertile

Hardiness Zones: 5–10

Ipomoea spp. (Moonflower)

Lablab purpureus (Hyacinth Bean)

Ipomoea spp. (Morning Glory)

Jasminum spp. (Jasmine)

Lagenaria siceraria (Bottle Gourd)

Ipomoea spp.
Morning Glory, Moonflower, Sweet Potato Vine, and others

The Ipomoea genus contains about 500 species classified as annuals and tender perennials. Most have showy colorful flowers that bloom mid- to late summer, but some, such as the Sweet Potato Vine, do not flower and are grown for their foliage. Moonflowers (I. *alba*) are large and so white that they seem to glow in the twilight conditions that stimulate buds to open.
Climbing Style: Twining stems
Soil Requirements: Moderately fertile
Hardiness Zones: 9–11

Jasminum spp.
Jasmine

to

Jasmines, which are perennials, are known for their fragrance, showy blossoms, and glossy, deep green leaves. Only J. *nudiflorum*, winter jasmine, and J. *humile*, yellow jasmine, tolerate freezing temperatures. Jasmine can be grown in heated sunrooms through the winter. Winter jasmine blooms in early spring, yellow jasmine in late spring to early autumn.
Climbing Style: J. *nudiflorum* and J. *humile* shoots are scandent; others have twining stems.
Soil Requirements: Fertile, well-drained
Hardiness Zones: 9–11

Lablab purpureus
(formerly *Dolichos lablab*)
Hyacinth Bean, Lablab, Egyptian Bean

This fast growing vine is a member of the pea family. Its pink flowers bloom from summer until autumn. The shiny, thick pods that follow them are a maroon-purple color.
Climbing Style: Twining
Soil Requirements: Fertile, high humus
Hardiness Zones: 10–11

Lagenaria siceraria
Bottle Gourd

This fast-growing annual vine with enormous (as large as a foot wide) heart-shaped leaves needs a strong support. Its white flowers bloom midsummer to late fall and have a crepe-paper quality. The gourds are pale green when mature but turn a cream color over the year or so that it takes for their skins to harden.
Climbing Style: Tendrils
Soil Requirements: Fertile, high humus

Lathyrus spp. (Sweet Pea)

Lycopersicon esculentum (Tomato)

Lonicera spp. (Honeysuckle)

Maurandella antirrhiniflora (Twining Snapdragon)

Lathyrus spp.
Everlasting Pea, Sweet Pea

Both everlasting peas (L. *latifolius*, a perennial) and sweet peas (L. *odoratus*, an annual) have ornamental leaves and lavish colorful blooms from midsummer to autumn. All 150 species of *Lathyrus* have flowers that look like those of edible peas. But, unlike the common garden pea, all parts of these plants are slightly poisonous.
Climbing Style: Twining tendrils
Soil Requirements: Fertile, high humus
Hardiness Zones: L. *latifolius*, 5–9

Lonicera spp.
Honeysuckle

There are about 180 honeysuckle species whose tubular to bell-shaped flowers vary in color: white, pink, yellow, bi-colored, red. They bloom from early to midsummer; the leaves turn red in the fall.
Climbing Style: Twining
Soil Requirements: Fertile
Hardiness Zones: 5 or 6–9

Lycopersicon esculentum
Tomato

These popular annual plants are grown for their fruit, not good looks. Some cultivars can grow to 8 feet high. Leaves are deeply toothed and somewhat hairy. Small, bright yellow flowers bloom from early summer to late fall.
Climbing Style: Scandent
Soil Requirements: Fertile, high humus

Maurandella antirrhiniflora
(formerly A*sarina antirrhiniflora*)
Twining Snapdragon

This plant grows vigorously enough to cover a trellis or screen by mid- to late summer in most regions. It is a tender perennial that is grown as an annual in most areas. The triangular, bright green leaves are decorative by themselves; the flowers add bright spots of color. Despite their name, the flowers are shaped more like trumpets than snapdragons. In warm regions this plant responds well to dappled shade during hot afternoons. It is a close relative to Chickabiddy (both were once considered members of the same genus), but differs in both size and color.
Climbing Style: Twining
Soil Requirements: Average fertility
Hardiness Zones: 9–12

Parthenocissus spp. (Virginia Creeper)

Rubus spp. (Red and Black Raspberries)

Rubus ursinus (Boysenberry)

Parthenocissus spp. (Boston Ivy)

Parthenocissus spp.
Virginia Creeper, Boston Ivy

Virginia Creeper (P. *quinquefolia*) and Boston Ivy (P. *tricuspidata*) are the best known species of the ten in this genus. These perennial woody plants are admired for their foliage rather than the flowers. Leaves of these vines are green or reddish green in summer, but they turn various shades of brilliant red in autumn. Boston Ivy leaf blades often drop before their stalks do, giving the plant a skeletal, spidery look. Black berries sometimes follow the inconspicuous summer flowers.

Climbing Style: Sometimes tendrils twine around supports, but more often they cling with small suckers on the tips of the tendrils.

Soil Requirements: Fertile

Hardiness Zones: P. *quinquefolia*, 3–9; P. *tricuspidata*, 4–8

Rubus idaeus, R. occidentalis
Red Raspberry, Black Raspberry

Leaves of these perennials are dark green with three leaflets; they turn dark red in autumn. The flowers are white or pink, and bloom from early to late summer. Fruits can be red, black, or yellow, and range in flavor from somewhat tart to very sweet.

Climbing Style: Scandent

Soil Requirements: Fertile

Hardiness Zones: 3–9

Rubus ursinus var. *loganobaccus* cv.
Boysenberry

Similar to other perennial bramble bushes, boysenberries have dusky green leaves and pink or pinkish white, five-petaled flowers with prominent centers. Bloom time is in early summer. Bred from blackberry, loganberry, and raspberry, boysenberries seem to combine the best of each of their flavors. They are also more drought tolerant than other brambles although they can't fruit well if they are severely moisture-deficient.

Climbing Style: Scandent

Soil Requirements: Fertile; can tolerate very sandy soils.

Hardiness Zones: 6–10

Schizophragma hydrangeoides (Jap. Hydrangea)

Vitis labrusca (American Grape)

Vitis spp. (Hybrid Grape)

Tropaeolum majus (Nasturtium)

Wisteria spp. (Wisteria)

Schizophragma hydrangeoides
Japanese hydrangea

Showy, dramatic flowerheads characterize this woody perennial in midsummer, but the plant is lovely at any time of year. It is particularly effective when grown against a wall or fence and is sometimes trained to grow up a large tree. Allow at least 2 feet between the stem of this plant and its support because it is extraordinarily vigorous.
Climbing Style: Aerial roots
Soil Requirements: Moderately fertile
Hardiness Zones: 6–9

Tropaeolum majus
Nasturtium

The brightly colored nasturtium flowers have a texture that is similar to crepe paper. Blooms of most cultivars are about 2 inches wide and spurred. Leaves are round with prominent veins fanning out from the center; edges can be lobed; and the color is a bright, clear green. Nasturtiums, which are edible, are annuals that bloom from early summer into autumn.
Climbing Style: Twining
Soil Requirements: Low to moderate nitrogen levels

Vitis labrusca
American Grape

The lobed leaves of these perennials are a dull, dark green with an almost quilted appearance. They turn yellow in autumn. Flowers form in small, green, inconspicuous clusters in spring; the grapes form in early summer and are harvested in late summer or fall.
Climbing Style: Scandent
Soil Requirements: Fertile, high humus
Hardiness Zones: 5–9

Vitis spp.
Hybrid Grapes

The dark green leaves of these perennials are lobed and about 6 to 8 inches long. In the autumn, they turn yellow rather than red. In the spring, the small green flowers are inconspicuous. Grapes begin developing in early summer and ripen in late summer or fall, depending on cultivar.
Climbing Style: Scandent
Soil Requirements: Fertile, high humus
Hardiness Zones: 7–9

Wisteria spp.
Wisteria

The blue, violet, pink, or white flowers are shaped like those of peas. Blooms of most species form in 6- to 12-inch-long clusters, but those of *W. floribunda* can be 2 to 3 feet long. The deciduous leaves of these perennial plants are decorative throughout the growing season; the sinuous, gray, rough-barked trunk and branches are dramatic during the winter months. Bloom time is spring or early summer; some *W. sinensis* plants bloom again in early autumn. Provide a very sturdy support for this vigorous plant because it will tear down anything that is insubstantial.
Climbing Style: Twining
Soil Requirements: Fertile, high humus
Hardiness Zones: *W. sinensis*, 5–8; all other species, 6–9

CLIMBING AND RAMBLER ROSES

No rose really climbs. Instead, they grow long canes that lean against supports. In the wild, they tend to weave themselves into trees and shrubs, but in the garden, they are tied to their supports.

The roses we refer to as "climbing roses" are divided into two categories: climbers and ramblers. Most ramblers bloom only once a season. Climbers, on the other hand, bloom more than once. Their canes are also stiffer and their flowers are generally larger than those of the ramblers. Despite this, ramblers can put on just as effective a show, even if it is for a shorter period of time. Many of them are so floriferous that the plants are literally covered with flowers for the two to four weeks that they bloom. By pairing them with another flowering climbing plant, such as a clematis that blooms from midsummer till fall, you can create a trellis that is covered with bloom from late spring until fall.

Choosing a Rose

If you have decided on a rose for your structure, you'll need to choose a cultivar that is well acclimated to your climatic conditions. If it is not, it is likely to suffer more than a fair share of problems with pests and diseases. For example, if you live in a humid climate, you'll want to choose a cultivar that is resistant to the fungal diseases that thrive there. In a cold climate, you'll want to pick a rose that is

Climbing and rambler roses, *cascading over a trellis, arbor, fence, or other open structure, can be the crowning touch to any yard or garden.*

winter hardy. Check the Rose Directory, pages 44 to 47, for information on the roses that you like, and ask advice at a nursery or garden club in your area.

You'll also want to be sure that the rose you pick suits the planned location. Does the color of the bloom complement the colors of the house or other nearby structures? Is there enough room so that the rose can grow wide as well as tall? Does the exposure match the plant's requirements? In general, you'll find that ramblers are more suited to arches, pergolas, and arbors because their canes are so flexible, while climbers are more suited to a trellis or fence.

Planting Your Rose

The most important factors are the depth of the bud union, or area where the rootstock was grafted to the top growth, the size of the planting hole, and sound contact between the roots and the soil. Many experts once advised planting a rose with the bud union an inch or so above the soil surface in warm, frost-free climates. In cold winter areas, they advised gardeners to place the bud union several inches below the soil surface. Today, however, almost everyone agrees that no matter where you live, it's best to bury the bud union a few inches below the ground.

Fences, *especially those with an open design and situated in a sunny location, are well-suited to the growing needs of climbing roses.*

A clematis vine is an ideal companion *for a climbing or rambler rose. Both types of plants need essentially the same soil, nutrients, and amount of water.*

Plant a rose so its bud union is at the prescribed depth, usually belowground.

If you are planting a bare-root rose, dig a hole at least 18 to 24 inches wide and 18 inches deep. Again, expert advice has changed. Gardeners used to mix the soil they removed from the hole and which they were going to put back around the roots with copious amounts of peat moss and compost. However, this isn't necessary if your soil is fertile and has a high humus content; amend only those soils that are not suitable for roses. See page 34 to learn how to handle a bare-root plant.

Bare-root roses must be planted in very early spring or, in Zones 6 and warmer, in autumn, about a month before the first frost. In contrast, you can plant a container-grown rose almost any time, as long as you keep the top growth shaded and the soil consistently moist while the plant is getting established. To make certain that the roots of your rose are in good contact with the surrounding soil, water well when half of the roots or root ball are buried and again when you finish burying them.

Pruning and Training

For the first two years, simply tie the canes to their supports. Because horizontal growth flowers more than vertical growth, spread out the canes as much as possible. The only pruning you need to do is removing dead, diseased, or damaged growth.

In the second or third year, your roses will begin blooming. Deadhead any flowers that form up to a month before the first expected frost by cutting just above the first pair of five-leaflet leaves below the bloom. Then stop deadheading, and let the plant form hips.

The best blooms on climbing roses are produced on one-year-old wood; in early

Wire is used to hold the canes of this rose to the column of its support.

TRAINING ROSES

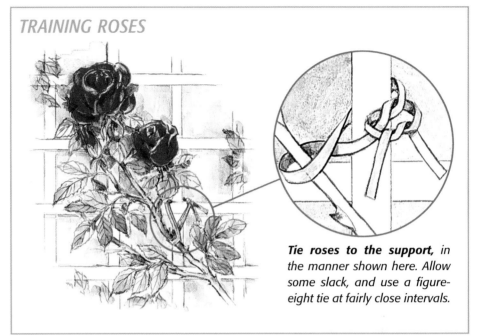

Tie roses to the support, in the manner shown here. Allow some slack, and use a figure-eight tie at fairly close intervals.

spring, cut back the canes that bloomed the year before to only 3 or 4 inches. New canes will grow to replace them. Roses in the wichuraiana group, such as 'New Dawn', are an exception to this. They are so free-blooming that you don't need to cut back two-year-old canes except when they crowd the plant.

Noisette roses are slow to produce new canes, so it's best to leave some of the canes that flowered the year before. Bend them to as far of a horizontal position as possible, and then tie them to the support to stimulate their blooming again the following year.

If your rose blooms only once, early in the season, cut back the flowering canes right after bloom. In addition to removing old canes, some climbers and ramblers need to be pruned to stay within bounds. Do this by cutting back the canes by several inches in late winter or early spring.

Care

It's important to choose a cultivar suited to your environment, care for its soil, and prune it enough to keep air circulation high. If all that is done, you probably won't have more trouble with your roses than you do with any other garden plant.

Natural beneficial insects are your best allies against many of the rose pests. To encourage these creatures, grow small flowered plants such as lavender, dill, garlic chives, and sweet alyssum under your roses and mulch with a well-made compost. The most common rose diseases are black spot and powdery mildew. Garlic chives are said to help protect against these fungus diseases, but a preventive spray made from 1 tsp. baking soda, 1 tsp. fine horticultural oil, and 1 tsp. liquid kelp to each quart of water is also effective. Spray every week starting early in the season, and continue until frost.

Most roses need winter protection in areas where it frosts. Some are hardy as far north as Zone 6b without protection. No matter where you live, however, you must mulch the crown of the plant to protect it from freezing.

ROSE DIRECTORY

Explanation of Icons

Light Requirements: Yellow sun means full sun; half-yellow/half-black sun means partial shade; black sun represents shade.

Water Needs: Full drop denotes high moisture requirements; half-full drop, moderate needs; low level (bottom third) means low water needs.

Thorns: Full thorn represents very thorny; a half-thorn means somewhat thorny; a one-quarter thorn means a few thorns.

Hardiness: Full snowflake denotes very hardy; a half-flake means some temperature resistance; a quarter-flake means not reliably hardy.

Fragrance: F means fragrant; F denotes that only some species or cultivars in the species are fragrant; F means the plant is not fragrant.

'Altissimo'

'America'

'Blaze'

'Blush Noisette'

'Altissimo'

The single blossoms of 'Altissimo' are 4 to 5 inches wide, deep blood-red with golden stamens; the petals are cupped when first open but quickly become flat. Its foliage is dark green, serrated, and leathery. It blooms in the summer and repeats again in fall. The flowers have long stems, making them an excellent choice for a cut flower. When in full bloom, the plant is spectacular.

Type: Climbing floribunda

Comments: This easy-to-grow climber is resistant to powdery mildew but susceptible to black spot.

'America'

The salmon pink blooms are 4 to 5 inches wide and shaped like hybrid tea flowers. They form in clusters. The semiglossy foliage is dark green. Plants bloom on new wood and flowers form until autumn.

Type: Large-flowered climber

Comments: 'America' received the AARS award in 1976, partially because it is such a beautiful plant and partially because it is so disease resistant and winter hardy. The fragrance is reminiscent of carnations. The plants are vigorous and cover arbors and trellises quickly.

'Blaze'

The crimson red semidouble blossoms of this rose are 2 to 3 inches wide and have 18 to 24 petals. They grow in clusters and have a somewhat cupped form. Bloom time is midseason, with good repeat performance. The foliage of this rose is medium green and semiglossy.

Type: Large-flowered climber, hybrid multiflora

Comments: Hardy to about Zone 7, this rose has excellent heat tolerance. It resists powdery mildew but is susceptible to black spot. The plant is a vigorous grower with strong, flexible canes that can be easily trained.

'Blush Noisette'

The double flowers of this rose form in loose clusters and are mauve, deep pink, or blush pink. It has dark green, abundant leaves, and blooms almost continuously from midsummer until autumn.

Type: Chinensis, noisette

Comments: Introduced in 1814, this is the original noisette rose. The fragrance resembles that of cloves. It is resistant to most fungal diseases if it grows in full sun in a spot with good air circulation.

'Cherokee'

'Dr. Huey'

'Constance Spry'

'Golden Showers'

'Cherokee'

☀ 🞂 ◢ ❋ **F**

The large single white flowers with prominent yellow stamens bloom late spring only—there are no repeat blooms. The leaves are bright green and large and are evergreen in mild climates.

Type: Rambler

Comments: This rose is a wild rose from China with origins so old that no one knows its parentage. Its thorns are a reddish, chocolate brown color and quite large. The fragrance is lovely. It does not tolerate frosts well and performs poorly in areas where winter frosts are common.

'Constance Spry'

☀ to 🞂 🞂 ◢ ❋ **F**

The flowers of this rose are large, clear pink, full, and globe-shaped; they bloom in early summer only. Its mid-green foliage is coarse.

Type: English rose

Comments: This is the first English rose that David Austin hybridized. It displays many of the qualities that make these cultivars so popular: vigor, hardiness, and disease resistance. It is very thorny and should be planted well away from paths and walkways or play and dining areas.

'Dr. Huey'

☀ 🞂 ◢ ❋ **F**

The deep maroon semidouble flowers with golden stamens and 12 to 15 petals are saucer-shaped and about 3 inches wide. They form in clusters and bloom midseason only. Its foliage is dark green and glossy.

Type: Large-flowered climber

Comments: 'Dr. Huey' has been used as a rootstock for many years because it confers good hardiness to roses grafted onto it. However, the top growth sometimes dies anyway, leaving the rootstock to grow.

'Golden Showers'

☀ 🞂 ◢ ❋ 🄵

The cupped, canary yellow blooms of this rose average 4 inches across and are double with 20 to 35 petals. It has dark green, glossy foliage. This rose blooms continuously throughout the summer and fall, stopping with the first frost.

Type: Large-flowered, floribunda climber

Comments: This plant is known for its vigorous, bushy growth. Its canes are flexible and easy to train. 'Golden Showers' is ideal for covering a wall or fence with its abundant flowers and attractive foliage. The brilliant yellow blooms make a great backdrop to a garden of yellow, white, and soft blue flowers. Its soft fragrance makes it a good choice for patios and seating areas.

'Iceberg, Climbing'

'Mme Alfred Carrière'

'Lady Banks Yellow'

'Mlle Cécile Brunner, Climbing'

'Iceberg, Climbing'

The cupped, double 3-inch-wide blooms are white with high centers and grow in clusters. Its light green leaves are semiglossy. This rose blooms in the summer, with good repeat throughout the season.
Type: Climbing floribunda
Comments: 'Iceberg' is justifiably famous. Its blooms have a lovely form, and plants are extremely floriferous. While it is reliably winter hardy in most of the United States and southern Canada, it is susceptible to both black spot and powdery mildew.

'Lady Banks Yellow'

This rose has multiple clusters of from 5 to 10 1-inch-wide yellow double blooms with 30 to 50 petals. It blooms in late spring; its evergreen leaves are dark green, small, and elongated.

Type: Climber
Comments: This plant spreads for a distance of 8 to 12 feet, so give it a great deal of room when you plant it. Although it won't live through frosts, it's quite disease resistant. 'Lady Banks White' differs from 'Lady Banks Yellow' in that it has fragrance and blooms throughout the summer.

'Mme Alfred Carrière'

Milky white, very fragrant double flowers, many of which are touched with a hint of pink, bloom from late spring with good repeat blooms until autumn. Its light green leaves are abundant.
Type: Chinensis climber
Comments: This rose is vigorous and will quickly climb any support it finds. It will grow to 20 feet or more and develop a trunk like a tree. 'Mme Alfred Carrière' can tolerate somewhat lean soils but grows better in good

ones. Similarly, it will grow in partial shade, although full sun promotes the best bloom.

'Mlle Cécile Brunner, Climbing'

The 1-inch-wide light-pink double flowers are shaped like miniature hybrid tea roses and are abundant. This rose blooms late in the season, repeating until frost. Its small, bright green leaves grow densely.
Type: Polyantha climber
Comments: A vigorous, strong grower, 'Mlle Cécile Bunner, Climbing' can become almost as wide as it is tall (can grow to 25 feet high). It grows well on walls and trellises in partial shade. While not reliably hardy in severely cold climates, it will overwinter in Zones 6 and 7 with winter protection. It also has good disease resistance. Because it has few thorns, you can grow it near a path or outdoor recreation or dining area. It is only mildly fragrant, however.

'Maréchal Niel'

'New Dawn'

'Souvenir de La Malmaison, Climbing'

'Phyllis Bide'

'Zéphirine Drouhin'

'Maréchal Niel'

☀ 💧 ◢ ❋ **F**

Soft, buttery yellow flowers open from pointed buds. Bloom time is from late spring with good repeat performance throughout the summer. The full flowers droop from their slender stems; the foliage is dark, copper-green.
Type: Chinensis climber
Comments: The softness of the flower color in combination with the superb fragrance and the way the blooms droop make this a wonderful rose. Unfortunately, it is not winter hardy. In Zones 7 and 8, place it in a very sheltered location. In colder areas, think about growing it in a greenhouse.

'New Dawn'

☀ to ◗ 💧 ◢ ❋ ⊡

Silvery pink blooms are wide, semidouble with 18 to 24 petals, and grow in clusters. When the flowers open, golden yellow stamens comple-ment the color of the petals. It flowers contin-uously from midseason until frost. The canes are upright; the medium green leaves are glossy; and the plant becomes bushy.
Type: Old-fashioned R. *wichuraiana* climber
Comments: This hardy plant resists most diseases, and grows well on cold, north-fac-ing walls. It tolerates soils with low fertility.

'Phyllis Bide'

☀ to ◗ 💧 ◢ ❋ ⊡

Clusters of dainty, double flowers in yellow, cream, pink, and red bloom summer until autumn and deepen in color as they age. Its foliage is light green in color.
Type: Polyantha climber
Comments: This plant tolerates partial shade and cool, north-facing walls.

'Souvenir de La Malmaison, Climbing'

☀ 💧 ◢ ❋ **F**

The double flowers of this rose are white with a pink blush, and they bloom in summer, reblooming in good environmental condi-tions. Its foliage is mid-green in color.
Type: Bourbon climber
Comments: This rose is extremely sensitive to wet soils and will languish in them. It thrives in warm weather but has difficulty in cold conditions.

'Zéphirine Drouhin'

☀ 💧 ◢ ❋ **F**

Large semidouble light-to-deep-pink flowers repeat over the summer amid mid-green, lush foliage.
Type: Chinensis climber
Comments: This hardy climbing rose can go without winter protection as far north as Zone 6b. Beyond that, the crown requires mulching. Because it is very susceptible to powdery mildew, it is best grown against a fence or up an arbor where air circulation is high.

TOOLS, TECHNIQUES & MATERIALS

You have some tools and know how to use them. But to tackle these arbors and trellises, you may need to expand your tool collection somewhat. The following information will assist you in both choosing and using your tools and materials.

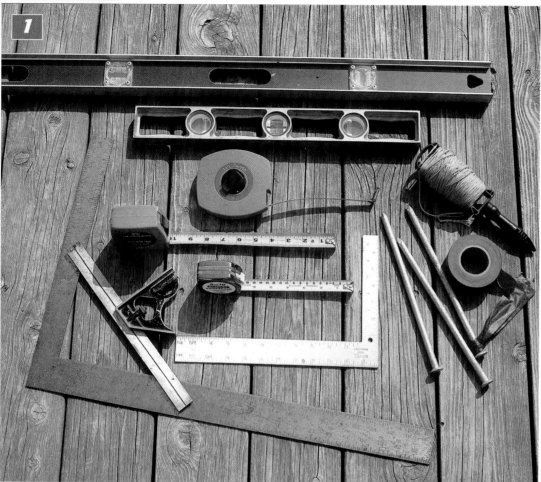

Layout tools (counter-clockwise from lower left): squares (framing, combination, steel), 10-in. nails, surveyor's marking tape, mason's string, levels (2- and 4-ft.), tape measures (100-, 25-, and 16-ft.).

TOOLS & TECHNIQUES

Layout Tools

The very first tool you are likely to use on any project is one for layout. **(Photo 1)**

Tape Measure. The most basic layout tool, a good all-around measure has a tape that's ½ inch or ¾ inch wide and 12 to 16 feet long; its scale will be readable. For large structures you'll need more than one tape, including a 25-footer. A longer tape—lengths range to 100 feet and more—can be useful in siting an arbor and laying out postholes.

Combination Square. All-purpose combination squares typically get a lot of use. The square shown has a 12-inch blade, but lengths range from 6 to 24 inches. The head, which can be moved and locked at any place along the blade, has machined edges at 90 and 45 degrees to the blade. The primary use of the combination square is as a try square—marking lines across boards, checking for flatness and squareness—but you can also use it as a marking gauge and a depth gauge.

Steel Squares. L-shaped steel squares have a long "blade" and a short "tongue," which meet in a right angle at the "heel." All of the edges of these squares are graduated in various scales. The largest of the steel squares is the framing square, used by builders for laying out parts of a house's framework. The smallest is handy for layout work of a smaller scale.

Level. A level is used to test for vertical and horizontal alignment. Many varieties are available, ranging from the tiny line level to the 6- or 8-foot carpenter's level. A long level spans surface irregularities to provide the most accurate reading, but for DIY projects, a tool between 18 and 36 inches will do.

String. Brightly colored mason's string is invaluable in laying out an arbor.

Site Tools

The tools you need to prepare the ground for an arbor or trellis are site tools. Many are garden tools, such as shovels, a rake, a mattock, or a wheelbarrow. Garden tools will be satisfactory for breaking up sod and leveling the ground. For digging postholes and mixing concrete you need more specialized tools. **(Photo 2)**

Posthole Digger. A clamshell type is the best all-around posthole digger. It has two long wooden handles mounted to a pair of scoops. The scoops are hinged together; spreading the handles closes their tips and captures soil between them so that it can be lifted from the hole.

Begin by clutching the handles together, lifting the tool, then driving it into the ground. Repeat this as necessary to loosen the soil. Then drive it into the ground; spread the handles; and lift the loose dirt to the side.

Digging Bar. Where the soil is compacted or stony, a digging bar is helpful. This heavy steel rod, 4 to 5 feet long, has a chisel tip, good for breaking up hard clay and splitting shale and porous stones, as well as for prying up boulders.

Mason's Hoe. For mixing batches of concrete to set posts, you need a hoe. A garden hoe will serve, but if you need to buy a hoe, get a mason's hoe, which has two or three holes in the blade.

Hand Tools

No matter how extensive your collection of power tools is, you need a few hand-powered tools. A basic handyman's kit **(Photo 3)** should include a few sizes of screwdrivers, both Phillips and flat-blade, a light claw hammer (12 ounces is about right), and a socket wrench with a selection of sockets. Pliers, a couple of adjustable wrenches, a hacksaw for metal, and a backsaw for wood will round out the kit.

A modest selection of traditional wood-

working hand tools will also come in handy for refining the fit of joints, trimming inside corners of rabbets, and dozens of other odd jobs. **(Photo 4)** Chisels and block planes are easy to find and don't cost a lot. Keep the blades sharp so that they'll always be ready to use.

Power Saws

In addition to basic handsaws, you will also need a few power saws.

Circular Saw. The circular saw is your basic wood-cutting power tool. **(Photo 5)** The saw's base has a notch in the front edge, which you can use to follow a cutting line or to make sure you line up squarely at the beginning of a cut. The saw doesn't gladly

Site tools: posthole digger; digging bar; hoe for mixing concrete; long-handle shovel; wheelbarrow.

change direction, even slightly, once a cut has begun. If you try to correct your course, the saw will shriek, maybe stall, and often burn the sides of the cut. A cutting guide may help you get started straight. With some practice, however, aligning the saw when starting a crosscut becomes second nature. A carpenter's square clamped to the work can also be a guide. A circular saw can also be used for ripping; for accurate rip cuts, use a guide.

Be sure to understand and follow all the manufacturer's safety instructions when you use a circular saw. Learn to set the depth of cut appropriately, and always clamp pieces that might move during the cut.

When you shop for a saw, look at the motor's amp rating; it's a fairly reliable indicator of power. For saws with 7¼-inch blades, a 13-amp motor should give plenty of power.

Power Miter Saws. The most basic model is the "conventional" miter saw, which looks like a circular saw mounted on a spring-loaded hinge above a small table. The saw body rotates from a straight crosscut to a 45-degree miter cut in either direction. To make a cut, grasp the handle, squeeze the trigger switch, and rock the blade into the stock in a chopping motion. The majority of the saws on the market use a 10-inch blade. Most will crosscut a 2x6 and miter a 2x4 at 45 degrees. It is a simple, functional saw.

To make compound miters, cuts that are simultaneously miters and bevels, you need the more sophisticated compound

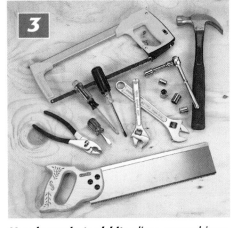

Handyman's tool kit: pliers, screwdrivers, wrenches, a hacksaw and backsaw, and a claw hammer.

Woodworker's tool kit: a set of chisels (¾-, ⅜-, ½-, and 1-in. widths) and a block plane.

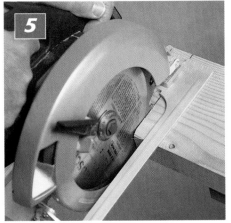

Circular saws make straight cuts, and it's difficult to alter your direction once you begin cutting.

Sliding compound miter saws offer a wide range of cutting capacities. The head rotates and tilts; it slides on a rail.

A table saw is essential for ripping stock to nonstandard widths. A good bench-top model is also suitable for many projects.

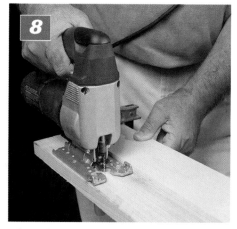

The saber saw is excellent for rip cuts and crosscuts, and is efficient at internal cuts. Its forte is the curved cut, made freehand.

miter saw. It has a rotating table but also a pivot to enable the head to be tilted 45 degrees (or more) to one or both sides. Size ranges up to 12 inches; cut capacities are similar to those of regular miter saws.

The most sophisticated of the miter saws is the sliding compound miter saw. **(Photo 6)** The head assembly rotates and tilts (some models both left and right) for compound cutting. But it also slides forward and back on a rail system, thus increasing the crosscutting capacity to about 12 inches. To make a cut, you pull the elevated blade toward you, pivot it down into the stock, then push it back toward the fence.

As you shop for one of these saws, look for smooth-working miter and bevel adjustments and easy-to-read scales. Miter-saw work will often require frequent setting changes. Large, accessible adjustment mechanisms make a big difference. In addition, detents (or stops) at common angles such as 0, 22½, and 45 degrees are useful.

On the safety front, look for a blade guard that retracts smoothly as you pivot the blade into the work. Look too for an electric brake that stops the blade when you release the on-off switch.

Table Saws. In the typical woodworking shop, the table saw is the boss. Buy a good one early on, and equip it with a first-rate blade, a good fence, and as big an outfeed table as your shop allows. For the occasional woodworker, consider a bench-top table saw. **(Photo 7)**

When shopping for a saw, look for sturdy handwheels, knobs, and locking devices that operate easily. The blade height and bevel should adjust without any play; a lock should hold the bevel setting. Degree scales should be easy to read, and there should be adjustable stops at 45 and 90 degrees.

On the safety front, the OFF switch must be large and easy to reach. The blade guard should swing out of the way during blade changing. Because the guard must be removed for some operations, look for one that's easy to remove and reinstall.

Buy a high-quality carbide-tip combination blade, and use it to do all your cutting.

Saber Saw. A saber saw cuts with a narrow blade. **(Photo 8)** The number of teeth per inch and the "set" of the teeth have a lot to do with the aggressiveness with which a particular blade cuts. But so does the oscillation setting of the saw.

When first introduced, the saber saw cut with an up-and-down action. Known as "straight-line" action, this is still best for smooth, tearout-free cutting, but it can be slow going on rip cuts and in dense materials. To accelerate the saw's cutting speed, orbital cutting action has been added. In this mode, the blade churns forward and backward as it strokes up and down, cutting more aggressively, but more roughly. On most saws, you can switch the orbital action on or off; on the best, you can ratchet it on by degrees.

When shopping for a saber saw, look for one that has variable speed, adjustable orbital action, a tilting base with stops at 45 and 90 degrees, and a blade-changing system with which you can deal.

Routers and Bits

The router is woodworking's most versatile power tool. It will surface stock, cut joints, profile edges, and knock out duplicate parts following a template or pattern. With a trammel, it will cut arcs and circles.

There are two types of routers: fixed-base and plunge. **(Photo 9)**

Fixed-Base Routers. The fixed-base model is the first you should buy. It is generally compact, has a low center of gravity, and is the more stable tool for the majority of the routing you'll do. Its handles are low enough that you can grip them firmly and still have the heels of your hands braced against the work. Any job that does not require on-the-fly changes in cutting depth should be done with a fixed-base router. This includes edge profiling and cutting dadoes, grooves, and rabbets.

Plunge Router. With the plunge router, you lower the spinning bit into the work in a controlled manner so that you can begin and end a cut in the middle of a board.

You will want to have two types of routers: a plunge router, left, and a fixed-base router, right.

Among the first router tips you should buy are straight bits, pattern and flush-trimming bits, and roundover bits.

A belt sander is usually best for smoothing rough boards and removing grading stamps and mill marks.

A pad sander is a finishing tool, intended to remove uniform scratches left by a belt sander. It uses regular sheet sandpaper.

The trade-off is balance. The motor rides up and down on a pair of spring-loaded posts rising from the router base. To plunge the router, you release a lock and push down on the handles. At rest, the handles are 4 to 6 inches above the work, and even in the middle of a cut, with the router plunged to the max, you may have trouble bracing the machine because the handles are so high above the work.

Attachments. An edge guide attaches to the router and slides along the edge of the workpiece to guide the bit. It is useful for cutting rabbets and grooves, and, with a plunge router, for cutting mortises.

Template guides, sometimes called guide bushings or guide collars, are essential for doing template work. You will need them to build some of the projects in this book.

Router Bits. The most important part of any routing operation is the bit. The more bits you have, the more jobs you can do with the basic machine. **(Photo 10)** In every performance aspect, bits with carbide cutting edges are superior to high-speed steel bits. An extremely hard material (close to the hardness of diamonds), carbide is relatively insensitive to heat, so it won't lose its temper when it gets hot.

Straight bits make most dadoes and mortise cuts. For trimming parts to match templates, you'll need pattern and flush-trimming bits. Roundover bits are used for softening edges and adding edge treatments.

Using a Router Safely and Effectively

First of all, never use a router without some sort of guide. The pilot bearing on the bit is a guide, and it is completely adequate. When using an unpiloted bit, you need an edge guide on the router or a fence or straightedge clamped to the work to guide the cut.

Even before you switch on the router, it's essential to know in which direction to feed it. (See "Router Feed Direction" drawings, this page.) You need to know so that you can put the fence in the correct place or stand in the right place and be prepared to move in the correct direction.

If you hold the router with the bit down, in standard hand-held operating orientation, the router bit will turn clockwise. With an unpiloted cutter and an unguided router, the rotation of the cutter will drag the tool to your left as you push it away from you. As you pull it toward you, it will veer to your right. You can use this dynamic to your advantage. Because you usually use a guide, feed the router so that the cutter rotation draws up against the guide.

Sandpaper and Sanders

Sandpaper is graded from coarse to fine in numbered grits. Start with 80-grit paper, and sand just enough to remove mill marks and the like. If a smoother surface is necessary, brush the dust from the workpiece before changing to a finer grit. (Perform this cleanup after each sanding cycle.) It is common to leapfrog grits when using a power sander. There's no benefit to sanding bare wood with grits finer than 150. Finer grits—180 or 220—will give it a more polished appearance, but once a finish is applied, it won't really look any better.

Many types of sanding tools are available. The three sanders, all portables, that make the most sense for these projects are

ROUTER FEED DIRECTION

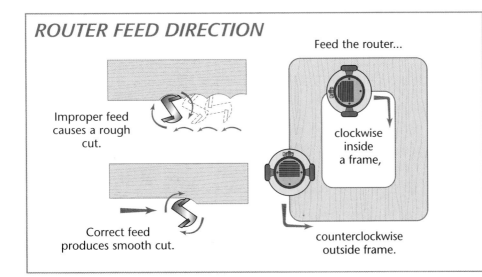

Improper feed causes a rough cut.

Correct feed produces smooth cut.

Feed the router...

clockwise inside a frame,

counterclockwise outside frame.

A random-orbit sander has a pad that rotates as well as oscillates, so it smooths a surface fast.

Bar clamps are the workhorses in most woodworking shops, and are available in a wide range of sizes and proportions.

Spring clamps are plenty strong for holding small parts together during assembly, and are great for holding stop blocks.

the belt sander, the pad sander, and the random-orbit sander (ROS). For the best results with the least effort, do as much of the sanding as possible before assembly.

Belt Sander. This common power tool has an abrasive belt mounted on rollers. **(Photo 11)** Between the rollers is a flat plate, and it is this plate that determines how much of the abrasive belt is in contact with the work. Belts and belt sanders are made in a variety of sizes, and the most common are 3 by 21 inches, 3 by 24 inches, and 4 by 24 inches.

Aggressive sanding is what a belt sander is all about. It can remove nicks and dents and other mill marks, and general roughness in no time at all. The trade-off is that belt sanders require your full attention; a lapse in concentration and a wobble can result in a sizable trough or swale instead of a flat, smooth surface.

Pad and ROS Sanders. These finish sanders provide a smooth-to-the-touch surface finish. The pad sander is much less effective at removing wood. It uses regular sheet sandpaper. Large ones take a third- or a half-sheet of sandpaper. Palm sanders typically take a quarter-sheet of sandpaper. **(Photo 12)**

The random-orbit sander is more effective than the pad sander. It combines rotary and orbital actions so that it can remove material quickly without being hard to control. The palm-grip sander is the favorite for finish sanding. It is compact and is designed to be held in one hand. **(Photo 13)**

Clamps

One of woodworking's oldest sayings is, "You can never have too many clamps." But there are so many styles and sizes and spe-

cialty designs on the market, it is almost impossible to keep track of them all.

Bar Clamp. The workhorse clamp in any workshop is the bar clamp. **(Photo 14)** You'll use them for assembly work, to secure workpieces to the workbench, to mount temporary fences to machines or workpieces, and for countless other tasks.

The two variables in sizing these clamps are the opening capacity and the throat depth. Typically, the clamp's overall bulk is proportional to the throat depth; as the throat gets deeper, both the jaw and the bar get beefier. A clamp having a thicker and/or wider bar can exert more pressure with less flex.

Spring Clamp. The jaws of the spring clamp are spread open simply by squeezing its two handles together, typically a one-handed operation. The jaws close firmly, even on work that doesn't have parallel faces. Spring clamps are strong enough for holding things together during layout and assembly, and for glue-ups on small objects too. **(Photo 15)**

C-Clamp. The oldest style of all-metal clamp, the C-clamp gets its name from its shape. **(Photo 16)** It can be tedious to apply and remove, but it exerts enormous clamping pressure. You need to use cauls to prevent damage to the wood.

Hand Screws. While not all-purpose clamps, hand screws are particularly good for laminations. **(Photo 17).** The jaws are long and flat, and thus you can apply intense pressure on broad areas (as opposed to isolated points). In the example shown, the pressure is applied evenly from edge to edge.

An all-metal C-clamp is the strongest style. Insert wood scraps between the jaws and the work to prevent dents.

Hand screws are particularly good for laminating stock face to face because the wooden jaws are long and flat.

Cordless drills can handle almost any job that their corded ancestors did, without the hassle of a cord.

If your drill has a ⅜-in. chuck, use larger-diameter bits with stepped-down shanks, so that they'll fit your drill's chuck.

Forstner bits cut flat-bottomed, smooth-walled holes. They are great for cutting counterbores in soft wood.

Drill-Driver and Bits

It's probably the least expensive power tool in the shop, but it's used on virtually every project. We call them drills but use them to drive screws as well. You'll need at least one; many woodworkers have three or more, in both corded and cordless versions. With a corded model, have long extension cords ready to reach the work.

Look at cordless models **(Photo 18)** because they have a better combination of features than corded models. Their power seems to be constantly increasing. The first cordless drills depended on 7.2-volt batteries for juice; now 18- and even 24-volt tools are available. With each increase in voltage, you'll find increases in speed and torque. The more work you expect from your drill, the more you will value the extra power of a big battery.

Other improvements include the elec-tronic brake and adjustable clutch. A keyless chuck allows you to loosen and tighten the chuck by hand.

Twist Drill Bit. The twist drill bit is the all-purpose hole-maker. **(Photo 19)** They are available individually and in sets, in fractional, decimal, wire, letter, and metric sizes, and in several different lengths. The all-inclusive sets run to 115 bits, but a 29-piece set of fractional sizes (¹⁄₁₆ through ½ inch) is more than adequate.

Forstner Bit. The design of the Forstner bit combines a tiny center point with cutting rims and chisel-like cutting edges. **(Photo 20)** The point locates the hole, the rims score its circumference, and the cutting edges essentially plane its bottom. The result is a flat-bottomed, smooth-walled hole. The Forstner does a great job on counterbores in the woods best-suited for outdoor uses (which tend to be soft).

Countersink Bits. The most expeditious way to drill pilot holes for screws is with a combination drill-countersink. **(Photo 21)** These assemblies have a countersink cutter fitted over a twist drill bit. The assemblies are labeled according to screw gauges, and for the projects in this book, you really need only No. 6 and 8 bits.

Plug Cutter. To conceal screws with wooden plugs, you need a plug cutter. **(Photo 22)** The cutter bores into the face or edge grain of wood scraps to produce plugs that blend right into the surrounding material. Because the plug is tapered, it's easy to insert into a counterbore. The cutter is not easy to use with a handheld drill. Try a drill mounted in a stand or a drill press.

Screwdriver Bits. Few people drive screws by hand these days. The cordless drill-driver does it for us, using special screwdriver bits. **(Photo 23)** The bits can

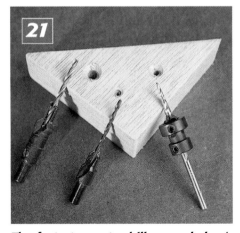

The fastest way to drill screw holes is with a drill-countersink combo. It has a countersink bit fitted over a twist drill bit.

Use a plug cutter to make wooden plugs. Best results come with a drill mounted in a stand or a drill press.

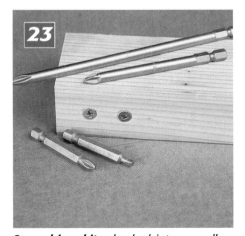

Screwdriver bits chucked into a cordless drill drive most of the screws today. It's helpful to keep some spares on hand.

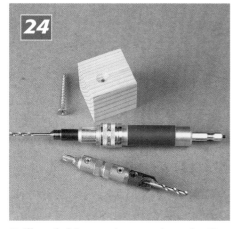

Drill-and-driver sets speed work. Use one end to drill a pilot, turn it end-for-end, and use the screwdriver to drive the screw.

Lumber quality is a key component of any outdoor project. You can sometimes work around minor defects.

Allow wood to acclimate to conditions in your shop. Use 2x4s to keep lumber off of the floor; add strips between layers.

get chewed up surprisingly fast, so it's a good idea to have spares on hand. When you shop for them, you'll find that a variety of sizes and lengths are available in three different drives. The most common are the Phillips and the square drive (called Robertson in Canada).

Drill-and-Driver Set. These sets are handy when assembling projects. **(Photo 24)** You chuck the tool socket in the drill. A bit holder, with a combination pilot drill-countersink at one end and a screwdriver bit at the other, fits into the socket. Drill the pilot hole; pop the bit holder out of the socket; turn it end-for-end; and reinsert it into the drill. The screwdriver bit will now be ready. You can easily make the switch with one hand, while holding the drill in the other.

MATERIALS

For your projects to survive outdoors, exposed to the sun and rain, you need to use sound construction techniques and build your projects with wood, glue, and fasteners that can stand up to the weather.

Wood

You need to work with wood that is strong, warp-free, and attractive. For these projects, the wood also has to stand up to fungi, insects, moisture, and sunlight. Some woods, such as redwood, cedar, and teak, have natural characteristics that make them good candidates for outdoor use. But you may not be able to find them in your local lumberyard or home center, or you

may be able to find only inferior grades.

Wood that's warped, cupped, and riddled with knots **(Photo 25)** is difficult to use. You can sometimes work around knots if the boards are straight and flat.

No matter what wood you select, try to use the heartwood, which comes from the core of the tree. This wood is denser, stronger, more stable, and generally more decay-resistant than the surrounding sapwood, which contains a lot of moisture. Heartwood isn't as laden with moisture and stays remarkably stable even through large swings in humidity. In the real world, many boards have both heartwood and sapwood in them, so be choosy and avoid boards that are all or mostly sapwood.

A lot of different grading systems are used for the lumber in home centers. The softwood and hardwood lumber systems use different classifications and names but grade lumber according to the volume and character of knots and blemishes. But you don't have to pore over grading charts. If what you want is the best stuff, just zero in on clear stock. You'll pay extra for this top-quality grade, but your project will look better and be easier to build.

Lumber Storage. Allow at least a few days for your lumber to adjust to the humidity level in your shop and reach what's called equilibrium moisture content. You don't want to cut tight joints only to have them open up as the wood gives off excess moisture and twists.

For best results, stack your lumber off the floor with strips of wood between each layer to maximize air circulation.

(Photo 26) Even a few days in a conditioned space can make quite a difference in wood that may have been stored under a shed roof.

Lumber Species

Here's a rundown of the species of woods I used, as well as a few you might choose. Generally, low-density woods, such as cedar and redwood, have less tendency to warp, check, and change dimensions than high-density domestic woods, such as white oak and southern pine. However, some remarkably dense tropical species are quite stable.

Cypress. (Photo 27) Cypress heartwood varies in color, but typically is a warm tan with some darker streaks. If left unfinished, it will weather to a charcoal or black color with tan highlights. This relatively light-weight wood is strong, moderately hard, and straight grained. The best grades have a smooth texture and an almost waxy feel.

Cypress

Standard, flat-sawn lumber has end grain roughly parallel with the board face, which makes the wood more likely to cup. More expensive quarter-sawn lumber has end grain roughly perpendicular to the board, which makes it more stable. Although cypress is resinous, it glues well, sands easily, and accepts finishes without a problem.

Douglas Fir. (Photo 28) A member of the pine family, Douglas fir is relatively hard and strong. The wood can be brittle and tend to splinter, but if you use sharp cutters, it machines well. However, drilling pilot holes for screws is essential to avoid splitting the wood. It also glues well, and finishes easily with stains and clear finishes. You might have more trouble getting paint to adhere to it.

Western Red Cedar. (Photo 29) Highly resistant to decay and rot, western red cedar is a dull red color when first cut, but it loses most of its reddishness and turns a handsome brown when exposed to the air. The sapwood is whitish, and cedar boards may contain both sapwood and heartwood. It has a distinctive spicy odor. Prolonged or heavy exposure to the dust can be irritating. The wood is light, very soft, and prone to split. Though it works easily, sharp tools are essential. Cedar is rich in tannins; hardware containing iron will turn the wood black.

Meranti Mahogany. (Photo 30) Not a true mahogany, Meranti is related to lauan (best known as a constituent of inexpensive plywood) and Philippine mahogany. The color of the best boards resembles South American (true and genuine) mahoganies. The texture is fairly coarse, and the color is highly variable. Stability doesn't match that of true mahoganies.

Pressure-Treated Southern Yellow Pine. (Photo 31) Treated wood is infused with wood-preserving chemicals to resist rot and insect damage. The preservatives are forced under pressure throughout the wood, which provides more protection than surface treatments do. Although some pressure-treated (PT) wood can be difficult to work (and a bit shy of standard lumber dimensions), its rot-resistance makes it popular for outdoor applications. It tends to twist, warp, and throw big splinters.

The main drawback is the chemical content. One ingredient of the most common treatment (chromated copper arsenate, called CCA) is arsenic, which is poisonous. One 12-foot-long 2x6 contains about an ounce of arsenic. Although most experts say it can't leach out, woodworkers are warned to wear a dust mask (and safety glasses, as always) to keep from inhaling the sawdust when cutting. Also, remember that you can't burn the scraps.

But there are several new preservatives, including ACQ, copper citrate, and a mix called the Kodiak formula, that increase the copper content (and raise cost about 10 percent) but decrease or eliminate the chromium and arsenic. Manufacturers say the new treatments give the wood a brownish color, which left to weather naturally turns gray. There should be no performance difference. Check the lumber tag to see whether the wood is CCA-treated or not. After December 2003, CCA will not be sold for residential use.

If you don't like the color of PT, you can stain it or even paint it. But it's difficult to conceal the grain of southern yellow pine, the wood most commonly treated. (You may find other treated species, including other pines, Douglas fir, western larch, Sitka spruce, western hemlock, western red cedar, northern white cedar, and white fir.)

Redwood. (Photo 32) Old-growth, all-heart redwood is expensive but an ideal outdoor wood. A bright red-orange when freshly cut, it darkens to a brownish red and weathers to a silvery gray. The wood is lightweight, soft, and easy to work, but also very stable with a smooth texture and straight grain. And it is highly resistant to insect and fungal invasion. Redwood contains tannins, so don't use iron hardware.

White Oak. (Photo 33) More than 50 oak species grow in North America and are divided into two primary groups: red oak and white oak. White oak is stronger, harder, more durable, and better suited for outdoor projects. Don't let iron hardware come in contact with white oak. Like cedar and redwood, it has a high tannin content, and iron will turn the wood black.

Adhesives

There are several water-resistant or waterproof glues to use. For the projects, I used two types. Here's a summary of them.

Yellow Glue. The polyvinyl acetates (PVAs), which include the familiar white and yellow glues, are popular because they're strong, versatile, and cheap. No mixing is required, the bottle that the glue comes in usually serves as an applicator, and required clamping times are short.

For outdoor projects, you want Type II yellow glue, which is highly water resistant (though not completely waterproof) and can be used at temperatures as low as 55 degrees F. It sets up fast, giving you only about five to ten minutes between

Douglas Fir

Western Red Cedar

Meranti Mahogany

application and clamping. Clamp the assembly for at least one hour. As the glue cures, the glue line becomes nearly invisible.

Before the glue cures, it can be cleaned up with water. A wet (not just damp) rag can be used to wipe away squeeze-out before it skins over; a chisel or scraper can do the job after that. The dried glue sands well and won't gum up sandpaper.

Polyurethane. Versatile, strong, and reasonably easy to use, polyurethane glue also has some peculiar characteristics.

It offers an unusually long open time but the glue needs moisture to catalyze. So unless the wood has a high moisture content, you have to moisten one of the joint surfaces with a damp cloth.

Clamping time is one to four hours, depending on the ambient temperature (minimum application temperature—68 degrees F), and the glue cures fully within 24 hours. The result is a strong, creep-resistant, and waterproof bond.

Remove squeeze-out by wiping the wet glue from the wood with mineral spirits or by scraping the dried glue. If you get some on your hands and don't remove it quickly (with rubbing alcohol) you'll carry stains for days. Note, too, that polyurethane glue may present a health hazard to asthmatics and those who tend to be highly allergic. Even if you don't have a problem, use it with ample ventilation.

Polyurethane glue expands as it sets up. It can fill an open seam, but can also push apart joints that aren't properly clamped.

Outdoor Fasteners

You need corrosion-resistant fasteners to make outdoor projects. In most situations, I prefer screws and bolts to nails. Here is a brief rundown of two of the options.

Coated Steel. Most of the stock exterior-grade fasteners are galvanized (coated). Hot-dipping is the best galvanizing method for nails, but not for screws because the process can clog the threads. Mechanically plated screws are generally suitable for decks and some furniture projects. But the iron content stains redwood and cedar. Electroplated screws have been improved with polymer coatings, but the coating is thin and can wear off even as you drive the screw.

Stainless Steel. Stainless-steel screws and bolts are the strongest and most durable on the market. While they'll eventually tarnish and develop a reddish cast, they won't stain wood or react with the tannins in redwood and cedar. They may cost twice as much as coated steel, but there really is no other sensible choice.

Wood Finishes

Most finishes provide some protection from moisture, the sun, and fungi, but each finish is better at some of these jobs than at others. Frequency and ease of maintenance also vary with types of finish. Here is a look at some of the options, aside from using a rot-resistant wood with no finish and watching it weather.

Paint. Paint does the best overall job of protecting wood outdoors because it has more pigments than other finishes. But while paint provides good protection on vertical surfaces, it is usually short-lived on horizontal areas. Once the film is ruptured, moisture, mold, and insects can penetrate.

If you do paint, use a good latex primer and top coat with mildewcide and fungicide additives. They are easy to apply, quick drying, and easy to clean up with water. Also, use a stain killer to hide knots.

Solid-Color Stains. Heavy-bodied stains (either latex or oil-based) have more pigment than other stains. They form a film similar to that of paint but thinner, and the oil-based stains can even peel like paint. But because the stain is thinner than paint, the surface can be recoated many more times before it needs stripping.

Semitransparent Stains. Moderately pigmented stains let some wood grain show through but still retard UV damage. Semitransparents do not form a paintlike film but penetrate the surface, which keeps them from peeling. Penetrating stains are oil- or alkyd-based. Latex stains also are available, but they don't penetrate wood surfaces as effectivley as oil-based stains.

Varnishes. Exterior-grade varnish uses blockers instead of pigments to reduce UV damage. Marine spar varnish formulated with a tung-oil phenolic resin is made to protect boats, so it's more than adequate for outdoor use. However, it darkens the wood.

Polyurethane spar varnish has the flexibility and light resistance needed for exterior use, and it's considerably less yellow than the marine spar varnish.

Water Repellents. Clear sealers contain a resin or drying oil, a small amount of wax, a solvent, and a fungicide. The fungicide won't prevent rot, only surface mildew and fungi. The first application may be short lived. After the wood has weathered, the treatments are more enduring.

Pressure-Treated Southern Yellow Pine

Redwood

White Oak

FAN TRELLIS

Classic in design, this graceful trellis is made from a single board. Assembly takes only a couple of hours. Just stake the trellis into the ground, and tie the top portion into a fence or wall.

EXPLODED VIEW

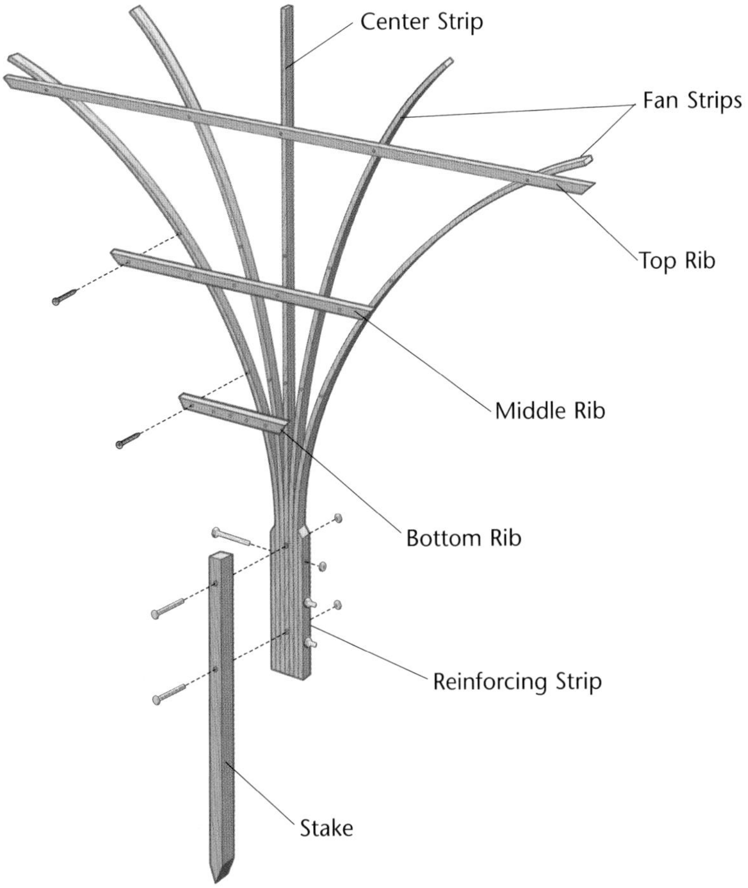

SHOPPING LIST

- 1 pc. 5/4×6 8' clear western red cedar
- 1 pc. 2×2 3' southern yellow pine (SYP)
- 3 stainless-steel hex-head bolts, 1/4" × 3 1/2", with washers and nuts
- 2 stainless-steel hex-head bolts, 1/4" × 3", with washers and nuts
- 15 stainless-steel flathead screws, #8 × 1"

CUTTING LIST

Part	Quantity	Thickness	Width	Length	Stock
Fan strips	4	3/8"	1"	72"	5/4×6 western red cedar
Center strip	1	1/2"	1"	72"	5/4×6 western red cedar
Reinforcing strips	2	3/8"	1"	16"	5/4×6 western red cedar
Top rib	1	1/2"	1"	64 1/4"*	5/4×6 western red cedar
Middle rib	1	1/2"	1"	35 5/8"*	5/4×6 western red cedar
Bottom rib	1	1/2"	1"	15"*	5/4×6 western red cedar
Stake	1	1 1/2"	1 1/2"	36"	2×2 SYP

*These are approximate finished lengths. When cutting the pieces, cut each about 6 to 12 inches longer and trim as needed after securing the fan strips.

FRONT ELEVATION

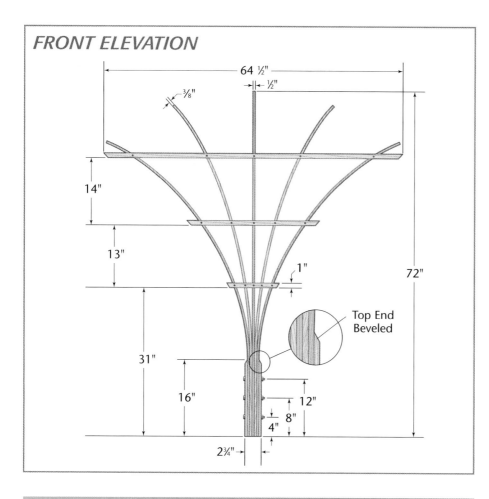

BUILDER'S NOTES

You can build this fan trellis fast using a table saw and a few shop tricks.

Materials
Any of a number of woods—cedar, redwood, cypress, and even treated types—can be used. You need only one board, but it must be straight-grained and free of knots. Otherwise, when you bend the fan strips, they could snap at a weak point.

The clear cedar shown requires the use of stainless-steel fasteners, because they won't react to the wood the way galvanized steel will. Regardless of the wood type, the extra couple of dollars spent on the stainless-steel fasteners are a worthy invest-

ment both for durability and looks. (They won't rust.)

Tools and Techniques
A table saw, even a bench-top model, is essential for ripping the board into the slats needed for the strips and ribs of the trellis. When ripping the stock, use a pusher to protect your hand from the saw blade. The heel of a pusher hooks behind the end of the stock, and the front holds the stock flat on the saw table. When the pusher gets too chewed up, replace it. You can buy a pusher, but I use a saber saw to cut push-ers from scrap plywood.

Having two drill-drivers, one ready with a pilot bit and the other with a screwdriver bit, is handy for this project.

As you're assembling the trel-lis, you'll need to bend a fan strip to a rib and pinch the two parts together while you drill a pilot hole and then drive a screw. A clamp would be in the way. Have the two separate drivers ready so that you can switch from one to the other without letting go of the strips.

Finish
If the trellis will support an enduring vine, the vine will prevent your renewing the finish. However, if you intend to prune back the plant suffi-ciently every few years, you could reapply stain or paint at those times.

Confident of the natural decay-resistance of cedar, I left my trellis unfinished.

STEP-BY-STEP

Cut the Trellis Parts
The first task is to rip the 8-foot-long board into thin strips. Because the board is actu-ally 5⅜ inches wide, it will easily yield the four ½-inch-thick strips for the ribs and center strip and the six ⅜-inch-thick strips for the fan and reinforcing strips. Use a pusher when ripping the board. The "Table Saw Pusher" drawing, below, shows a simple but effective one you can cut with a saber saw from scrap ½-inch plywood.

Unfortunately, on most table saws the standard blade guard interferes with thin rip cuts. The guard knocks against the rip fence and prevents you from getting a pusher between it and the fence. You need to either remove the guard or calculate a new fence setting for each cut and have the thin strip fall to the outside of the blade. Photo 1 shows the guard removed.

With the saw set up and pusher in hand, rip the board into the strips needed for the trellis. **(Photo I)** Next, using a saber saw, a circular saw, or a power miter saw, cross-cut the strips to their proper lengths. Crosscut the center and four fan strips to 72 inches each. Cut each of the two rein-forcing strips to 16 inches, and then bevel the top end of each at 45 degrees (detail, "Front Elevation" drawing). Cut the three ribs, leaving them 6 to 12 inches longer than specified in the Cutting List. The fin-ished lengths of the ribs, particularly the middle and bottom ones, will depend on the placement of the bends of the fan strips, so you don't want them to be shorter than what you'll need.

TABLE SAW PUSHER

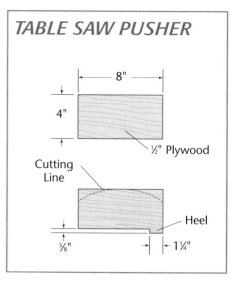

Rip the board into strips of the proper thicknesses: ⅜ in. for the fan and reinforcing strips; ½ in. for the ribs and center strip. Use a table saw pusher for protection.

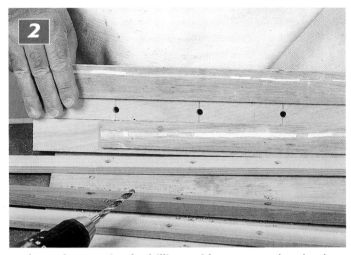

Make and use a simple drilling guide to ensure that the three bolt holes in each strip will line up with one another. Make the guide from scraps of plywood. Drill the strips one by one.

Arrange the strips so that the center one is flanked on each side by two fan strips and one reinforcing strip. Line up the bolt holes, and then tape and bolt the strips together.

DRILLING GUIDE

⁹⁄₃₂" Diameter Hole

¾" Plywood

12"

8"

4"

5"

16"

24"

1"

¼" Plywood Fence

Bolt the Strips Together

First, drill three bolt holes into the lower end of each strip. In order for the strips to join tight and be flush against each other, these three holes must line up from one strip to the next. Unless you have a drill press, which can facilitate precise positioning of these holes, you'll need to use a simple drilling guide. (See the "Drilling Guide" drawing, this page.)

To make the guide, cut a 5 x 24-inch piece from a scrap of ¾-inch plywood, and then mark and drill three holes 4 inches on center, along its center, as shown in the illustration. Center the guide under the lower, unbeveled end of a reinforcing strip so that the holes fall on the centerline of the strip, the first

hole 4 inches up from the end of the strip. Butt scraps of ¼-inch plywood against the strip—most importantly along both edges and at one end, as shown—and tack them to the thicker plywood with brads. **(Photo 2)** The strips need to be exact in placement rather than in their length.

Protect the bench top with expendable wood because it will be marred by drill-bit penetration. One-by-one, position the guide face down over the end of each strip and use the holes as guides for drilling three holes into the end of each strip.

Next, assemble the strips and bolt them together, first bundling them with masking tape. This frees both your hands for

assembly and tightening of fasteners; no clamp is needed. Be sure that the beveled end of each reinforcing strip is face up; use the 3½-inch bolts. **(Photo 3)**

Clamp the Strips to the Workbench

During assembly, clamp the components to the workbench so that they won't shift and the center strip won't bend or flex. The center strip is a reference that must remain straight during the construction of the trellis.

Position the strip bundle on your workbench close to an edge. (Or, lacking a large enough workbench, place the bundle on a sheet of plywood or an old flush door laid across a pair of sawhorses.) Clamp the bottom of the strip bundle to

Clamp the strip bundle to the edge of the workbench. *Also clamp the middle and top of the center strip in place, making sure it is straight.*

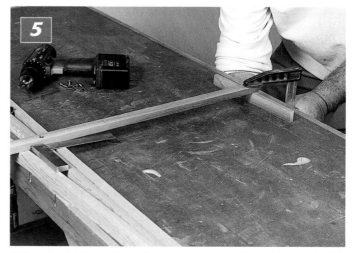

Align the bottom rib *to the center strip at the 31-in. mark. Slip a scrap piece of stock under its end, and clamp both to the workbench.*

Offset the middle rib from the bottom one, *using a 12-in. spacer. Center and screw it to the center strip, drilling a pilot hole first. Repeat for top rib, using a 13-in. spacer.*

Carefully bend the outer fan strip *to its mark at the end of top rib. Hold it in place while drilling a pilot hole and then driving a screw through both pieces.*

the bench, as shown. Then clamp the middle and top portions of the center strip in place. **(Photo 4)**

In clamping the middle of the center strip to the bench, you'll need to carefully bend the fan strips out of the way. While tightening the clamp, sight along the center strip, ensuring that it remains straight.

Attach Ribs to the Center Strip

Next, fasten the three ribs to the center strip. For now, don't worry about how long the ribs are.

With its 1-inch-wide face up, locate and mark the center point of each rib. While working with the top rib, consult the "Top Rib Layout" drawing, and measure and mark the specified strip intersections in relation to the center of the top rib.

On the center strip, make a mark 31 inches up from the bottom, as shown in "Front Elevation," page 60. Center the bottom rib over the center strip, aligning its lower edge with the 31-inch mark on the strip. While holding them together, countersink a pilot hole through the rib into the strip, and then drive a screw through both. Use a square to align the rib at a right angle to the strip, pivoting the rib on the screw to line it up. To hold that angle, slide a scrap of working stock under the end of the rib, and clamp both to the opposite edge of the workbench. **(Photo 5)** This will keep the rib square with the strip, even while you are bending the outer strips in the next step.

Before placing the middle and top ribs, cut two plywood spacers, one of them 12 inches wide, the other 13 inches wide. Place the 12-

inch spacer onto the strips, its lower edge tight against the bottom rib. Lay the middle rib, marked side up, against the top edge of this spacer, aligning the center points of the rib and center strip. Drill a pilot hole, and drive a screw, fastening the rib to the center strip. **(Photo 6)** Check that the middle rib is square to the center strip, and then clamp one end to the workbench, just as you did the bottom rib.

Placing the 13-inch spacer tight against the middle rib, attach the top rib, marked side up, in the same way described for the middle rib. Check it for square, and clamp its end to the bench.

Fasten Strips to the Top Rib

Let the bending begin! You need to flex the four fan strips into position in relation

Bend the next strip over to the second mark on the top rib, and fasten it in place as you did the outer fan strip. Repeat the process, securing the strips to the top rib's other half.

Attach the middle and bottom ribs. Center each rib to the center strip; screw them in place; and check for square. Where ribs cross strips, screw them together.

to markings on the 1-inch-wide face of the top rib. (See "Top Rib Layout," below.) Exactly where the strips will intersect the lower two ribs depends upon the flexibility of the wood. For now, be concerned only with attaching the strips to the top rib.

Grasp the top of an outer fan strip, and slowly bend and slide it toward the outermost mark on that half of the top rib. **(Photo 7)** Avoid yanking the strip, which could snap it near the bottom, at the reinforcing strip. When the fan strip reaches the mark, hold the pieces together tightly while you drill a pilot hole through the the center of the rib into the center of the strip. Still holding the pieces together, lay the drill aside and use the driver to screw the two parts together.

Bend and fasten the next fan strip to the next mark on the top rib. **(Photo 8)** Here the risk of breaking this strip is not as great because it doesn't have to bend as much as the outside strip did. Repeat this process to fasten the remaining fan strips to the other half of the top rib. Remove the rib spacers.

Fasten Strips to Remaining Ribs

Fasten the strips to the middle and bottom ribs, at whatever points they cross, again drilling pilot holes and driving screws. **(Photo 9)** Unclamp the trellis from the workbench.

Trim rib ends parallel with the contour of the strip. With the rib side down, measure and mark the cutting lines as indicated in the text, and then use a saber saw to make the cuts.

Trim the Ribs

With the trellis rib side down, trim the rib ends parallel with the outer strips. In trimming them, progressively increase, from the bottom rib to the top one, the measurement between the outer strip and the end of the rib. These measure about 1½ inches at each end of the bottom rib, 3 inches at the ends of the middle rib, and 4½ inches at the ends

of the top rib. The angle of each cut roughly parallels the angle of the strip.

To make these cuts, measure and mark the specified distance out from the strip along both the top and bottom edges of every rib; connect these marks; and cut along those lines. **(Photo 10)**

Install the Trellis

Many times a fan trellis is staked into the ground a few inches from a wall with its upper portion fastened to the wall. A few screws set along the center strip of the trellis are usually adequate.

Make a stake from a 3-foot-long piece of pressure-treated 2x2, shaping one end to a point. Drive it into the ground, and have an assistant hold the trellis against the stake while you clamp it to the stake. Drive holes through both the trellis and stake for the 3-inch assembly bolts. Bolt the trellis to the stake, and then screw it to the wall using wall anchors as necessary.

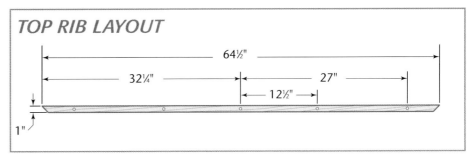

TOP RIB LAYOUT

64½"
32¼"
27"
12½"
1"

SIMPLE TRELLISES

A trellis on the side of a house, like a white picket fence, is an American icon. Sure, a simple base of thin strips is a good way to support climbing plants. But even without a vine on it, a trellis is a decorative element. Here are three simple trellis designs. One is contemporary in feel; the other two use a diamond pattern in their layout.

CONTEMPORARY TRELLIS EXPLODED VIEW

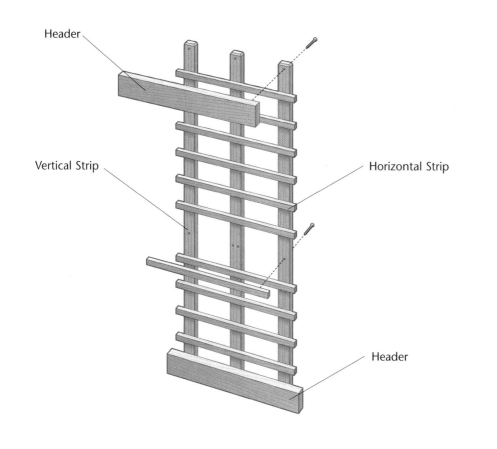

Header

Vertical Strip

Horizontal Strip

Header

SHOPPING LIST

CONTEMPORARY TRELLIS
- 1 pc. ⁵⁄₄×6 8' cypress
- 1 pc. 1×6 8' cypress
- 1 pc. 2×4 8' western red cedar
- 50 flathead stainless-steel screws, #6x1"

DIAMOND TRELLIS
- 1 pc. 2×6 8' Douglas fir
- ¾" stainless-steel brads

DOUBLE-DIAMOND TRELLIS
- 1 pc. 2×6 8' Douglas fir
- ¾" stainless-steel brads

CUTTING LIST

Part	Quantity	Thickness	Width	Length	Stock
CONTEMPORARY TRELLIS					
Horizontal strips	11	½"	1"	21½"	⁵⁄₄×6 cypress
Vertical strips	3	¾"	2"	49¾"	1× cypress
Headers	2	1½"	3½"	24½"	2× western red cedar
DIAMOND TRELLIS					
Horizontal strips	6	½"	1¼"	24¼"	2× Douglas fir
Vertical strips	5	½"	1¼"	48"	2× Douglas fir
Diamond strips	4	½"	1¼"	14⁹⁄₁₆"	2× Douglas fir
DOUBLE-DIAMOND TRELLIS					
Horizontal strips	6	½"	1¼"	24¼"	2× Douglas fir
Vertical strips	5	½"	1¼"	54¾"	2× Douglas fir
Diamond strips	8	½"	1¼"	8⅜"	2× Douglas fir

FRONT, SIDE, AND BACK ELEVATIONS

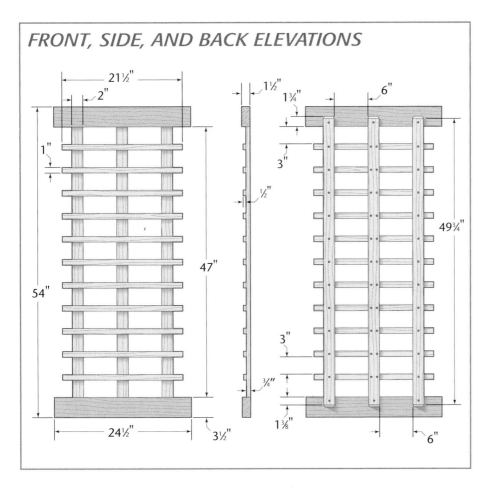

BUILDER'S NOTES

The three trellises in this section feature basic joinery and straightforward construction techniques. With good stock and the right tools, each project should require no more than a few hours of work.

Materials
Home centers don't carry the wood strips that these trellises require, so you'll need to rip stock or have the home center do it. Use stock that is straight-grained and free of defects. Do not use scrap wood. Scrap tends to be twisted and bowed, making square, flat trellis patterns difficult to achieve. Split or damaged scrap wood simply looks bad.

Many types of wood are suit-able for trellises. If you plan to paint a trellis and maintain its finish over the years, even pine can last. But an unfin-ished trellis will weather well only if it is made of weather-resistant wood such as western red cedar, redwood, cypress, and white oak, or tropical woods such as teak, mahogany, and ipé.

Tools and Techniques
You'll use a table saw to make any of these trellises (a bench-top model is perfect). For the Contemporary Trellis, you'll also need to use a plunge router to cut dadoes into the headers of the trellis. Constructing and using a dadoing jig (pages 68-69) will make this step easier and more accurate.

Using the table saw, you'll rip the stock into thin strips and then crosscut them to length. (Reminder: Rip cuts run with the grain. Crosscuts run across the grain.)

Other tools include: a ham-mer, miter saw, saber saw, framing square, drill-driver, and a few clamps. You'll save time if you have two drill-drivers—one fitted with a countersinking bit, the other fitted with a screwdriver bit. To create a large flat work surface, you can use a sheet of plywood or a flush door supported by two sawhorses.

Finish
I did not finish the Contem-porary Trellis. I used white paint for the other two.

STEP-BY-STEP

Here you'll find instructions for building three trellises: the Contemporary Trellis, Diamond Trellis, and Double-Diamond Trellis. All are easy to make. When you're constructing either the Diamond or Double-Diamond Trellis, you'll need to refer back to some of the instructions given here for the Contemporary Trellis.

CONTEMPORARY TRELLIS

Cut the Parts
Rip and crosscut the stock to produce all of the pieces to the dimensions given in the Cutting List. **(Photo 1)** Cut the 11 horizontal strips from ¾-by cypress stock, the three verticals from one-by cypress stock, and the two headers from two-by western red cedar stock. When ripping the stock, use a pusher to feed the wood near the blade. (See "Table Saw Pusher," page 60.)

Prepare for Assembly
From ¾-inch scrap, cut two gauges, each having square corners and measuring 3 inches wide by 9¾ inches long. Clamp one gauge to the workbench as shown in Photo 2. Place horizontal strips against both long sides of the gauge, and align the ends of the strips flush with its end. Apply a clamp across the strips and gauge, thereby immobilizing them. Next, place the center vertical strip across the slats. Because there are 11 horizontal slats, one of the first two that you clamp to the work-bench should be the middle slat, and it should sit equidistant from the ends of the vertical. Adjust the alignment of the verti-cal accordingly.

Drill pilot holes for two screws through the center vertical and into each horizontal. Space the screw holes as far apart as practi-cal so that the screws will hold the pieces square and tight to each other. Be careful not to split the wood. Before driving the screws, lift the vertical strip and apply a dot of con-struction adhesive to the horizontal. Re-lay the vertical, and drive the screws. **(Photo 2)**

Add the Remaining Horizontal Strips
Keeping the gauge clamped in place and stepping the trellis assembly over it, posi-

Here is a way to crosscut several strips at a time. Clamp them together with all their ends aligned. Clamp a guide piece across them, and cut them to length using a saber saw.

Clamp two horizontals against the gauge, their ends flush with its narrow end. Lay the center vertical across the horizontal pieces, tight against the gauge. Fasten with glue and screws.

To add more horizontals, unclamp and step the trellis assembly over the gauge, and position and align the next strip. Clamp the new strip in place, and glue and screw it to the vertical strip.

Shorten the gauges, and use them to place the outer verticals. Set the gauges tight against the center vertical and the new verticals against the gauges. Fasten verticals to horizontals.

tion and join the rest of the horizontals to the center vertical in the same manner as the first two. **(Photo 3)** If you want, you can clamp the second gauge to the workbench and place more slats at one time.

Attach the Remaining Verticals

To help you position the two remaining verticals, recut the gauges to measure 6 inches long. Fit the shortened gauges tight against the center vertical and between the last two horizontals on each end of the trellis. Lay the outside vertical on the horizontal slats, and push it firmly against the gauges. (They are slightly higher than the slats.) Position the vertical to ensure that it extends the same distance above and below the last horizontal at each end. With

a pencil, scribe along both sides of the vertical onto each slat.

Remove the vertical; apply adhesive to each horizontal between the pencil lines. **(Photo 4)** Carefully reposition the vertical between the pencil marks, taking care not to smear the adhesive on portions that will show from the front of the finished trellis. Drill a pilot hole, and drive one screw through the vertical into each horizontal.

Move the two gauges to the other edge of the center vertical strip, and repeat the process to attach the last vertical.

Cut Dados into the Headers

The two headers are dadoed (grooved) to fit over the ends of the three verticals so that when joined, the back of each header is flush with the backs of the verticals.

Each dado should be ¾ inch deep by 2 inches wide by 1¾ inches long.

Typically, dados are made by guiding the router along a T-square or a straight-edge clamped to the work. That's fine, if the cut extends from edge to edge on the work and is no wider than the bit diameter. But the Contemporary Trellis calls for six stopped dados that, at 2 inches wide each, can't be cut in a single pass. Also, four of the cuts are close to the ends of the headers.

The solution is to make a dadoing jig like the one on pages 68–69. Set up with a ¾-inch template guide and a ½-inch straight bit, the plunge router rides on the broad fences. The router's cylindrical template guide slides along the insides of the fences, preventing the router from

Attach the first fence to the crossbar with a single screw, pivoting the fence on the screw until it is square with the crossbar. Then drive additional screws to lock it in place.

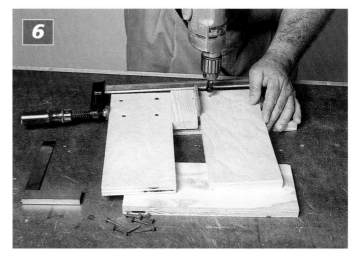

To position the second fence, secure a scrap of the stock used for the verticals and a piece of ¼-in. hardboard between the fences. Clamp the fence, and fasten it to the crossbar.

Mark the positions for the dados on each header. Wrong side up, center and butt the trellis against a header. Scribe locations of verticals onto the header, extending the lines as needed.

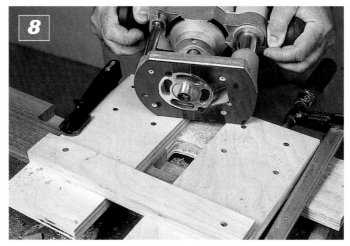

Cut dados into each header using a plunge router and the dadoing jig. The cylindrical template guide rides along the jig's fences. The bit plunges through the guide to make the cut.

Attach a header to each end of the trellis. Add adhesive in each dado; gently push verticals into them, using a mallet if necessary. Measure to keep the gap between the header and first strip equal.

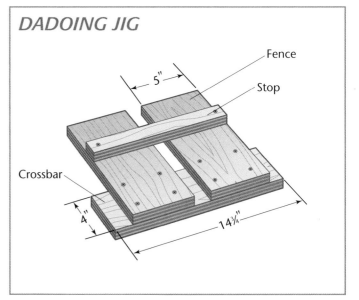

DADOING JIG

Fence
Stop
5"
Crossbar
4"
14¾"

making the cut too wide. A wooden stop screwed to the fences stops the router from cutting too far and making the cut in the header too long. With the first dado cut, you will also cut out the jig's crossbar, matching the width of the dado. Use this cutout to position the jig against layout lines for other header cuts.

To make the dadoing jig, cut the crossbar, fences, and stop to the dimensions specified in the drawing. Attach the first fence to the crossbar, making its guide edge perpendicular to the crossbar. **(Photo 5)**. Position the second fence to make the dados the correct width. (The distance between fences is the width of the dado plus two times the offset distance.) Use a scrap of vertical stock plus a piece of ¼-inch hardboard as a spacer when mounting the second fence. **(Photo 6)**. Then screw this fence to the crossbar.

Next you will position the stop. Make a test cut along the guides. You will cut into the crossbar. This cut will help determine where to position the stop so that you can make dados that are the correct length for

this project. (See Photo 8.) Its position will vary depending on the dimensions and configuration of your router. If your test dado is the correct width and length, you're ready to make the dados in the trellis headers.

Begin by locating the position of the stopped dados. Working with the back side of the trellis facing up, center a header at one end of the trellis, butting it against the ends of the vertical strips. Scribe along both sides of each vertical, marking its position on the header. Use a square to extend the pencil marks as needed. **(Photo 7)** Repeat this process with the other header at the opposite end of the trellis.

Set up your plunge router with a ¾-inch-diameter template guide and a ½-inch straight bit. Align the edges of the cut in the jig's crossbar with the pencil layout lines. Place the jig over the header so that the header's penciled cut lines align with the insides of the jig's two fences. Clamp the jig and the header to the bench top; then clamp the header against the crossbar.

Set the router onto the jig; bottom the bit against the header; and zero out the depth of cut. Then dial in a ¾-inch plunge depth. Make the cut, guided by the jig, in depth increments of about ⅛ inch. **(Photo 8)** Upon completion, shift the jig to the next dado layout,

and cut it as you did the first one. When the three dados are cut into the header, repeat this process on the second header.

Attach the Headers

Lay a header on the workbench, with dados facing up. Apply a little construction adhesive in the bottom of each dado. With the back side of the trellis facing up, fit the ends of the vertical strips into the dados. If the fit is snug, use a mallet to gently drive the parts together. Because the corners of the dados are rounded, you won't be able to seat the vertical strips all the way into the dados. **(Photo 9)** Instead, make the gap between the header and the first horizontal strip equal to those between the other strips. Then fasten the header in place, using one screw per vertical strip. Repeat this process for mounting the second header to the other end of the trellis, and you're finished.

DIAMOND TRELLIS

Although different in design from the Contemporary Trellis, the Diamond Trellis is constructed using some of the same methods.

Begin by ripping and crosscutting all of the parts needed for the Diamond Trellis, referring to the Cutting List for measurements and quantities. **(Photo 10)** Use a framing square and precisely cut spacers to position the horizontal and vertical pieces for the trellis. Refer to the measurements given in "Building the Diamond Trellis," page 70, for placing them. Cut ten 3-inch-square spacers

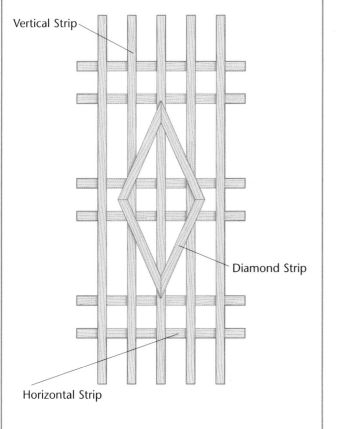

DIAMOND TRELLIS ELEVATION

Vertical Strip

Diamond Strip

Horizontal Strip

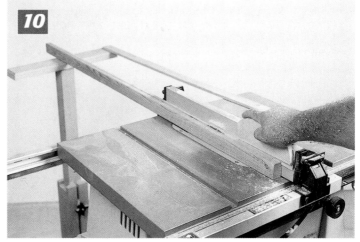

10

When ripping stock for the long trellis pieces, position an outfeed stand to support the work as you cut it. This way you won't have to struggle to hold the work down while finishing the cut.

BUILDING THE DIAMOND TRELLIS

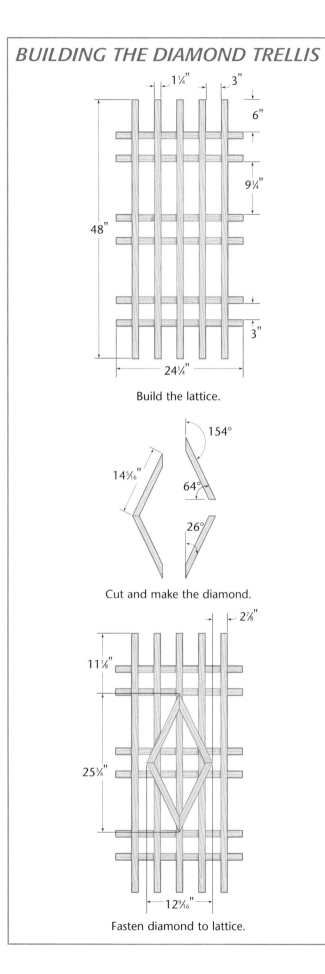

Build the lattice.

Cut and make the diamond.

Fasten diamond to lattice.

Assemble the lattice. *Set a vertical against a framing square; use spacers for placing the others. Fasten sets of horizontal slats square with the verticals. Flip the trellis to attach the diamond.*

Use caution when cutting *the steep miters for the diamond. Clamp a square guide to the table and the workpiece to the guide. Tape two pieces together and cut to speed the process.*

Attach diamond to the lattice. *Glue and tape it together; position it on the lattice; and add glue at the points where it will sit on the verticals. Fasten it in place. Remove tape when glue's dry.*

from scrap; use them to help in placing the strips. Assemble the trellis one joint at a time, using glue and brads rather than screws. **(Photo 11)**

The new element in this trellis is the diamond. Its dimensions and proportions require two different miters, as shown in the second drawing of "Building the Diamond Trellis." The steep-angled one is a challenge to cut, but all of the miters can be cut on a power miter saw or with a saber saw. **(Photo 12)** Once you cut them, you glue them together and hold them in place with masking tape until the glue sets. Then you can center the assembled diamond onto the front of the trellis, as shown in the third drawing, and fasten it in place. **(Photo 13)**

DOUBLE-DIAMOND TRELLIS

To build the Double-Diamond Trellis, use the same techniques given for making the Contemporary and the Diamond versions. Refer to the Cutting List on page 65 for the measurements and quantities of pieces. Place the pieces as shown in the drawings below.

Its design is similar to that of the Diamond Trellis. What differs is that the middle horizontal slats are placed farther apart; there are two diamond shapes on the lattice; and most of the vertical strip behind the diamonds is removed using a backsaw or dovetail saw. **(Photo 14)**

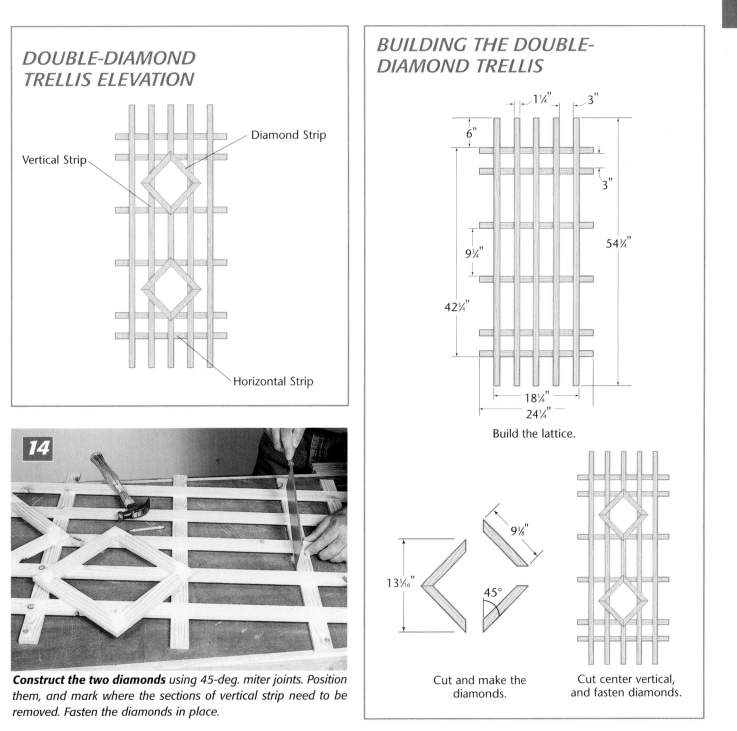

DOUBLE-DIAMOND TRELLIS ELEVATION

Diamond Strip

Vertical Strip

Horizontal Strip

14

Construct the two diamonds using 45-deg. miter joints. Position them, and mark where the sections of vertical strip need to be removed. Fasten the diamonds in place.

BUILDING THE DOUBLE-DIAMOND TRELLIS

1¼" 3"

6"

3"

9¾"

54¾"

42¾"

18¼"

24¼"

Build the lattice.

9⅜"

13⁵⁄₁₆"

45°

Cut and make the diamonds.

Cut center vertical, and fasten diamonds.

DESIGNER TRELLIS

Graceful curves at top and bottom and vertical lines set at a slight angle might lead you to assume that this trellis is tricky to build. After all, multiple arcs and oblique angles aren't as easy as square framing and a "tic-tac-toe" latticework. Yet, with basic power tools and methodical work, you can create this elegant trellis in just a few hours.

EXPLODED VIEW

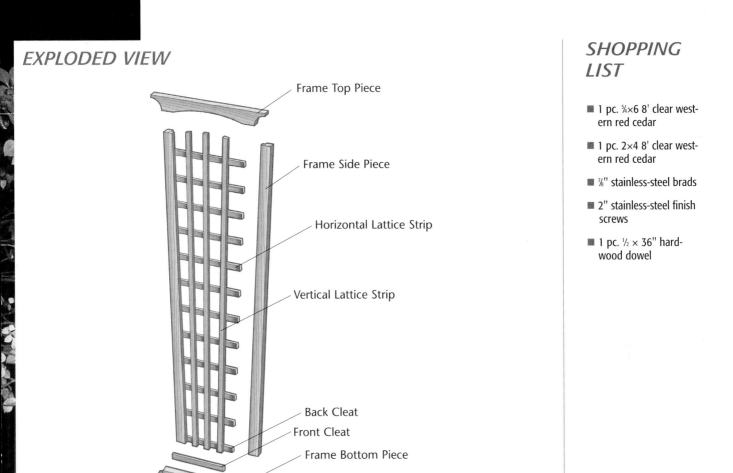

Frame Top Piece

Frame Side Piece

Horizontal Lattice Strip

Vertical Lattice Strip

Back Cleat

Front Cleat

Frame Bottom Piece

SHOPPING LIST

- 1 pc. ¾×6 8' clear western red cedar

- 1 pc. 2×4 8' clear western red cedar

- ⅞" stainless-steel brads

- 2" stainless-steel finish screws

- 1 pc. ½ × 36" hardwood dowel

CUTTING LIST

Part	Quantity	Thickness	Width	Length	Cedar Stock
Frame side pieces	2	1"	1½"	48½"	⁵/₄×6
Frame top piece	1	1½"	2½"	21¼"	2×4
Frame bottom piece	1	1½"	1½"	15"	2×4
Horizontal lattice strips	11	¼"	1"	13¾"*	⁵/₄×6
Vertical lattice strips	3	¼"	1"	50"*	⁵/₄×6
Back cleat	1	½"	½"	10³/₁₆"*	⁵/₄×6
Front cleat	1	½"	½"	9³/₁₆"*	⁵/₄×6

*Will be trimmed to fit later on

FRONT AND BACK ELEVATIONS

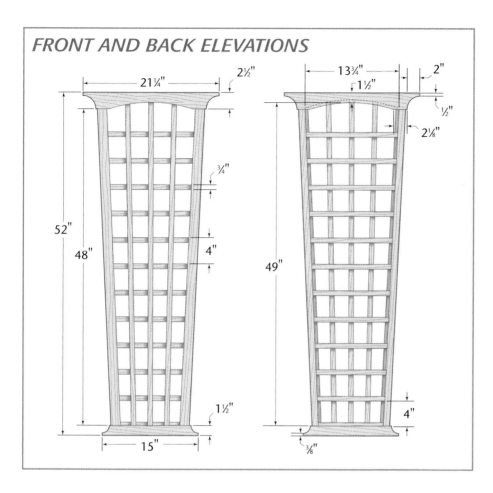

BUILDER'S NOTES

Even though some of the techniques may be new to you, they are relatively easy to execute. Just address them one at a time. Begin by making and using templates for the shaped top and bottom pieces. Then fasten them to the trellis's side pieces, and add the horizontal and vertical lattice strips.

Materials

I built this trellis from widely available western red cedar. Other suitable woods include redwood, cypress, white oak, mahogany, and teak. For best results, select clear stock. If you choose redwood, cedar, or white oak, also use stainless-steel fasteners. Tannins in these woods react with iron and produce black stains.

Because the side pieces are narrow, I needed to space closely the assembly screws that enter the end grain of the sides. To accomplish this, I used finish screws, which have small heads. These allowed me to get by with ¼-inch-diameter counterbores. Self-drilling screws are ideal for this; the point bores a pilot and the threads pull the screw into the wood.

For the top and bottom templates, I used medium-density fiberboard (MDF) because it doesn't warp and it yields crisp, smooth edges on which router-bit pilot bearings can ride. You probably won't need to buy a full 4x8 sheet of MDF; most home centers stock 2 x 4-foot pieces.

Tools and Techniques

You'll need a table saw, a router, a saber saw, and a drill-driver. One simple but effective construction technique that is used in this project deserves note here:

You will assemble the trellis's frame with screws that pass through the top and bottom pieces and penetrate the ends of the sides. Screws, however, don't hold well in end grain, so to ensure that they get a secure hold, you'll need to put dowels into the sides. You'll set the dowels perpendicular to the grain of the sides, so that when a screw bites into one, it holds. The dowels are ordinary, but in this instance, they add strength to the joint.

STEP-BY-STEP

Make the Top and Bottom Templates

The shaped top and bottom pieces of the trellis frame are cut from pieces of 2×4 cedar. The most reliable and accurate way to cut out these parts is with a router guided by a template that is the exact shape you want.

Begin by cutting template blanks to the rectangular dimensions shown in the drawings "Making Top Template" and "Making Bottom Template," opposite. Mark pivots for the end arcs. At each pivot, drill a ⅛-inch-diameter hole through the template. Clamp the template and an underlying piece of scrap wood to the workbench.

For the end arcs, use either a fixed-base or a plunge router. The radius of each cut (2 inches for the top piece and 1⅛ inches for the bottom piece) is shorter than the router baseplate's radius, so the center point of the arc is on the router's baseplate. Hook your tape over the bit, and measure off the radius for each arc. (Be sure the router is unplugged first.) At each spot, drill a hole into the baseplate just large enough to firmly hold a finishing nail. When you are ready to actually cut a radius, drive or press a nail (as in Photo 1), from which you have cut the head, into the pivot hole.

Rout the end arcs. **(Photo 1)** If you use a fixed-base router, set the bit for a cut ⅛-inch deep. Mount the router base pivot pin, and while placing the router on the template, insert the pin into the template pivot hole. Switch on the router, and guide it through the arcs. After switching off the router and adjusting the bit deeper, cut again. Repeat this process until you've cut through the template. (If you use a plunge router, you increase depth at each end of the arc without shutting it off.)

With the end arcs cut, prepare to cut the long center arc for the top template. For this you'll need to create a trammel from a long strip of ¼-inch plywood, as shown in Photo 2. Drill a hole at one end of the trammel for the bit to protrude through. Then apply several patches of double-faced carpet tape to the router's baseplate to affix the baseplate to the trammel.

The trammel pivots on a screw driven into scrap wood clamped to the worktable. Mark the pivot point, as in "Making Top Template"; drill a pilot; and screw the trammel to the scrap. To cut this arc **(Photo 2)**, employ the

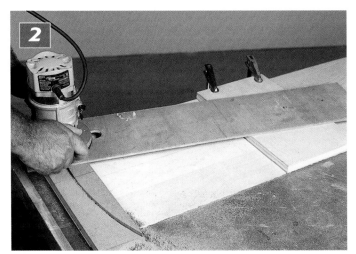

Cut end arcs with a router, *guided by a pivot pin (headless nail) set in the base. To locate pivot point, measure the length of the arc's radius from the unplugged router's bit. Drill the hole for pin.*

Cut the center arc of the top piece *with a router and simple trammel. Screw the trammel to a scrap plywood base, and swing it back and forth on the pivot to make the cut.*

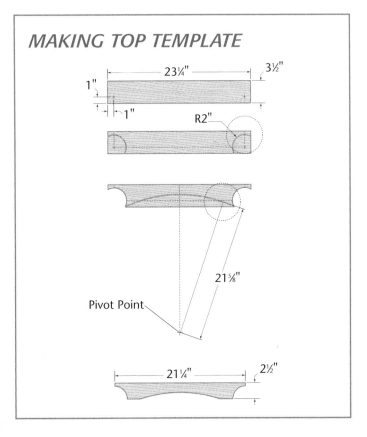

MAKING TOP TEMPLATE

MAKING BOTTOM TEMPLATE

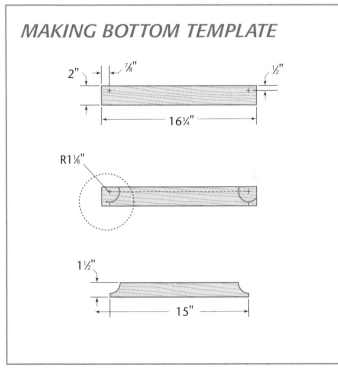

same incremental ⅛-inch increases in cutting-depth that you used for the end arcs.

To complete each template, cut it to final dimensions trimming equal amounts from each end.

Shape the Frame Top and Bottom

With the templates completed, ready the cedar blanks for cutting into the top and bottom pieces. Crosscut them from a 2x4,

and rip each to the correct width. Trace the shape of the template onto the appropriate blank. Then cut reasonably close to the arcs with a saber saw. (You'll use a router for the finish cuts.) Next, use screws to temporarily attach the template to the blank.

To set up your router, tighten the longest pattern bit you have into the router collet. Place the router on the template, and adjust it so that the bit's bearing makes contact only with the template, because you'll want its cutting

edges to cut only the cedar workpiece.

To prevent the router from tipping off of the work, use carpet tape to stick a scrap of MDF to a scrap of the two-by stock, and then stick both of them to the router's baseplate. This will support the "off board" portion of the router, holding it level and ensuring that you get a good cut.

In the unlikely event that you have a bit that is long enough to address the full edge in a single pass, set the work on an expendable piece of plywood or MDF and secure it with at least two clamps placed at one end of the work. What is more likely is

Rout the top piece flush with the template. *To support the router and keep it from tipping while you work, carpet-tape scraps of cedar and MDF to it.*

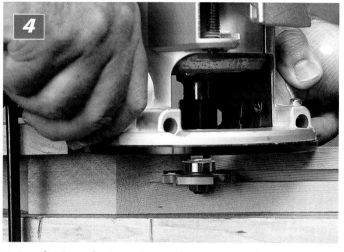

Cut a slot into the top piece *with a router and slot cutter, first clamping a piece of scrap to the work to stop the router where you want the cut to end.*

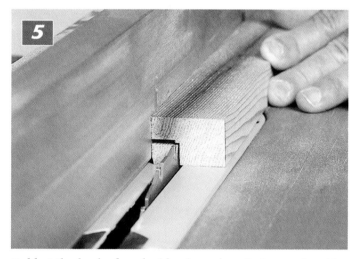

Rabbet the back of each side piece *along its inner edge. After a first cut with the work on edge, turn it onto its face and make a second cut at the same setting to complete the rabbet.*

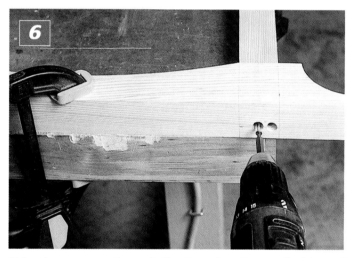

Drive two screws through the top piece *into each side and screw-holding dowels. Drill counterbores and pilot holes first. Clamp the parts to the benchtop to hold them while you work.*

that you will need to make the cut in two passes. Make one, and then remove the template. On the second pass, the bearing rides along the cut part of the edge while the bit trims the remainder of it.

When all is ready, plug in the router, set it on the work, and rout. **(Photo 3)** Cut as much of the part as you can, and then move the clamps and complete the part. Shape both the top and bottom pieces this way.

Prepare Top Piece for Lattice

In the arch of the top piece of the trellis, create a slot about 10 inches long to hold the vertical lattice strips. Rout the slot using a ¼-inch slot cutter, first adjusting the cutter so that it is ½ inch from the baseplate and the back face of the top piece of the trellis.

Lay out the slot by measuring out about 5 inches from each side of the middle. With its back side facing up, clamp the workpiece to the bench, and cut the slot. **(Photo 4)** The bearing on the cutter guides the router while ensuring a ½-inch-deep cut.

Make the Frame Sides

Cut the side pieces to their 1½-inch width from the ¾-by stock (which actually measures 1 inch thick.) Then use a power miter saw to crosscut the pieces to length, cutting each end at an 88-degree angle. Be sure to cut the ends of each side parallel to each other. These angled cuts are what produce the trellis's taper.

Before rabbeting the side pieces, install the screw-holding dowels mentioned in "Builder's Notes," page 74. Start by laying

out the sides, one canting to the left, the other to the right, and mark the faces and backs. Measure 1¼ inches up from the end of the inner edge of each side. At each of these spots, drill a hole 1¼-inch deep to receive a ½-inch-diameter dowel. Make sure that you don't drill all the way through to the outer edge of the side. Crosscut the dowel to produce four dowel pieces, each about 1½ inches long, and glue one into each hole. Drive the dowels, seating them. Cut off the protruding ends, and sand them flush with the side pieces.

Finally, rabbet the inner, back-face edges of the sides, using a table saw or a router with rabbeting bit. **(Photo 5)** The ½-inch-wide and -deep rabbet extends from top to bottom and cuts through the ends of the dowels.

Fasten the horizontal lattice strips to the trellis's sides with construction adhesive and stainless-steel brads. Hold the brads with a needle-nose pliers to drive them.

Install the center vertical strip first. Adjust the tops and bottoms of the outer strips until each visually splits the space between the center strip and its adjacent side piece.

TOP-TO-SIDE FASTENING

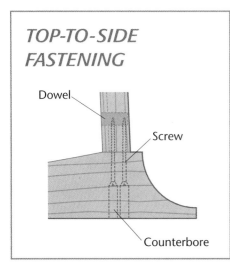

Dowel

Screw

Counterbore

Assemble the Trellis Frame

Lay the top piece and one side piece of the frame, face sides up, along adjoining edges of the workbench. Clamp the side, and then apply a bit of adhesive to its top end before firmly butting the top piece to it and clamping the top to the workbench. (The top piece is ½ inch thicker than the side piece, and so the plane of its face side will be ½ inch above the face of the side piece.) Lightly scribe screw-alignment lines on the face and top surfaces of the top piece. Then lay a screw on the lines to establish how deep your counterbores must be in order to allow three to four of the screw's threads to penetrate the dowel. (See illustration "Top-to-Side Fastening.") To make your counterbores, first mark the desired depth on the drill bit by wrapping it with a little masking tape.

Drill counterbores for two finish screws

at each end of the top piece. Then use a smaller-diameter bit, matching the screw's gauge, to extend the pilot holes into the dowels. Make sure the pilots are heading straight for the center of the dowel. Drive the screws with a long-shank screwdriver or screwdriver bit. **(Photo 6)** After joining the second side to the top in the same manner, join the bottom to the sides in the same way. Using a plug cutter, cut eight plugs from cedar scrap. Glue them into the counterbores; trim them flush.

Cut the Lattice Strips

Rip all of the ¼ × 1-inch horizontal and vertical lattice strips from ¾-by stock. Position an outfeed stand to receive stock and strips as they move off the saw table. For safety, use a pusher to clear the strips past the blade, keeping your hands well clear of it. (Typical blade guards need to be removed before cutting thin strips because they would otherwise conflict with the saw's rip fence and your pusher.)

Fit the Horizontal Strips

Because the frame is tapered, each horizontal lattice strip must be a different length. Position the top strip 4 inches from the crest of the arch and the remaining strips 4 inches on center. One by one, crosscut the strips to fit, first stepping back and looking to make sure that the strips will fit the taper of the trellis. Apply construction adhesive at the points where the strips will sit, press each into place, and drive a ⅛-inch stainless-steel brad at each end. **(Photo 7)** Before driving the

brads, slide an extra strip of lattice stock under the sides for support.

Fit the Vertical Strips

Cut the front and back cleats. Measure across the frame's back side from rabbet to rabbet, and trim the back cleat to fit. Apply adhesive to the bottom of the strip; fit it into the rabbets, pressing it firmly to the trellis's bottom piece. Fasten in place, using three or four stainless-steel brads.

Fit the vertical strips. Measure the distance from the center of the arch on the frame's top piece down to the frame's bottom piece. Cut the center vertical strip ½ inch longer than this measured distance (to account for the ½-inch-deep slot in the top piece). With the trellis face down, fit this strip into the slot, dead center and perpendicular to the top and bottom pieces. Then drive a brad through the back of the top piece, securing the strip in place. Turn the trellis face up; drive a brad, at a slight angle, through the lower end of the vertical strip and into the bottom.

Position the remaining verticals parallel with the sides of the trellis and equidistant between the trellis's side and center vertical strip. Cut the strips, angling their top ends to fit. Attach them to the top and bottom pieces as you did the center strip. **(Photo 8)**

Measure across the front of the frame along the bottom, and trim the front cleat to fit. Glue the front cleat in the same manner as the back cleat. Round out the ends of the cleats at the frame's sides.

More Wall-Mounted Trellis Ideas

The area around a trellis is often as important as the trellis itself. Simple wall-mounted trellises, above left, get a boost from colorful hydrangeas planted at their base. While waiting for the climbing plants to take hold, the owners added a hanging basket to help decorate the blank wall at left.

Use trellises to frame windows and doors. Simple lattice panels placed between windows, above, serve as a path for climbing roses. A basic lattice pattern, above right, matches a simple climbing ivy. Combine trellises and window boxes to surround a bank of windows with plants, right.

An old window frame placed in the center of a trellis, top left, becomes a unique garden decoration. The lines of the trellis, top middle, will make an interesting pattern when the plant dies back during the winter. Wall-mounted trellises, such as the one shown top right, let you cover an entire wall with plants. An interesting design technique is to combine trellises with garden statues and other accents, right. In the end, it's the plant you choose to grow on your trellis that becomes the focal point of your yard, left.

TRELLIS WALL

trellis wall is an elegant way to screen in space— under a deck, as shown here, between posts of a pergola, or even between free-standing posts set in a specific spot of a yard. This trellis is strong enough to support the heaviest of climbing plants, and its two "windows" provide spaces for hanging flowering plants as color accents.

EXPLODED VIEW

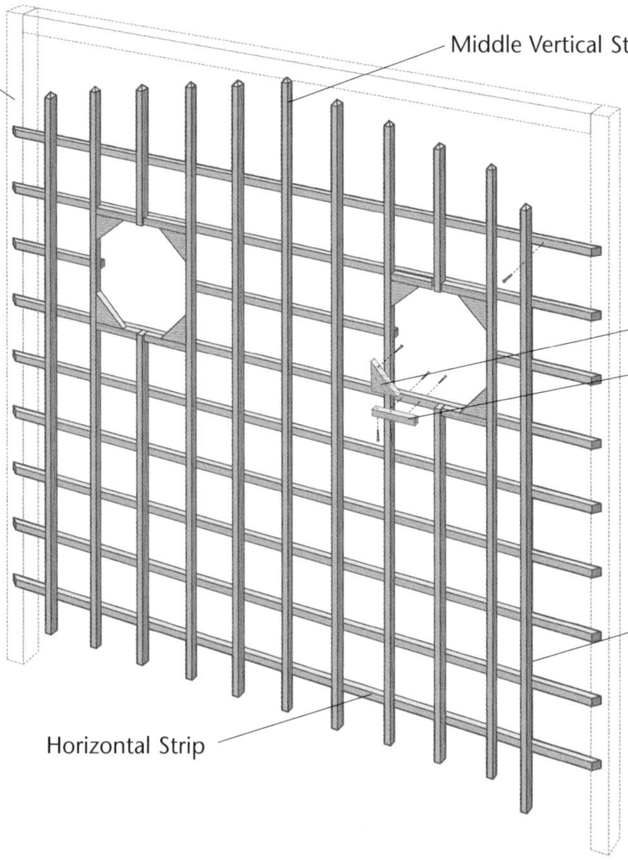

SHOPPING LIST

- 7 pcs. $\frac{5}{4}$x6 8' treated southern yellow pine
- 3" deck screws
- 2" deck screws
- $1\frac{5}{8}$" deck screws

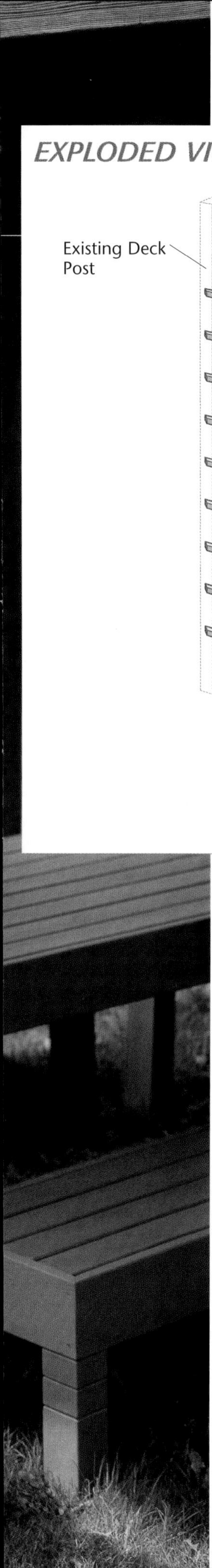

CUTTING LIST

Part	Quantity	Thickness	Width	Length*	SYP** Stock
Horizontal strips	9	1"	$1\frac{1}{2}$"	96"	$\frac{5}{4}$×6
Middle vertical strip	1	1"	1"	$86\frac{1}{4}$"	$\frac{5}{4}$×6
Vertical strips	2	1"	$1\frac{1}{2}$"	$84\frac{15}{16}$"	$\frac{5}{4}$×6
Vertical strips	2	1"	1"	$83\frac{7}{16}$"	$\frac{5}{4}$×6
Vertical strips	2	1"	$1\frac{1}{2}$"	$81\frac{15}{16}$"	$\frac{5}{4}$×6
Vertical strips	2	1"	1"	$80\frac{7}{16}$"	$\frac{5}{4}$×6
Vertical strips	2	1"	$1\frac{1}{2}$"	$78\frac{15}{16}$"	$\frac{5}{4}$×6
Blocking strips	8	1"	$1\frac{1}{2}$"	7"	$\frac{5}{4}$×6
Triangles	8	1"	4"	4"	$\frac{5}{4}$×6

*These are the lengths for this particular project. Yours will depend on the spacing of the deck posts and the height of the deck.

**Southern yellow pine

FRONT ELEVATION, PLAN VIEW

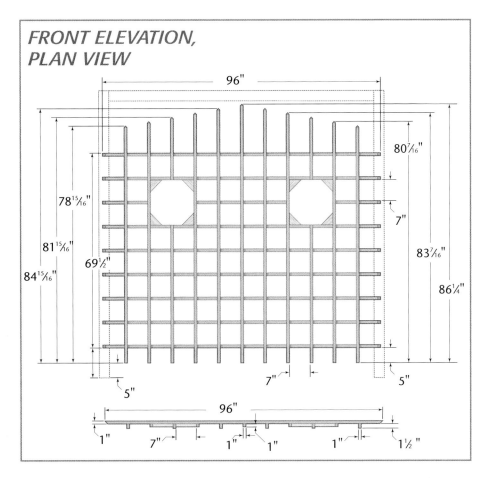

BUILDER'S NOTES

The trellis wall made for this project is large enough to screen an 8 × 8-foot space under an existing deck, and is mounted to the deck posts. If the area you want to screen is of a different height or width, adjust the dimensions and number of slats accordingly.

Materials
The horizontal and vertical strips (or slats) for the lattice can be ripped from a number of woods. Those shown here are from ¾ pine decking, which is 1 inch thick and 5½ inches wide and has eased (rounded) edges. (Actual measurements may vary slightly from one board to another.) Because the slats for the trellis will be no wider

than 1½ inches, be sure to select boards that are free of big knots.

Treated southern yellow pine is prone to bowing, crooking, and twisting, especially when ripped into thin strips. To minimize the chance of this happening, rip the stock and install the strips the same day. Galvanized mounting screws will keep them from warping; for additional holding power you can apply construction adhesive.

Tools and Techniques
You'll need a table saw or a bench-top model to rip the stock, and a power miter saw (preferred), circular saw, or saber saw for the crosscuts. You may be tempted to think

that you can crosscut the slats on a table saw, but it's neither practical nor safe to attempt to hold one end of an 8-foot-long piece against a miter gauge while sliding the wood to make the cuts. Instead, hold the strip in position and cut it with a moving saw.

To assemble the trellis wall, you'll need a level, a drill-driver or two, several clamps, spacer gauges, and a vertical gauge. (See illustration on page 86.)

Finish
The trellis shown has no finish. You can, however, apply a water repellent, solid-color stain, or paint, but it will be difficult to refinish once a vine has been established on the latticework.

STEP-BY-STEP

Rip Stock into Strips
The biggest job in this project is ripping the stock into the vertical and horizontal strips that will form the lattice of the trellis wall. For strip measurements and quantities, refer to the Cutting List, page 83.

Rip the stock into slats, and assemble them the same day. If you let even a day pass, at least one or two will dry and twist and become unusable.

I worked outdoors using a bench-top saw mounted on a portable table; 4 feet away from that I set up an outfeed stand as a support for the stock. **(Photo1)** To begin with, I ripped the eased (rounded) edges from each piece of stock as waste. Then I ripped the stock into the required number of 1½-inch-wide horizontal strips and some of the verticals. After that I ripped the stock into enough 1-inch-wide strips to produce the total number necessary for the verticals.

Shape Ends of Strips
The tops of the vertical strips have four miters each, somewhat like tiny hip roofs. This looks good and helps them shed water. To provide a pleasing transition where the horizontal strips end against the posts, I mitered their tips, as well.

For miter cuts, use a power miter saw—a chop saw, a compound miter saw, or a sliding compound miter saw. (A saber saw or a circular saw would be a satisfactory alternative.) All are faster and safer than attempting miter cuts on a table saw. Because the workpieces are all 8 feet long, you will also need an outfeed support, beyond the saw's small table. **(Photo 2)**

Cut an opposing 45-degree miter at each end of every horizontal strip. Keep the strips the same length but as long as possible.

Begin the quadruple miter on the top end of each vertical strip with a 45-degree miter cut. Square a guideline across the edge of the strip from the shoulder of the miter. For the second cut, line up the saw blade at the square line, and cut, forming a miniature "gable roof." **(Photo 3)** Then turn the vertical strip one-quarter turn; line up the blade at the shoulder line; and make a third 45-degree miter cut. Give the board a half-turn to cut the fourth miter.

Leave the bottom ends of the vertical strips uncut for now. You will trim them to length during assembly.

Attach the Bottom Horizontal Strip

On one post, establish the location for the bottom horizontal strip. For this project there is a 5-inch ground clearance under the trellis assembly, and the vertical strips will extend 5 inches below the bottom horizontal strip for a total of 10 inches. (See "Front Elevation," page 84.) But you can determine your own measurements. In any case, working from the ground up, transfer that combined measurement to the one post, marking it with a horizontal line.

Determine the exact placement of the ends of the horizontal strips on the posts. If the strips aren't long enough to extend from one post's outside edge to the other, which is the situation I faced here, center one between them and mark those vertical lines on both posts to align the ends.

Clamp a scrap of wood under the horizontal mark to support one end of the bottom horizontal strip. Slide it over until its end reaches the vertical mark. Hold the strip approximately level, and secure its end to the post so that it won't fall.

Move to the opposite, free end, and with a level resting on the strip, raise or lower this end until the strip is level. **(Photo 4)** Drill a set of pilot holes, and then drive 2-inch mounting screws to fasten the horizontal strip to the post. Two drill-drivers, one with a pilot hole bit and the other with a screwdriver bit, will make the rest of the assembly process much easier.

Return to the other end of the horizontal strip; remove any clamps; drill pilot holes; and drive the mounting screws. Remove the temporary supports. The bottom strip is in place.

Install Remaining Horizontal Strips

With the bottom horizontal strip level, the remaining eight strips can go up quickly. To accurately space the distance between them, you'll need two scrap-wood gauges, each 7 inches square, as illustrated on page 86.

Place a gauge atop each end of the bottom horizontal strip, aligning the vertical edge of each gauge with the end of the strip and clamping each gauge to its post.

Set the next horizontal strip on top of the two gauges, aligning their ends with

Ripping treated stock *into strips is best done outdoors. Several feet away from the saw, set up an outfeed stand on which the stock can rest. Weight the stand's base.*

Miter the ends of the strips. *If possible, use a power miter saw; a saber saw is a good substitute. These cuts are easier and safer to make with a moving blade rather than a stationary one.*

Shape the top *of each vertical with four miter cuts. For the second cut, align the blade on a line squared from the shoulder of the initial miter across the edge.*

Level the bottom horizontal strip *before fastening it to the posts. Prop its far end on a block clamped to the post; monitor the level as you raise then fasten the near end to its post. Fasten the other end.*

Position subsequent horizontal strips using 7-in.-square gauges. Set one on each end of the strip just installed, clamped to the post. Put the new strip atop the gauges, and fasten both its ends.

Hang the middle vertical strip on the top horizontal, using as a catch a clamped-on block at the set distance the vertical is to project above the horizontal. Plumb the vertical, and clamp it in place.

the outside edges of the gauges. Clamp the one end of the strip so it won't fall off while you drill and fasten its other end. **(Photo 5)** Then unclamp the free end, and fasten it in place. Remove both gauges.

Repeat the above process for the other horizontal strips. Every two or three strips, check for level to ensure that you aren't inadvertently moving out of level.

Attach the First Vertical Strip

The vertical strips are mounted to the fronts of the horizontal strips and the middle (tallest) one is the first to be secured. As shown in the illustration "Plan View," page 84, the middle vertical strip and every other one of them measures 1-inch-square. The remaining strips are 1½ inches wide. To avoid

mix-ups, arrange the verticals on each side of you in the order that you will install them.

Before mounting the middle vertical strip to the horizontals, determine its exact length. Hook your measuring tape onto the lower edge of the bottom horizontal strip, and measure to the top of the top horizontal strip. To that dimension, add the distance you plan to have the verticals extend below the bottom horizontal and the distance you want the middle vertical to project above the top horizontal strip. Crosscut the bottom of the middle vertical strip to the length you just calculated.

Measure and mark the top projection of the vertical strip. On that mark, clamp the end of a small scrap of slat, extending toward the tip.

Measure from post to post along the top horizontal strip, marking its midpoint. Offset this center mark equally, ½ inch on each side, which establishes edge marks for aligning the middle vertical strip.

Hang the vertical strip on the top horizontal, employing the scrap cleat as a hook, and clamp it in place just snugly enough so that it doesn't fall off while you plumb it, using a level. **(Photo 6)** Confirm plumb at the bottom of the vertical strip and there apply a second clamp.

So the screw heads won't show, move around to the back side of the assembly to drill pilot holes and drive a 1⅝-inch galvanized screw through each horizontal strip and into the middle vertical. **(Photo 7)**

Install Remaining Vertical Strips

To position and mount the remaining vertical strips to the horizontals, cut a vertical gauge 7 inches wide by 2 to 3 feet long with one end mitered at 79 degrees, as in the illustration at left. **(Photo 8)**

Position the gauge on the lattice with the high corner of its mitered end flush with the mitered shoulder of the middle vertical strip. Then clamp the gauge to two of the horizontal strips. You'll need to position these clamps over the middle vertical so that they won't interfere with the positioning of the next vertical strip against the opposite edge of the gauge.

In determining the length of the second vertical strip, you already know the measurement from the top horizontal to the bottom one (top to bottom) and the distance the

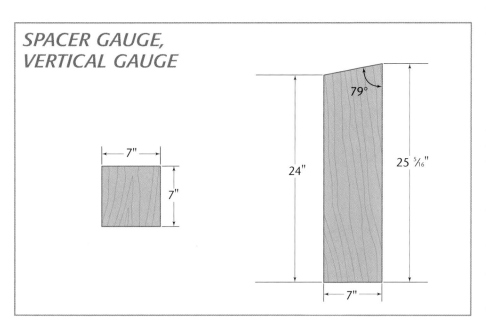

SPACER GAUGE, VERTICAL GAUGE

7"

7"

79°

24"

25 ⁵⁄₁₆"

7"

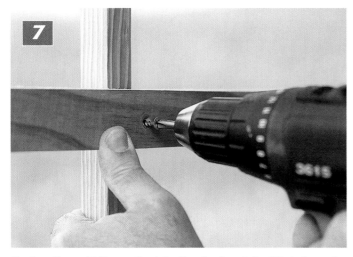

Fasten the middle vertical to the horizontals. *Work from the back side of the lattice, driving 1⅝-in. screws through the horizontal into the vertical. Always drill pilot holes first.*

Make and use a gauge *for placing the remaining vertical strips. Use ½-in. plywood, and cut it 7 in. wide by 2 ft. long. Miter one 7-in.-wide end at 79 deg.*

Clamp vertical gauge *to horizontals, its upper corner at shoulder of fastened vertical's miter, its lower at shoulder of next vertical's miter. Use a 7-in. gauge to align lower part, and clamp in place.*

Make openings *by removing a piece from a horizontal and a vertical strip. Use the rocking motion described below. Cut the vertical from the front of the lattice; the horizontal, from the back.*

verticals will extend below the bottom horizontal. You still need to determine the amount that the second vertical strip will extend above the top horizontal. For that, measure from the top horizontal to the lower corner of the mitered end of the gauge. Add that to the other measurements to arrive at the length of the next vertical strip.

Again, alternating cross-sectional dimensions, the second vertical strip is placed with its 1-inch face to the horizontals. After measuring and cutting it, position it with its 1-inch face against the horizontals, tight against the gauge, the shoulder of its "hip roof" tip aligned with the lower of the mitered corners of the gauge. Clamp the vertical to a couple of horizontals. Then clamp a 7-inch-square spacer gauge farther down. **(Photo 9)** With some verticals, it may

be helpful to apply clamps across the gauges in order to pull the vertical strip to align with the one adjacent to it.

When you've lined up the vertical strip, move around to the back side of the lattice for fastening. Drill pilots, and drive 2-inch screws through all the intersections of the vertical with the horizontals. Use longer screws on the wider verticals.

All of the remaining vertical strips are sized and mounted in the same way. Remember to alternate the 1-inch-square verticals (and 1⅝-inch screws) with the 1½-inch-wide verticals (and 2-inch screws).

Cut the "Windows"

In this project, the two square openings, "windows" for hanging plants, are at about eye level and equidistant from the posts.

But you could position them anywhere on the lattice—one high and one low, for example. Or you could make them rectangular instead.

To form a "window," just cut away the segments of the horizontal and vertical slats that cross the space. In marking the pieces you will cut, use a square to scribe cut lines across the three sides that will be visible to you while cutting.

Use a saber saw to cut one vertical in two places and the intersecting horizontal in two places. Save the removed pieces for the blocking of the window brackets. To cut the vertical from the front of the lattice, place the base of the saber saw on the narrow side of the strip. **(Photo 10)** Rock the saw back so that the blade initially cuts the back corner. As the blade creates a kerf, you can

Assemble corner brackets. *Hold parts, blocking side up, in a work-bench vise. It helps to first tape parts together. Drill two pilot holes; then drive 3-in. screws through the blocking into the triangle.*

Install corner brackets. *From the back side, drive 1⅝-inch screws through horizontal strip into the blocking, then a 2-in. screw diagonally through triangle into the vertical. Drill pilots first.*

press the saw's baseplate against the strip. But as you approach the end of the cut, tilt the saw forward a bit to keep the blade and its tip in the kerf. This will help keep the blade from catching the adjacent strip and pushing the saw toward you abruptly.

Move around to the back side of the lattice to cut the horizontal, following essentially the same procedure used to cut the vertical.

Make the Corner Brackets

Corner brackets in the openings provide a design accent, breaking the predictable pattern created by the slats. The brackets are triangles of ¾ stock that seat against the vertical strips. However, to support them on the horizontals you'll need additional blocking.

For the blocking, cut eight 7-inch-long strips from the stock used for the horizontal strips. You can recycle the waste you cut from the openings, though you'll need a bit more than that.

For the eight triangles, rip a 24-inch-long piece of ¾ stock to 4 inches wide, removing the rounded edges. Swing your miter saw to 45 degrees and cut a triangle from each end of this piece, giving you two triangles with two 4-inch edges. Return the saw to 90 degrees, and moving the stock up 4 inches, crosscut both ends of the stock to give you two more triangles. Repeat to get four more triangles.

Assemble the brackets by screwing a strip of blocking to each triangle. There's no convenient way to clamp these parts together. With the grain of the triangle

parallel with that of the blocking, I held them together with masking tape and, blocking side up, secured the unit in a workbench vise. I drilled two pilot holes and then drove 3-inch screws through the blocking into the triangle. **(Photo 11)**

Install the Brackets

One by one, clamp each bracket into place and fasten it. Mount each bracket onto the back side of the lattice by drilling two pilot holes and driving two screws through the horizontal strips into the blocking. Then drill a pilot hole and

one screw through the edge of the triangle into the vertical strip, as shown. **(Photo 12)** Use 1⅝-inch screws to fasten the blocking to the horizontal strip and a 2-inch screw to join the triangle to the vertical.

With all the brackets in place, the trellis is done—except for hanging some plants in the "windows" or planting some vines or climbing roses. If you wish to apply a finish, consider the fact that renewing it in a few years may be difficult once a network of vine has been established.

CORNER BRACKET DETAIL

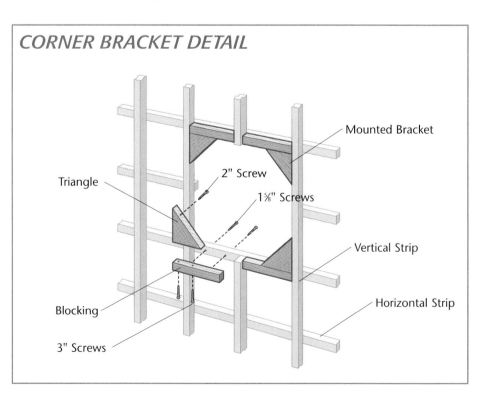

Mounted Bracket

Triangle

2" Screw

1⅝" Screws

Vertical Strip

Blocking

Horizontal Strip

3" Screws

Trellis Wall on Freestanding Posts

Besides serving as screening under a deck, this trellis wall can be supported by freestanding posts and be a focal point or a backdrop for a flowerbed. Here are some guidelines for making a freestanding trellis wall. To construct the lattice, refer to the specific step-by-step instructions within this project. For more complete instructions on installing posts, see "Grape Arbor," pages 142–149.

• Use 4x4 treated posts that are long enough for the needed wall height plus the depth into the ground.

• Follow local building codes when digging the postholes.

• The measurement between the outside edges of the posts should equal the length of the horizontal strips. If the posts are slightly farther apart, adjust by centering the strips back from the post edges. If they're slightly closer together, trim excess beyond the posts.

• Stand each post in its hole, and extend a temporary brace from about midheight to a stake driven into the ground about 5 feet from the post. Use one screw to fasten the bottom of the brace to its stake, but don't yet attach the brace to the post. Install a second brace at a right angle to the first, attaching it to the post about a foot above or below the first. After plumbing the post with a level, fasten the braces to the post.

• Set the posts in concrete. Use a small trowel to slope the top of the concrete away from the post. This will ensure proper rain runoff.

• After the posts have set, trim their tops. To do this, mark one post and carry the line across to the other post using a line or water level. Chamfer the tops to a point in the manner described for the verticals so that water doesn't collect there. (See "Shape Ends of Strips," page 84.)

• Let the posts set at least overnight before constructing the latticework.

TRELLIS WALL

TRELLIS WALL FASTENED TO FREESTANDING POSTS

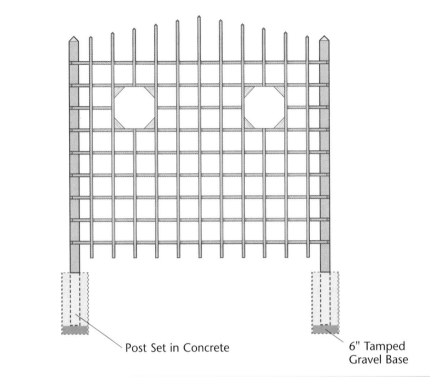

Post Set in Concrete

6" Tamped Gravel Base

TEMPORARY BRACING OF A POST

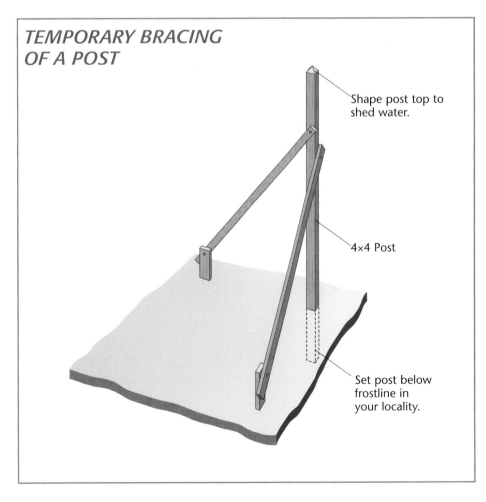

Shape post top to shed water.

4×4 Post

Set post below frostline in your locality.

TOWER TRELLIS

Shaped like an obelisk, this tower serves both as a plant trellis and a garden focal point, its pyramidal copper cap requiring just a little "tin knocking." The dark meranti mahogany of the frame contrasts pleasingly with the cypress of the woven stock, although you could use other woods to achieve a similar effect.

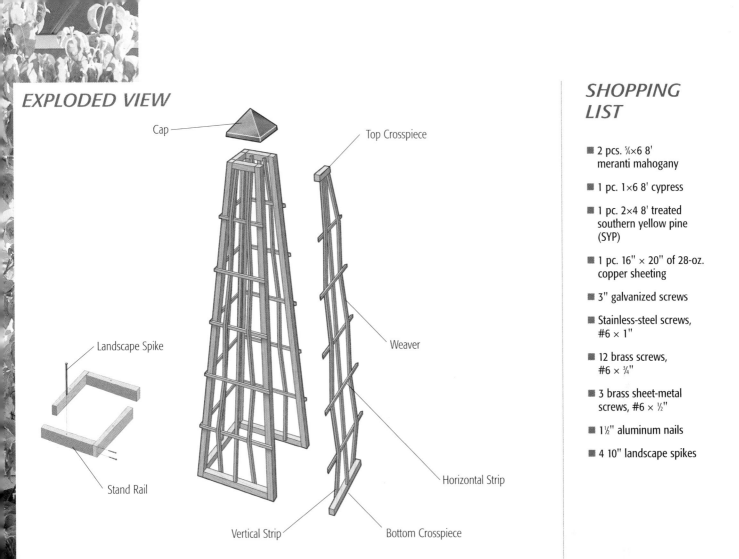

EXPLODED VIEW

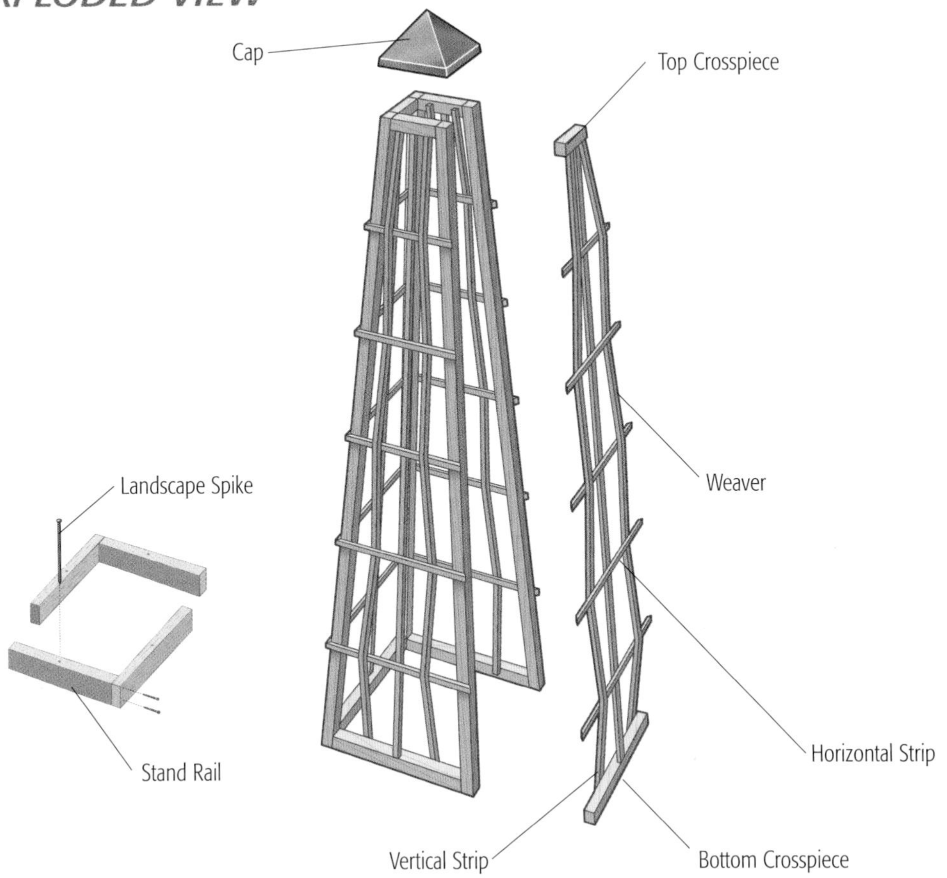

SHOPPING LIST

- 2 pcs. 5/4×6 8' meranti mahogany
- 1 pc. 1×6 8' cypress
- 1 pc. 2×4 8' treated southern yellow pine (SYP)
- 1 pc. 16" × 20" of 28-oz. copper sheeting
- 3" galvanized screws
- Stainless-steel screws, #6 × 1"
- 12 brass screws, #6 × ¾"
- 3 brass sheet-metal screws, #6 × ½"
- 1½" aluminum nails
- 4 10" landscape spikes

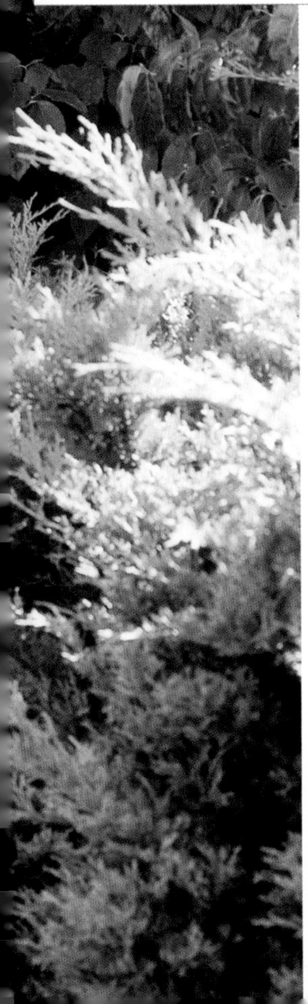

CUTTING LIST

Part	Quantity	Thickness	Width	Length	Stock
Corner posts	4	1 1/16"	1 1/16"	73"	5/4×6 meranti
Top crosspieces	4	1 1/16"	1 1/16"	7¾"	5/4×6 meranti
Bottom crosspieces	4	1 1/16"	1 1/16"	18"	5/4×6 meranti
Horizontal strips	4	½"	½"	12⅜"*	5/4×6 meranti
Horizontal strips	4	½"	½"	14⅛"*	5/4×6 meranti
Horizontal strips	4	½"	½"	15⅞"*	5/4×6 meranti
Horizontal strips	4	½"	½"	17⅝"*	5/4×6 meranti
Horizontal strips	4	½"	½"	19⅜"*	5/4×6 meranti
Vertical strips	2	½"	⅝"	69¾"*	5/4×6 meranti
Vertical strips	2	½"	⅝"	70⅝"*	5/4x6 meranti
Weavers	8	⅜"	½"	96"**	1×6 cypress
Stand rails	4	1½"	3½"	19½"	2×4 SYP

*Most likely finished measurement; will be trimmed to fit

**Working length and trimmed once in place

FRONT AND SIDE ELEVATIONS

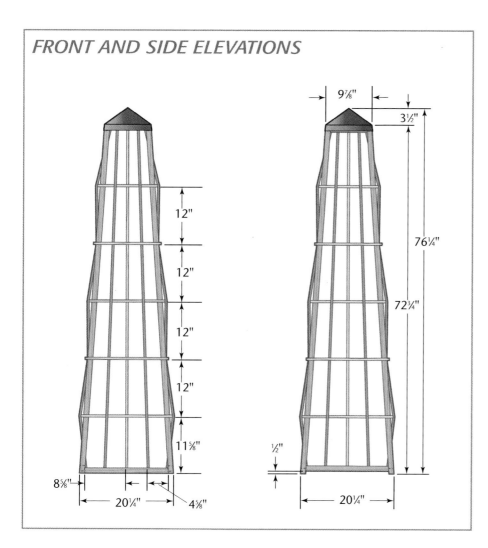

BUILDER'S NOTES

There are no elaborate joinery cuts in this project, but it does require miters and compound miters.

Materials

This project employs woods of contrasting hues that are relatively decay resistant. Most of the tower is of meranti mahogany; the weavers are of cypress. You could instead use redwood for the meranti or combine western red cedar and white oak.

I chose to use 28-ounce copper sheeting for the cap. I checked roofing and building supply entries in the classified section of the phone book to locate a source. You could instead use other sheet metal, such as aluminum flashing. Before tackling the pricey copper, I practiced cutting and bending on less expensive aluminum flashing. If you use copper, diligent shopping should also lead you to copper escutcheon pins (nails, really) to fasten the cap to the tower.

Tools and Techniques

All parts in the tapered frames are mitered, and most of the lattice pieces are compound-mitered. You can cut all the pieces using a table saw, but a compound miter saw will make the crosscutting easier.

The only special tool required for making the copper cap is a pair of straight-cutting aviation snips. I used a special sheet-metal seamer to fold the tabs, but you can fold against a scrap piece of hardwood, the same way you will make other bends.

Finish

The tower can be varnished, stained, or painted, but do it before you install the cap. The trellis may be hard to refinish once it's covered with vines.

STEP-BY-STEP

Rip the Frame and Lattice Stock

The majority of the tower's parts are cut from two 8-foot lengths of ¾-by stock. The tower frame, consisting of four posts and eight crosspieces, comes from one of these 8-footers; the horizontal and vertical strips for the lattice are ripped from the second 8-footer. At this point in the process, cut the stock into strips of the correct thickness and width, not length.

Most table saws, especially bench-top models, have a blade guard that interferes with ripping the stock into narrow strips. And while ripping stock, you need to use a pusher that is narrow enough to pass between the blade and fence to clear the work as you complete the cut. If the blade guard prevents this, you will need to remove it. (For help in making a table saw pusher from scrap wood, see page 60.)

Cut the first board into five square strips for the framing. Because of the length of the board, you must have good outfeed support for the stock behind the table saw. Measure the thickness of the stock, and set the rip fence that distance from the blade. **(Photo 1)** Methodically rip the board into the five square strips. Set these aside.

Using the second 8-footer, rip the lattice material next. Each of the horizontal strips will be ½ inch square. Simply rip ½-inch strips off the ¾-by board, and then one by one, turn a strip on its side and rip it in half. If your strips end up being slightly off, it will be okay.

Set the rip fence ½ inch from the blade. Rip at least eight strips from the board and be sure to use the pusher. Next, lower the blade and rerip only four of the strips in half. You probably will need to reset the fence for this cut. From the resulting eight strips, each 8 feet long, you should be able to cut all of the horizontal lattice pieces, but set them aside for now.

Use the four remaining ½-inch-by-¾ strips to produce the four vertical strips for the lattice, each ½ inch by ⅜ inch. Reset the rip fence to ⅜ inch, turn each strip on its side, and rip them to a ⅜-inch width.

You need eight weavers of a contrasting wood, ripped slightly thinner than the lattice strips you just cut. Rip these eight ⅜-inch-by-½ strips from the cypress.

Cut five square framing lengths by first measuring the stock thickness and setting the rip fence that distance from the blade. Use an outfeed stand to support the stock as it travels off the saw table.

Cut the posts and crosspieces. Use a sliding compound miter saw with its blade tilted to bevel the end of the stock. Cut each piece individually, or clamp four together and cut all in one pass.

Crosscut the Framing Strips

Next, crosscut four of the five framing strips to produce the four corner posts and the four bottom (long) crosspieces of the tower trellis. Use the fifth framing length for the four top (short) crosspieces.

Because each side of the tower frame is tapered, none of the frame pieces is cut square across. The angle is slight, but every post and crosspiece is crosscut on an angle, which allows the ends of the posts to be parallel with each other. Cut the ends of all the crosspieces at opposing angles so that they can fit flush against the four corner posts.

Using a compound miter saw, tilt the blade to 86 degrees, just 4 degrees off plumb. For each of the first four post pieces to be cut, begin by making a trim cut to clean the end and introduce the angle. Then slide the workpiece 73 inches across the saw table, and cut again to get one post. Roll the remaining piece 180 degrees, and slide it 18 inches across the saw table. Cut it, and the 18-inch-long piece becomes a bottom crosspiece. You can cut the four strips individually, or you can gang them together and cut them all at the same time. **(Photo 2)** Cut the fifth framing length into the four 7¾-inch-long top crosspieces, again cutting the ends at opposing 86-degree angles.

Assemble the first tapered frame, with crosspieces clamped between posts and assembly clamped to the bench. Countersink pilot holes through each post into the crosspiece; drive in screws.

Assemble the First Tapered Frame

Lay two corner posts on your workbench, positioning a top and a bottom crosspiece between them. Make sure that the parts are oriented properly, with the posts butted flat against the angled ends of the crosspieces. Apply dabs of glue to the ends of the crosspieces, and then press the posts against them. Clamp across the posts at the top and bottom of the tapered frame, pinching the crosspieces. Make sure that the clamp positions allow you room to drill pilot holes and drive screws.

Clamp the assembly to the bench top before drilling a pilot hole through each corner post into each crosspiece. **(Photo**

3) Then drive 3-inch galvanized screws. The clamps keep the assembly fixed when you drill and drive, while also holding it flat after you remove the clamps.

Cut and Attach Horizontal Lattice

Attach the horizontal lattice strips before fully assembling the tower. Fasten five cut-to-fit strips to each of two tapered frames, parallel with the bottom crosspieces and spaced 12 inches apart on center. Once the two tapered frames are joined by the remaining top and bottom crosspieces, set the remaining lattice strips across those two sides.

Lay out, cut, and then attach each horizontal lattice strip in sequence, beginning at the bottom of the first tapered frame. To make the positioning easy, especially after the first strip is in place, use a spacer gauge. From scrap plywood, cut a piece 11½ inches (the height of the gap between horizontal strips) by about 22 inches. If the piece isn't large enough to span the corner posts at the bottom of the tapered frame, as was mine, use a scrap piece of the post stock as a support between the two posts.

Align the gauge against the previous horizontal strip (or the bottom end of the frame for the first strip). Lay one of the ½-inch-square horizontal strips across the posts, tight to the top edge of the gauge. Using a pencil or a marking knife, scribe along the outside faces of the two corner posts onto the strip. **(Photo 4)**

Make a compound miter cut on each end of the strip. Tilt your compound miter saw to 45 degrees. For one end, you swivel the saw table to the right and lock it at 4 degrees. For the other end, you leave the blade tilted, but you swivel the saw table to the left 4 degrees. When you make the cuts, remember which way the miter is supposed to angle. **(Photo 5)** Cut the strip and check its fit on the frame. Trim it as needed. When it fits exactly, attach it to the frame.

Apply a little glue at each end of the strip; then set it in place, aligned with the post edges and seated against the gauge. Drill a pilot hole, countersinking it. **(Photo 6)** Make sure the hole is big enough for the screw. Otherwise, it is very easy to split the end. Then drive a mounting screw.

Work your way up the frame in this fashion until all five horizontal strips are fitted and mounted to the frame.

Assemble the Second Tapered Frame

Make the second frame duplicate the first one. Lay out the corner posts and top and bottom crosspieces for the second frame on top of the first one. Clamp the second frame's parts to the first frame and to each other. **(Photo 7)** Then add dabs of glue, drill pilot holes, and drive the four screws to join the ends of the crosspieces to the posts.

When that's done, separate the two frames. Then cut and mount the five horizontal strips one by one to the second tapered frame.

Join Frames to Form Tower

To form the full tower structure, join the remaining top and bottom crosspieces to the two tapered frames. For this, an extra pair of hands is helpful.

You'll need to stand the two frames on edge, but the projecting mitered corners of the horizontal strips make this impossible unless you rest the frames on two or three blocks to raise up the frames. Place a crosspiece between the frames at top and bottom, making sure that these pieces are dropped down from flush at the frame top and bottom, as in "Assembly Sequence," below, and Photo 8. Clamp the frames to capture the crosspieces.

Carefully turn the tower over 180 degrees, and clamp the last two crosspieces. If you rest the crosspieces on the blocking, it is easier to align them and apply clamps. Drill pilot holes, and drive the assembly screws. **(Photo 8)**

Cut and Attach Remaining Lattice Strips

Most of the lattice strips remain to be cut to length and attached to the tower, including half of the horizontal strips and all of the vertical ones. Cut the remaining horizontal lattice strips first.

At this stage, you need to change your marking method slightly. You can't rest the lattice stock across the posts to mark it because of the already attached horizontal strips. Placing the stock on either side of the fastened strips wouldn't give you an accurate mark. So rest the stock on the tips of the installed lattice strips, and use a pencil to scribe along them. **(Photo 9)** Now you have the outside face of the cuts marked rather than the inside. But you will be able to see the marks as you operate your saw. Again, lay out, cut, and fasten the horizontal lattice strips one by one.

Cut and Install the Vertical Lattice Strips

With all of the horizontal lattice strips attached, cut and then install the four vertical strips to the inside of the structure, placing one in the center of each side of the tower trellis. Don't cut any of the strips without first measuring them in place on the structure.

Slide a vertical strip between the top and bottom crosspieces, and seat it

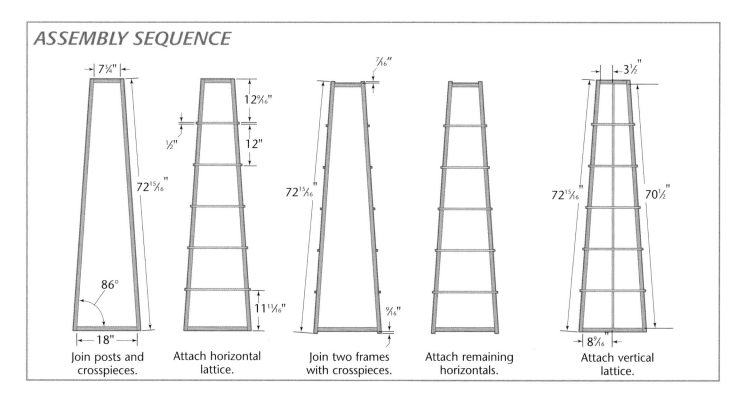

ASSEMBLY SEQUENCE

| Join posts and crosspieces. | Attach horizontal lattice. | Join two frames with crosspieces. | Attach remaining horizontals. | Attach vertical lattice. |

Position horizontal lattice strips using the 11½-in. spacer gauge. Butt the strip against the gauge, and scribe a cutting line onto the piece where it falls along the outside edge of each post.

Cut compound miters on ends of strips. To make the cuts, tilt the saw blade to 45 deg. Swing the saw table 4 deg. to the left to cut one end, and the same amount to the right to cut the other end.

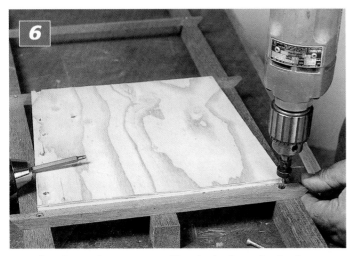

Use the plywood spacer to position the horizontal strips for mounting. Drill a countersunk pilot hole for one screw in each end, and fasten the strip. A pilot is needed so the screws won't split the wood.

Use the first tapered frame as a pattern for the second, clamping their posts together. Dab glue on the ends of the top and bottom crosspieces for the second frame; clamp and fasten them in place.

Position opposing tapered frames, and inset new crosspieces a bit low, so their screws will clear those in the assembled frames. Tape and clamp pieces together; drill pilots; and drive assembly screws.

Mark these horizontal lattice strips a bit differently than the first two sides of the tower. Rest the stock across the frame, and scribe along it to mark the outside ends of the cuts for the miters.

Position vertical strip, and then drill pilots for 1½-in. aluminum nails down through crosspieces into the ends of the vertical strip. First, dab glue on horizontal strips crossed by the vertical.

Rip thin weavers from a wood of a different hue, and weave them over and under the horizontal lattice strips. Use one hand to weave the lead end while feeding with your other hand.

against the horizontal strips. Make sure that the ½-inch-wide face is turned face out. Center the strip between the posts. Mark the inside face of each horizontal strip so that you can apply a dot of glue to each intersection with the vertical strip.

Move the vertical lattice strip aside enough to apply the glue to the horizontal strips, and then move the vertical strip back into position. Then, drill pilot holes and drive 1½-inch aluminum nails though the top and bottom crosspieces and into the top and bottom ends of the vertical lattice strip. **(Photo 10)** Repeat the process for the remaining vertical strips.

Install the Weavers

The weavers are lattice strips cut from wood of a contrasting hue. For this project they were cut from cypress stock. They are cut thin so that they will be flexible enough to bend under and over the rigid horizontal strips. The weavers were cut along with the other pieces. (See page 92.)

Start by placing a weaver inside the top or bottom cross-piece, and feed its lead end over the first horizontal lattice strip, under the next, over the third, and so on. Keep pushing the weaver, guiding it over and under the horizontal lattice pieces. When you've threaded the lead end under the cross-piece at the far end of the tower, stop.

Repeat the same process

with each of the seven remaining weavers. **(Photo 11)**

As you weave these strips on each side of the tower, slide the weavers left and right a bit to space them so that they look good. Trim the ends of the weavers flush with the top and bottom of the tower structure, and then tack them in place at each of the crosspieces.

Make the Cap

The cap for this tower trellis is made from a copper sheet purchased from a local roofing contractor. But you could use a less expensive sheet metal, such as aluminum, instead. In brief, you lay out the cap, make a few cuts using aviation snips, fold on the appropriate lines, and then drive screws into the metal to form a low pyramid. (Because copper is expensive, you might want to use aluminum sheeting to practice cutting and folding a cap first

before working with the copper sheeting.)

Begin by making a pattern using thin cardboard or office file folders. Refer to the drawing below, "Making the Cap." Cut four single segments to size, and then tape them together. For the last tab, the one that will slide under and become part of the final "hip" of the cap, you can either tape a 1⅛-inch-wide strip of paper onto the pattern or draw that tab onto the sheet metal itself.

Fold the pattern into a cap shape, and tape it so that it fits properly on the top of the tower trellis. If it does fit, you can unfold it and use it to mark the sheet metal. If not, make the necessary adjustments and test-fit it until it's right.

Lay the pattern flat on your sheet metal and, using a felt-tip pen, draw its shape onto the metal. These are your cutting lines. Set the pattern aside. Now, referring to the pattern, mark the hip fold lines and the tab fold lines with the aid of a 1⅛-inch-wide straightedge. This side of the sheet metal will be inside the cap, so the lines won't show. **(Photo 12)**

To separate the cap from the sheet, score and break the metal along the cutting lines. Place a straightedge along a cutting line, and draw the point of a utility knife along the marked line several times. Then carefully bend the metal on the scored line, wiggling it back and forth until it breaks. Use aviation snips to cut the wedge of waste from the cap.

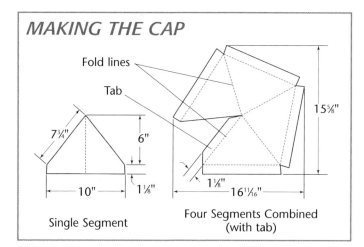

MAKING THE CAP

Fold lines

Tab

7¾"

6"

10"

1⅛"

Single Segment

15⅝"

1⅛"

16¹¹⁄₁₆"

Four Segments Combined (with tab)

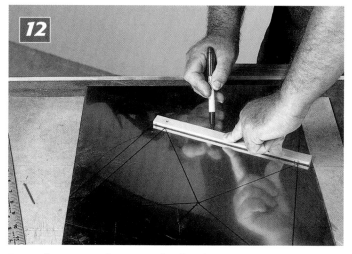

Draw the cap on sheet metal, *using the pattern you made. Use a felt-tip pen to mark cutting and fold lines and a 1⅛-in.-wide straightedge to check tab widths and draw lines between key points.*

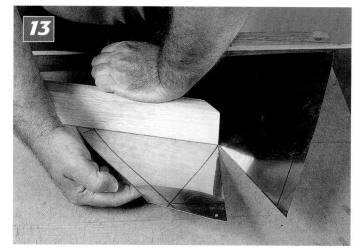

Fold the cap into shape using a straightedge. *Hold the straightedge firmly in place along a marked foldline, and use your other hand to lift up the sheet metal, bending it along the straightedge.*

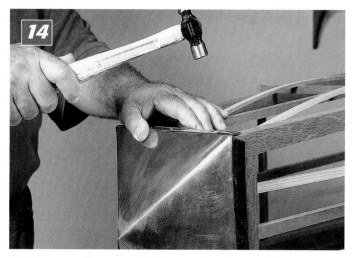

Fit the cap to the tower *with its eaves lapping over the crosspieces. Support the tower on a block of wood so that the weavers aren't damaged. Drill pilot holes; then drive the fasteners.*

Make and install a stand. *Cut the rails, and butt them up to each other, forming a simple frame. Secure with screws. Drill and countersink a hole for a spike in each rail. Spike the stand to ground.*

Next, bend roof hips into the cap, without folding the tabs yet. Start with the three main hips, using a straight mitered piece of hardwood as a brake. Lay the wood directly on the fold line of a hip, and hold it firmly in place while you work your free hand under the sheet metal and carefully bend the metal upward, along the line, creating a sharp hip. **(Photo 13)** To fold the tabs, I used a metal-bending tool called a seamer (similar to pliers), but you should be able to bend them against the piece of hardwood.

Fold the cap carefully to its intended shape, closing the open wedge and sliding its joint tab under the adjoining edge. Hold this joint together; rest it on a block of wood held in a vise; and then drill through the two layers of metal. To hold the joint closed, drive sheet-metal screws into the holes.

Fit the cap onto the top of the tower trellis; drill pilot holes through the metal and into the crosspieces; and nail or screw the cap to the tower. **(Photo 14)**

Make the Tower Stand

Unless you used treated wood to make the tower trellis, direct contact with the ground will significantly shorten its life. To ensure that the tower will last many years, create and install a stand of treated wood to buffer it from the ground. Use landscape spikes to hold the stand firmly to the ground.

Use an 8-foot-long 2x4 for the stand rails. Cut the stock to produce four rails, each measuring 19½ inches long. Given the true dimensions of this type of lumber,

each rail will be approximately 1½ inches thick by 3½ inches wide.

Stand the rails on their 1½-inch wide planes, and butt them up against each other to form a simple frame. Secure each butt joint with a pair of 3-inch screws, drilling pilot holes first. Then, at the center of each of the four rails of the frame, drill and countersink a hole for a landscape spike.

Set the frame on the ground, leveling it as necessary. Insert a landscape spike in the center of each rail, and then using a mallet, drive each spike into the ground. **(Photo 15)**

Set the tower trellis atop the buffer stand; center it; and screw the stand to the frame, drilling pilots in the bottom crosspieces first to avoid splitting the wood.

TRELLIS BENCH

With sheltering lattice and climbing vines, this bench can serve as both a garden focal point and a cozy, shaded retreat. Simple to make, the entire project consists of treated wood connected with galvanized screws.

EXPLODED VIEW

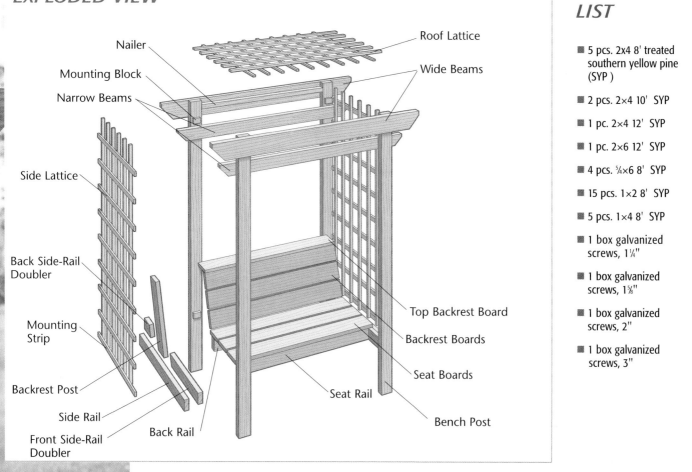

Nailer

Mounting Block

Narrow Beams

Roof Lattice

Wide Beams

Side Lattice

Back Side-Rail
Doubler

Mounting
Strip

Backrest Post

Side Rail

Front Side-Rail
Doubler

Back Rail

Seat Rail

Top Backrest Board

Backrest Boards

Seat Boards

Bench Post

SHOPPING LIST

- 5 pcs. 2x4 8' treated southern yellow pine (SYP)
- 2 pcs. 2×4 10' SYP
- 1 pc. 2×4 12' SYP
- 1 pc. 2×6 12' SYP
- 4 pcs. ⁵⁄₄×6 8' SYP
- 15 pcs. 1×2 8' SYP
- 5 pcs. 1×4 8' SYP
- 1 box galvanized screws, 1¼"
- 1 box galvanized screws, 1⅝"
- 1 box galvanized screws, 2"
- 1 box galvanized screws, 3"

CUTTING LIST

Part	Quantity	Thickness	Width	Length	Treated SYP Stock
Bench posts	4	1½"	3½"	84"	2×4
Wide beams	2	1½"	5½"	69½"	2×6
Narrow beams	2	1½"	3½"	61¾"	2×4
Side rails	2	1½"	3½"	33⅝"	2×4
Back rail	1	1½"	3½"	47½"	2×4
Seat rail	1	1½"	3½"	47½"	2×4
Backrest posts	2	1½"	3½"	23⁷⁄₁₆"	2×4
Back side-rail doubler	2	1½"	3½"	4⁹⁄₁₆"	2×4
Front side-rail doubler	2	1½"	3½"	26⁵⁄₁₆"	2×4
Seat boards	3	1"	5½"	50½"	⁵⁄₄×6
Backrest boards	3	1"	5½"	47½"	⁵⁄₄×6
Top backrest board	1	1"	5½"	47½"	⁵⁄₄×6

Cutting list continues on page 104

TRELLIS BENCH ELEVATIONS

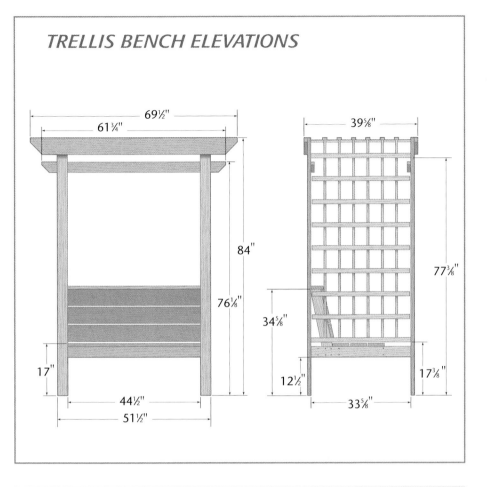

BUILDER'S NOTES

You can build this project in a weekend using materials that are readily available at most home centers.

Materials
I used treated southern yellow pine. You need 2x4s, a 2x6, some ¾ boards, and one-by stock for the lattice strips.

Where I shopped, I found 1x4s, 1x6s, and 1x2s. Some home centers, however, do not stock one-by lumber because it warps readily. So, bear potential warping in mind when you shop and when you work. Remember also that commercial lumber designations indicate dimensions before milling. For

example, nominal 1x2s are actually ¾ x 1½ inches, the same dimensions as several of the pieces for this project. Using 1x2 stock will save the time needed to rip larger boards. For the ¾-inch-square parts, I ripped 1x4s (actually ¾ x 3½ inches). If you can't find one-by stock, you can rip two-by stock into the ¾-inch strips.

During assembly, you will need to make several gauges from plywood or hardboard to act as spacers when placing the strips that make up the lattice. I used scraps of various thicknesses. If you need to buy material for spacers, buy a precut quarter-sheet of hardboard. It's flat and inexpensive.

Tools and Techniques
I didn't need many tools. I used a circular saw, a drill-driver, a pair of sawhorses, several clamps, and typical layout tools, such as measuring tape, square, and pencil. If you can't buy one-by lumber for the lattice strips, you will need a table saw to rip larger stock.

Except for the lattice strips, you can crosscut all the parts with a circular saw or a saber saw. For this, you'll appreciate an adjustable speed square. The speed square was designed primarily for layout work. But clamped to the workpiece, it is sturdy enough to serve as a saw guide, both for crosscuts and the project's miter cuts.

STEP-BY-STEP

Construct Post-and-Beam Assemblies

You need four bench posts cut from 2x4s, two narrow beams cut from 2x4s, and two wide beams cut from 2x6s.

Miter the top corners of the four beams at 45 degrees, offsetting the miters as specified in "Post-and-Beam Assembly," next page.

You need two post-and-beam assemblies—one for the front of the trellis bench and a second for the back. To set up, position two sawhorses about 6 feet apart. If the sawhorses are less than 5 feet long, extend the length of one sawhorse by laying an extra 2x4 on top of it.

Scribe square lines across the wide beam 9 inches in from each end. Lay a bench post to the inside of each line, with its top end flush with the top edge of the 2x6 beam. Square each post to the beam, and clamp each post to the beam and sawhorse. Check the assembly for square by measuring from the outside top of one post to the outside foot of the other post. Repeat this measurement for the other diagonal. If the measurements are equal, the assembly is square. **(Photo 1)**

To fasten the bench posts to the beam, drill pilot holes for four 2-inch screws at each joint, countersinking deeply.

Then place a narrow 2x4 beam on top of the posts, aligning it in relation to the post tops and the post edges as specified in "Post-and-Beam Assembly," next page. Attach it with four countersunk screws. Build the other post-and-beam assembly

Cut the Seat Frame Parts

Cut all seat frame parts from 2x4 stock: the two side rails, the back and seat rails, the two backrest posts, and the four doublers. (Refer to "Backrest Post Layout" and "Seat Frame Construction," page 102.)

Square-cut the rail ends to the lengths specified on the cutting list. Square cut the ends of the side rails and the back and seat rails, but cut the ends of the backrest posts and one end of each doubler to a 78-degree angle. Twelve degrees on a speed square or power miter saw gives you the desired 78-degree cut (90 − 12 = 78). **(Photo 2)**

As shown in the drawing "Backrest Post Layout," page 102, trim the corner of each backrest post to provide a flat surface where the posts will meet the bench posts.

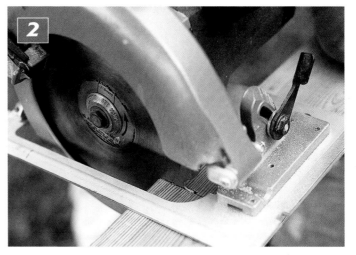

Check that posts are square to the beams. *Measure diagonals between their upper edges, adjusting post bottoms until diagonals are equal. Screw the squared parts together.*

Cut the seat frame pieces, *cutting some ends at a 78-deg. angle and others square. For safety and control, start with the shortest lengths and hold each board squarely on the sawhorse.*

POST-AND-BEAM ASSEMBLY

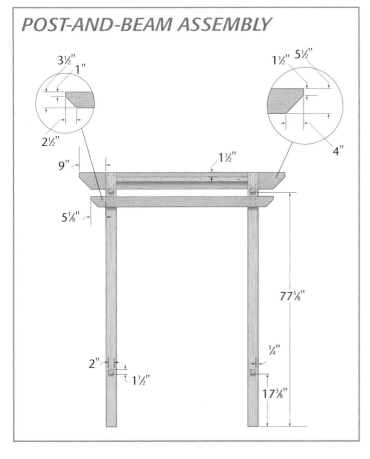

Clamp and fasten the backrest post *to the side rail, tight against the back side-rail doubler. Drill pilot holes, and drive assembly screws. Then mount the front side-rail doubler to the side rail.*

Make the cut with a circular saw, or flatten the corner with a file, a sander, or a surface-forming tool.

Assemble the Seat Frame

Assemble the seat's two side frames. (See "Seat Frame Construction," page 102.) Then join them to the back rail and the seat rail, completing the seat.

Begin each side frame by clamping one side rail to a sawhorse. Clamp a short piece of scrap 2x4 on end to the back end of the rail. This scrap temporarily represents the back rail, which you will attach later. Butt the back side-rail doubler against the scrap, and fasten it to the rail with two 2-inch screws.

Align the backrest post tight against the back side-rail doubler, making sure its end is flush with the bottom of the side rail. Clamp the backrest post in place, checking its alignment with a framing square to ensure that the short flat plane at the top of the backrest post aligns with the back end of the scrap 2x4 clamped to the end of the side rail. (That flat plane and the back rail need to be flush with the bench post when all is assembled.) Drill pilot holes, and drive four 2-inch screws through the backrest post into the side rail. **(Photo 3)**

Place the front side-rail doubler on the side rail, its mitered end against the backrest post. Drill countersunk pilot holes, and drive four 2-inch screws through it into side rail. Remove the scrap 2x4.

Assemble the second side frame in the same manner. The other frame should be a mirror image of the first, not a duplicate.

Complete the seat frame by screwing the back and seat rails to both side frames. To do this, clamp one of the side frames to the sawhorse. Then, stand the back and seat

Attach the back and seat rails to each side frame *by putting them into position and driving several 3-in. screws diagonally through the rails and into the frames.*

Set the back post-and-beam assembly on sawhorses, *and position the seat frame on it. When it is aligned, drive screws through the backrest posts, the side rails, and the back rail into the posts.*

BACKREST POST LAYOUT

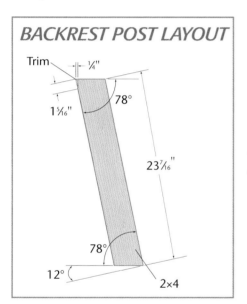

SEAT FRAME CONSTRUCTION

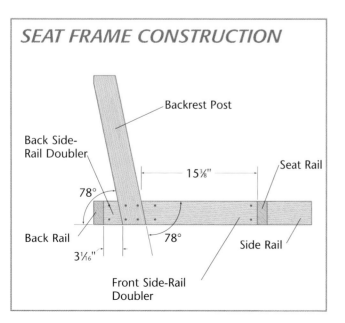

rails on end in position. Because screws driven straight into end grain do not hold as well as screws driven into long grain, drill pilot holes and drive 3-inch screws on angles through the top and bottom edges of the rails. **(Photo 4)** For extra holding power, drill through the doubler into the rails.

Attach the Seat Frame to Post-and-Beam Assemblies

Return one of the post-and-beam assemblies to the sawhorses, supporting it just as you did when assembling it. Position it so that the wide beam is lying face down. This assembly will be the back of the trellis bench. Measure from the foot end of each bench post, and mark the positions of the side rails as indicated in "Trellis Bench Elevations," page 100. Position one of the side rails and back post assemblies on the post-and-beam assembly, aligning it with your marks. Clamp it so that it can't shift as you drill pilot holes and drive screws for the assembly. Screw the frame to the post-and-beam assembly. Attach the second side rail to the assembly. **(Photo 5)**

The next step is to position the front post-and-beam assembly on top of the seat frame's front end.

Again, measure from the foot end of each bench post, and mark the position of the side rails. (Refer to "Trellis Bench Elevations," page 100.) You also need to cut a pair of temporary supports to hold the front beam end of the project in place. Cut these supports to match the lengths of the side rails (33⅝ inches), and clamp them to the back post-and-beam assembly. Working on one side at a time, stand a temporary support on the wide beam tight against the post, and clamp the support to its bench post. **(Photo 6)**

With the supports firmly clamped, lift the front post-and-beam assembly into place. Make sure the assembly is properly oriented, with the wide beam up and the narrow one down, and that the side rails are aligned with the marks. You might need someone to help you with this procedure.

Clamp the temporary supports to the posts of the front post-and-beam assembly. Drill pilot holes in the side-rail edges, and fasten the rails to the posts. **(Photo 7)**

Attach the Seat and Backrest Boards

Stand the completed framework for the trellis bench on its feet.

Next, you will attach three seat boards, three backrest boards, and a backrest top. Cut all from ⅞x6 stock, which measures 1 inch thick and 5½ inches wide with eased (rounded) edges.

Using the outside distance from side rail to side rail as a guide, cut the three seat boards. Position the front board so that it overhangs the front of the seat rail by ¼ to ½

Clamp a temporary support to each bench post behind the wide beam. These will support the top end of the front post-and-beam assembly while it is being fastened to the front of the seat frame.

Set the front post-and-beam assembly atop the temporary supports and the seat rails. Clamp the assembly to each support. Then drive screws through the side-rail edges into the bench posts.

Cut and install the seat boards. Fasten the front board first and the rear board second, drilling pilots and using 2-in. screws as fasteners. Center the third board between them, and then fasten in place.

Install the upper and then the top backrest boards. Notch the top backrest board at its back corners so that it fits between the bench posts. Use 2-in. screws for fastening the boards.

inch. Drill pilot holes, and drive two 2-inch screws at each end. Drive a few screws along the length of the front seat board down into the seat rail, and countersink them well so that they won't scratch anyone sitting on the bench. Next, butt a seat board against the backrest posts, and fasten it. Center the third seat board midway between the other two, and fasten it. There should be a small space between each seat board to allow for drainage. **(Photo 8)**

Using the outside distance from backrest post to backrest post, cut the three backrest boards and the top backrest board. All of these boards should measure 3 inches shorter than the seat boards. Fasten the uppermost backrest board flush with the tops of the two backrest posts using a pair of 2-inch screws at each end.

Notch the top backrest board at its back corners so that it will fit between the bench posts. Locate these cutting lines as follows: rest the board on the backrest posts, and scribe lines at each end, parallel with the inside faces of the bench posts. Then measure from the face of the already-installed backrest upper board to the bench post, and transfer that measurement to the top board. Clamp the top board to a sawhorse or workbench, and cut the notches along the guidelines using a saber saw. Test your work. You may have to use a file to get the notched boards to fit snugly against the bench posts. When satisfied, set the top backrest board in place. **(Photo 9)** Then screw it to the tops of the backrest posts.

Attach the other two backrest boards, first resting the lower one on a couple of scraps

to establish an even gap between it and the seat board. Then screw it to the backrest posts. Position the middle board in a similar way, using scraps to establish even gaps between the boards.

Cut the Side Lattices

Crosscut the horizontal strips from 1x2 stock. For each of the two side lattices, cut seven horizontal strips 32⅞ inches long and two mounting strips 33⅜ inches long. The longer ones are for attaching the completed lattice to the framework.

Rip the ¾-inch vertical strips from whatever width of one-by stock you can get. Crosscut them an inch or two longer than the 65⅞-inch length specified in the cutting list. You will mark

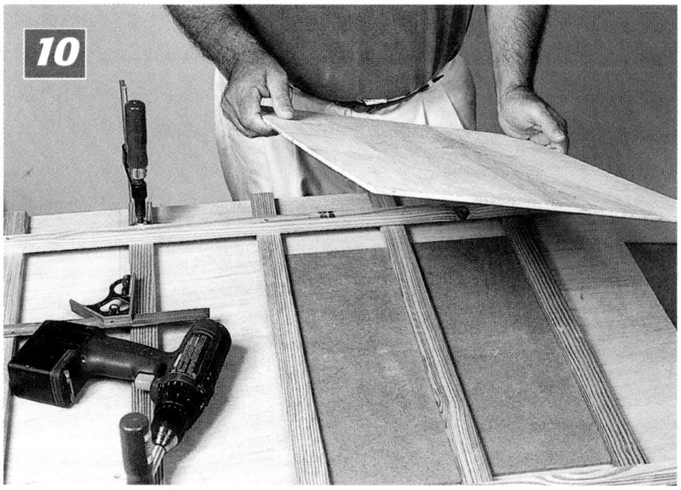
10

***Use the two 6-in.-wide spacers** to make sure that the horizontal strips are parallel and the space between them is correct. Use the 23 ¼-in. spacer to position the two outer vertical strips.*

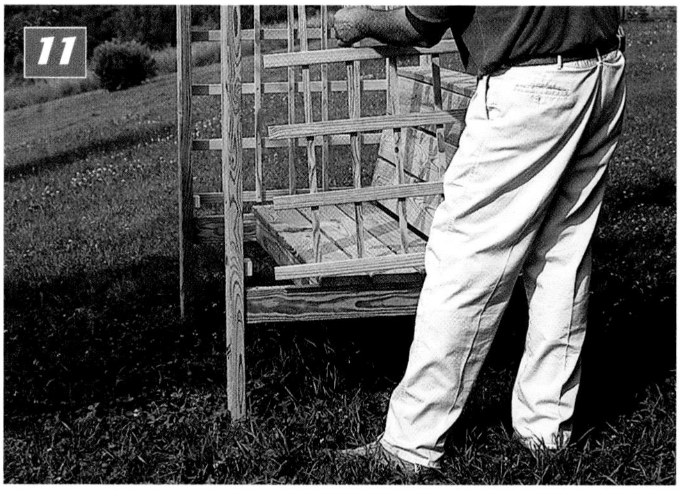
11

***Install a lattice to each side of the project,** positioning each so that the ends of its top and bottom mounting strips seat squarely against the four mounting blocks.*

them for trimming after you mount the lattices to the bench posts.

Before assembling the lattices, cut several spacers (gauges) from scrap hardboard or plywood. Cut two spacers to be exactly 6 inches wide each (the distance between horizontal strips) by 12 to 18 inches long. The width is the critical measurement. Cut a large spacer exactly 23¼ inches (the distance between the two outer vertical strips) by 18 inches or so. Then cut a couple of small spacers exactly 4 1/16 inches by 6 inches to use when fastening the verticals. Be sure to make these spacers square.

Assemble Side Lattices

Work on a large flat surface. For side latticework dimensions and spacing, refer to the drawing "Side Lattice Layout," below.

Lay a mounting strip and then two or three of the shorter horizontal strips on the work surface, with their 1½-inch-wide faces up. Mark lines across the mounting strips 4 7/16 inches in from each of its ends. On the shorter strips, mark lines 4 1/16 inches in from each end. Line up the strips and their marks, positioning a 6-inch-wide spacer in between them as follows: the mounting strip, a spacer, a horizontal strip, a spacer, a horizontal. Over them, place the large spacer, its longer edge along the outside edge of the mounting strip and its ends even with the marked lines on that strip. Clamp it and the mounting strip to the work surface.

Now, introduce the two outer vertical strips to the assembly. Place a vertical strip over the horizontals, tight against one end of the large spacer and flush with the bottom edge of the mounting strip. Drill a pilot hole, and drive a 1¼-inch screw, fastening the vertical to the mounting strip. Install the other vertical strip along the opposite end of the large spacer.

Align the second and third horizontal strips, using the spacers to ensure that they will be parallel and properly spaced. Align the marked lines on them with the outside edges of the fastened verticals. Drill pilot

LATTICE CUTTING LIST

Part	Quantity	Thickness	Width	Length	Stock
Side lattice horizontal strips	14	¾"	1½"	32⅞"	1×2
Side lattice mounting strips	4	¾"	1½"	33⅝"	1×2
Side lattice vertical strips	12	¾"	¾"	65⅞"	1×4
Side lattice mounting blocks	8	1"	2"	1½"	5/4×6
Nailers	2	¾"	1½"	44½"	1×2
Short roof slats	9	¾"	¾"	36⅝"	1×4
Long roof crosspieces	6	¾"	1½"	50"	1×2

SIDE LATTICE LAYOUT

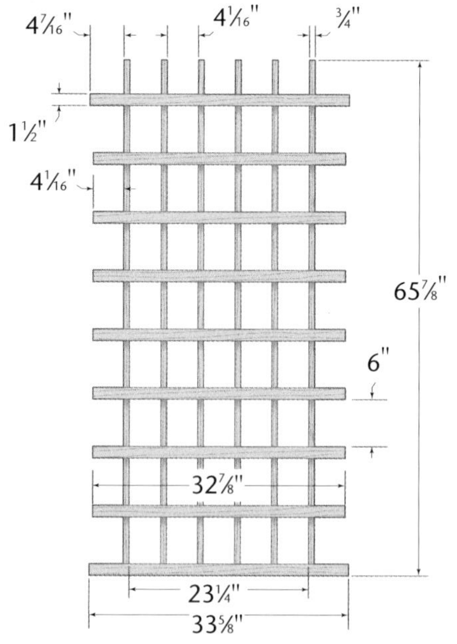
4 7/16"
4 1/16"
¾"
1½"
4 1/16"
65⅞"
6"
32⅞"
23¼"
33⅝"

Mark the vertical strips for trimming using a gauge made from scrap 1x2 stock. Rest the gauge on the wide beam and scribe along its underside on each vertical strip. Trim as needed.

Lay the crosspieces over the short slats, aligning their ends over the tops of the vertical strips of the side lattices. Screw both ends of each crosspiece to the verticals.

holes, and drive all of the assembly screws.

Working from the bottom up, continue to assemble the lattice, using this routine: **(Photo 10)** Place a 6-inch-wide spacer against the last horizontal strip you attached, and then slide a new horizontal strip into place. Slide in the other 6-inch-wide spacer and another horizontal strip. Shift the large spacer up the lattice to ensure that the outside verticals remain square with the horizontals. Fasten the horizontals to the outer verticals, ending with the other mounting strip at the top. The verticals will extend above it.

Once all of the horizontals strips are fastened to the two outside vertical strips, position and install the four remaining verticals. Use the small 4¹⁄₁₆- x 6-inch spacers to establish the space between them. Reference them to the outer ones already

installed, and align the bottom edge of each vertical so that it is flush with the lower edge of the bottom mounting strip. Repeat the process to build the second lattice.

Mount the Side Lattices
Make eight mounting blocks, and attach two to each of the four bench posts. Using scraps of ¾- or one-by boards, cut a 2-inch-wide strip that is at least 24 inches long. Then crosscut that into eight 1½-inch-long blocks.

On each bench post, measure up 17⅜ and 77⅜ inches as shown in the "Post-and-Beam Assembly" drawing, page 101. Just above each of those marks, measure in ¾ inch from the outer edge of the post, and mark to intersect the first mark. Attach a mounting block at each pair of marks, orienting the block so that the two block-mounting screws and the eventual single lattice mounting screw will penetrate into the block's edge grain, not its end grain.

To install the lattice, place its top and bottom mounting strips against the mounting blocks. **(Photo 11)** Drill pilot holes, and drive a 1⅜-inch screw per block. You might need a helper.

With both side lattices installed,

mark and trim the tops of the vertical strips. Use scraps of horizontal-strip stock to make a two-ply gauge for marking. **(Photo 12)** Make the top ply long enough to span the tops of the wide beams and the bottom ply equal to the thickness (¾ inch) of the long roof crosspieces. Lay this gauge across the beams, and set it against the vertical strips. Scribe along its underside onto each vertical strip, and trim to the scribed lines using a saber saw.

Mount the Trellis Roof
Begin by cutting two nailers, each 44½ inches long, from 1x2 stock and fasten one to the back of each of the wide beams, 1½ inches from the top, as shown in "Post-and-Beam Assembly," page 101.

Rip the short roof slats ¾ inch wide from one-by stock, and then crosscut them to length. The ends of these strips will rest on the nailers. Crosscut the 1x2 stock to produce the roof crosspieces, which will rest across the short roof strips.

Install the short roof strips first. Measure from the ends of the wide beams 34¾ inches to locate the centerline position for the center one. Then fasten each of the strip's ends to a nailer using 1¼-inch screws. Work out from there, using 4¹⁄₁₆-inch-long spacers.

Lastly, install the crosspieces with their 1½-inch dimension up. Their ends rest atop the vertical strips of the side lattice panels. **(Photo 13)** Drill pilot holes, and use 1¼-inch screws to fasten the crosspieces to the verticals. Then connect the crosspieces and the short roof strips with screws.

TRELLIS ROOF LAYOUT

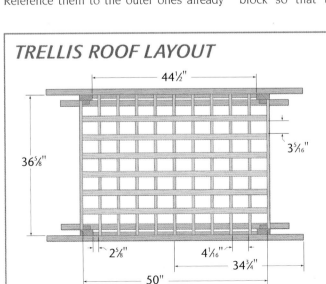

44½"

36⅝"

3⁵⁄₁₆"

2⅝" 4¹⁄₁₆"

34¾"

50"

MODULAR CORNER TRELLIS

Here's an ideal trellis to place at the corner of your property or at the intersection of a walk and driveway. Its decorative posts resemble gate or fence posts, and its airy latticework modules suggest elegant fencing. Festooned with a flowering vine or climbing roses, the trellis can be a highlight in any landscape. This project takes a day or two to complete.

EXPLODED VIEW

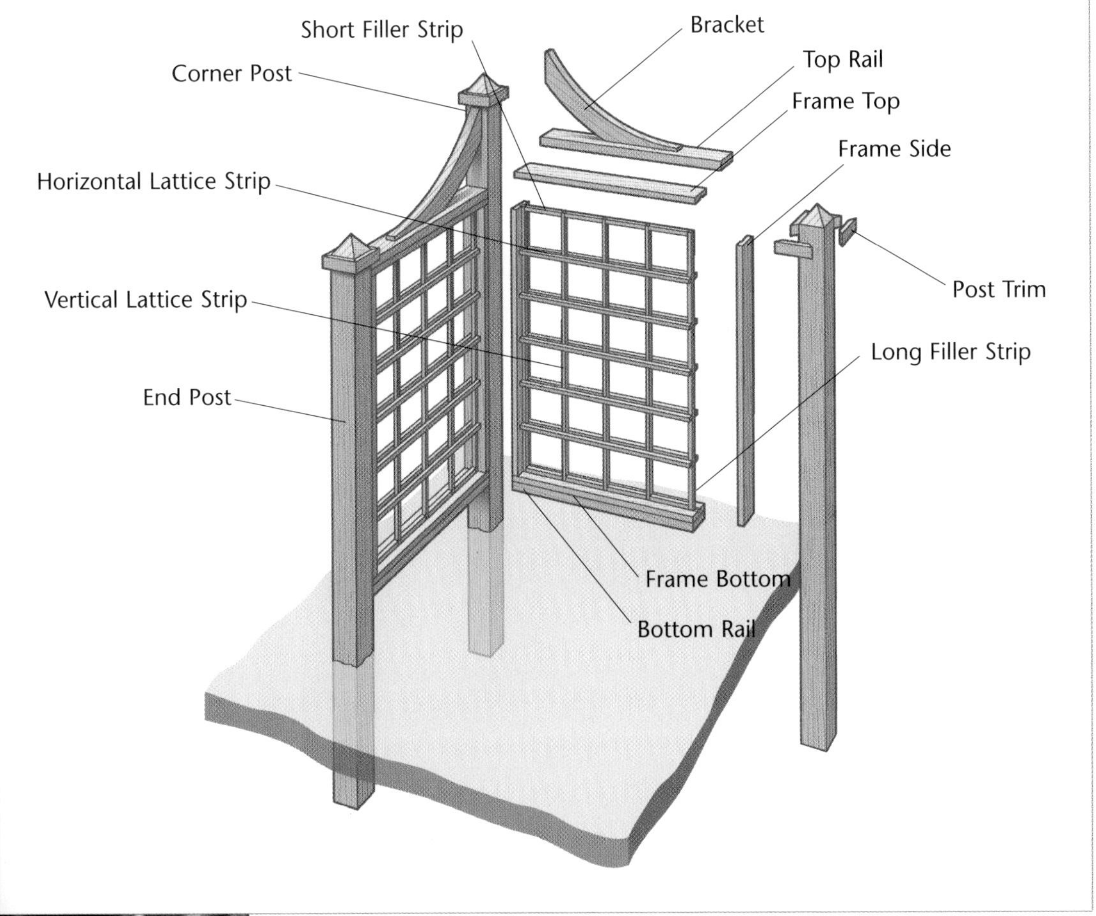

Short Filler Strip

Corner Post

Horizontal Lattice Strip

Vertical Lattice Strip

End Post

Bracket

Top Rail

Frame Top

Frame Side

Post Trim

Long Filler Strip

Frame Bottom

Bottom Rail

SHOPPING LIST

- 4 pcs. 1×6 8' white oak
- Half sheet of ¼" hardboard
- 1 pc. 4×4 12' western red cedar
- 1 pc. 4×4 8' western red cedar
- 1 pc. 5/4×4 12' western red cedar
- 1 pc. 2×8 8' western red cedar
- 1 pc. 1×6 8' western red cedar
- Stainless-steel screws, #8 × 1 5/8"
- Stainless-steel screws, #8 × 2"
- 2 stainless-steel screws, #10 × 3"
- 17-gauge, ¾", 1", and 1¼" stainless-steel brads

CUTTING LIST

Part	Quantity	Thickness	Width	Length	Stock
Frame tops/bottoms	4	¾"	2¼"	27¾"	1×6 white oak
Frame sides	4	¾"	2¼"	39¼"	1×6 white oak
Vertical lattice strips	6	½"	½"	39½"	1×6 white oak
Long filler strips	4	½"	½"	39½"	1×6 white oak
Horizontal lattice strips	20	½"	½"	26¾"	1×6 white oak
Short filler strips	16	½"	½"	6"	1×6 white oak
Corner post	1	3½"	3½"	96"	4×4 8' red cedar
End posts	2	3½"	3½"	72"	4×4 12' red cedar
Bottom/top rails	4	1"	3⅛"	27¾"	5/4×4 12' red cedar
Brackets	2	1½"	5⅞"	24 3/16"	2×8 8' red cedar
Post trim	12	1 1/16"	1 ½"	4⅞"	1×6 8' red cedar

SIDE ELEVATIONS

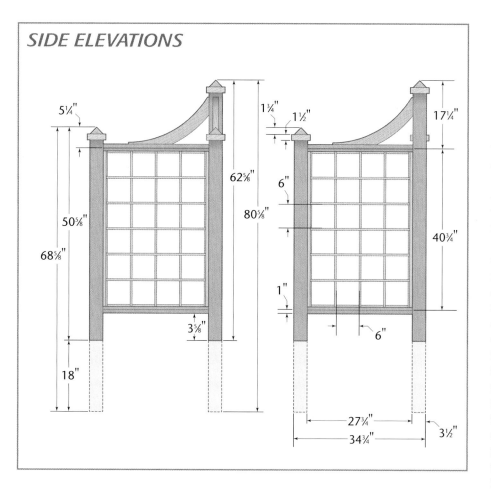

STEP-BY-STEP

Cut and Prepare the Frame Pieces

Rip and crosscut the stock to produce the pieces that make up the frames for the two latticework modules. Arrange the top, bottom, and side pieces to form two frames, and mark the inside face of each piece.

Equip the router with an edge guide and a ½-inch-diameter straight bit. Then, along the full length of the inside face of each frame piece, center and cut a groove that is ½ inch wide by ⅛ inch deep. Because the cut is shallow, you should be able to make it in a single pass. To make the cut, secure a frame piece with its marked side up, on the bench top with two clamps near one end. Rout from the free end toward the clamps, making sure that the guide is on the far side of the board and that you are moving the router from right to left. Turn off the router, and set a third clamp to hold the end that's been routed. **(Photo 1)** Resume cutting, and when you reach the other two clamps, turn off the router. Shift the clamps to the other end of the board, and complete the cut. Repeat this process for the other frame pieces.

Cut Lattice Pieces

Using a table saw, produce the vertical and horizontal lattice strips and the long and short filler strips. All are ½ inch wide. Start by crosscutting the oak 1x6s into two pieces that are 39½ inches long and three that are 26¼ inches long.

The ½-inch-wide strips should just fit into the ½-inch-wide grooves routed into the frame pieces, so you should cut a test strip and check its fit. (Remove the saw's standard blade guard. Otherwise, it would

BUILDER'S NOTES

Contrary to appearances, this modular corner trellis is easy to make. In addition, it doesn't require a great deal of material or an extensive array of tools.

In brief, the sequence is to first build two framed latticework panels (modules), and then join the panels to the posts and add the rails, curved brackets, and trim. When the modular corner trellis is assembled, you take it to the site and set it into the ground.

Materials
For woods, I chose western red cedar and white oak. Both are durable outdoors, and they provide a contrast in hues, with the generally dark cedar framing the blond oak.

I also needed the strength of white oak for the slender lattice strips. White oak is probably a material you'll have to order, as it is not always in stock. Red oak is widely available, but it fares poorly in the outdoors and will deteriorate quickly. You could use other woods, of course. For the darker hue, redwood, mahogany, teak, or ipé would be appropriate; for the lighter hue, cypress would work well.

Be sure to use stainless-steel (or aluminum) fasteners with the cedar and oak. Both woods contain tannins that react with iron to produce black stains.

Tools and Techniques
More than any other tool, you

will need a table saw to construct this trellis. It is essential for ripping the stock for the latticework.

You also need a router and an edge guide. It is nice to have a fixed-base model with the edge guide for cutting the grooves in each of the frame pieces for the lattice, and a plunge router for cutting out the curved brackets. But one or the other can be used for both tasks. You will also need assorted clamps, a drill-driver, and small hammer.

Finish
I finished the structure with a penetrating oil formulated for outdoor use. It is easy to apply, cleans up with water, and can be renewed annually.

PLAN VIEW

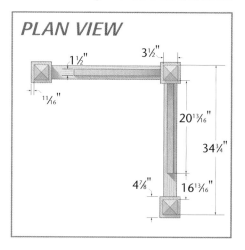

Groove the frame pieces with a router equipped with an edge guide. Secure the work with clamps, and rout up to them; then shift them to the other end, and complete the cut.

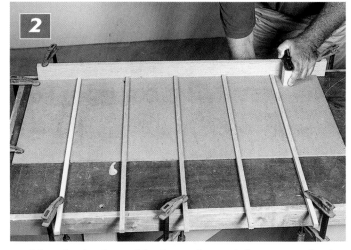

Position the horizontal lattice strips and the gauges, butting them against a side piece of the frame clamped to the bench. Apply clamps to key parts to keep them from shifting.

Set the gauge strip against the base, over the horizontal lattice strips, and abut a 6-in. gauge next to that. Align the centers of a vertical lattice strip to the middle horizontal lattice strip.

Apply a dot of glue on each horizontal lattice strip where it contacts a vertical. A gel formulation is preferred because it doesn't spread on its own (but may be hard to squeeze from the bottle).

prevent your using a pusher, which is a safety essential. (See "Table Saw Pusher," page 60.) Set the table saw's rip fence to ½ inch; adjust the blade barely higher than the stock's thickness; and carefully make a test cut. As the end of the board approaches the blade, use a pusher to clear the narrow strip between the blade and fence.

Insert the end of the test strip into the groove of a frame piece—the fit should be snug. If the strip is too narrow, slightly increase the space between the saw fence and blade. If it's too thick, move the fence closer to the blade. Make another test cut, and recheck the fit. When the strip fits the groove tightly, cut all the strips.

Rip the stock pieces to produce the total number of ½-inch-wide strips needed. Cut one extra, and put it aside. One by one, flip all of the remaining strips, and rerip each of them to ½ inch thick, thereby producing the ½-inch-square strips. Crosscut some to produce the short filler strips. Flip the extra strip, and rip it to be ⅜ inch thick. Label this strip; it will be used as a gauge during assembly.

Cut Latticework Gauges

From a half-sheet of ¼-inch hardboard, cut three strips 6 inches wide. Crosscut two of them into 16-inch-long pieces. Crosscut the third strip of hardboard into one 16-inch-long piece and one 32-inch-long piece.

Assemble the Latticework

Clamp a frame side on edge to the bench top. Starting with a 16-inch-long gauge set at the top of the side piece, alternate five horizontal lattice strips with the other 16-inch-long gauges, butting each tight to the frame side. Clamp the outer gauges and a few of the strips to the bench. **(Photo 2)**

Select three vertical lattice strips, and mark the center on them, equidistant from each end. Position the clearly labeled ⅜-inch-thick gauge strip against the base, crossing all the horizontal strips. Tight against the gauge strip, position one of the 32-inch-long gauges. Then lay the first of the vertical lattice strips in place, tight against the gauge, centering its center mark over the middle horizontal lattice strip. **(Photo 3)** Scribe along both edges of the vertical lattice strip onto each horizontal one. Then set the vertical strip aside, and apply only a dot of glue to each horizontal strip within these marked areas. **(Photo 4)**

Drill a pilot hole for each brad to avoid splitting the thin wood. For your bit, use a brad with its head nipped off and chucked so that it projects just ½ in.

Brad driving does not require much force. A small hammer and a deft touch are all you need. Use ¾-in.-long brads to fasten the lattice strips.

Position the second layer of horizontal strips, aligning them by eye directly over the first layer. Use glue and brads to fasten them to the vertical lattice strips, removing clamps as you progress.

Partially assemble the frame by joining a side piece to the top and bottom pieces of the frame. Clamp other side piece between the top and bottom members to help hold the angle at the corner.

Reposition the vertical lattice strip, and drill a pilot hole at its intersection with the first horizontal strip. To make a hole that exactly matches the brads, use a brad as a bit. For this, nip its head off and chuck it in the drill so that it projects just ½ inch. **(Photo 5)** Then insert a brad into the pilot hole and hammer it in. Fasten the vertical lattice strip to each of the remaining horizontal lattice strips. **(Photo 6)**

Place the second vertical lattice strip after repositioning the 32-inch-long hardboard gauge, tight against the other edge of the first vertical lattice strip. Scribe its intersections with the horizontal strips; remove the vertical strip; and then apply dots of glue to the horizontal strips as you did before. Reposition the second vertical strip, and fasten it to each horizontal one. Then

mount the third vertical lattice strip to the horizontal lattice strips in the same way.

Before mounting the second layer of horizontal lattice strips to the vertical strips, remove the long gauge so that you can see the fastened horizontal strips below them. Lay five new horizontal lattice strips over these, aligning each directly over a fastened horizontal. **(Photo 7)** One by one attach them to the vertical lattice strips with glue and brads, moving each strip aside to see where to apply the glue. With the strip glued in place, drill pilot holes and drive brads. Take care not to hit the brad that is in the joint underneath.

After assembling the first latticework, unclamp it from the frame's side piece, set it aside, and build the second in the same manner.

Mount Lattice into Frame

To start, glue a long filler strip in the groove cut into each of the frame's side pieces. The strips are ¼ inch longer than the side pieces, so position each strip so that its ends overhang an equal amount. These projections are meant to sit in the grooves in the top and bottom frame members.

Join the top and bottom pieces to one of the side pieces, using waterproof glue and a couple of 2-inch stainless-steel screws in each joint. Position the side piece so that the filler strip fits in the grooves of the top and bottom pieces. To hold the angle at the corners, clamp the other side piece between the top and bottom pieces. **(Photo 8)**

Once the glued joints dry, remove the clamps and slide the lattice panel into place. The ends of the vertical strips

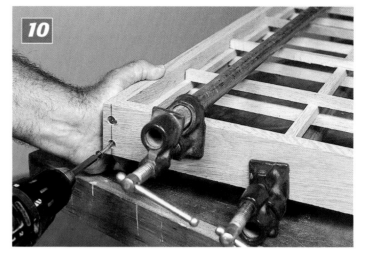

Slide the latticework into the partial frame. *The vertical lattice strips fit into the frame's grooves. The horizontal lattice strips fit to each side of the filler strip glued into the side piece.*

Fit the second side piece *into place, completing the frame and trapping the latticework within it. If necessary, use one or two pipe clamps to hold pieces in place.*

MODULE ASSEMBLY

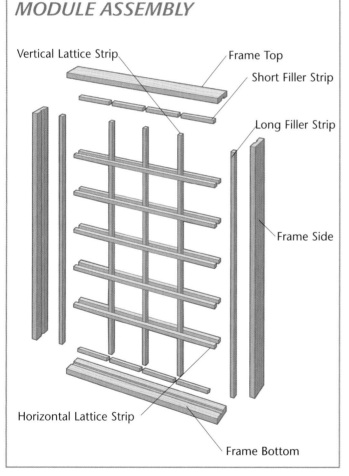

- Vertical Lattice Strip
- Frame Top
- Short Filler Strip
- Long Filler Strip
- Frame Side
- Horizontal Lattice Strip
- Frame Bottom

Stabilize the vertical lattice strips *by gluing short filler strips into the grooves of the top and bottom frame pieces. One spring clamp per filler provides sufficient pressure.*

should travel in the grooves cut into the frame's top and bottom pieces. As you seat the panel into the side piece, the double layer of horizontal lattice strips should fit around the long filler strip glued there. **(Photo 9)**

Apply glue to the free ends of the top and bottom pieces, and then fit the second side of the frame into place, fitting the horizontal lattice strips to each side of the long filler strip glued into its groove. Secure each joint with a pair of stainless-steel screws, checking to be sure that the frame is square and readjusting as necessary. **(Photo 10)**

Finish the assembly by driving stainless-steel brads through the horizontal lattice strips into the long filler strips. Then glue the short filler strips into the top and bottom grooves between the vertical lattice strips. **(Photo 11)**

Set aside the first completed lattice-work module, and assemble the second one in the same manner.

Cut the Posts

The modular corner trellis has three 4x4 posts. Two, the end posts, are made by crosscutting a 12-foot-long 4x4 in half. The taller corner post is an 8-foot-long 4x4. Work with these lengths, and shorten the posts as needed when you are setting the trellis into the ground.

The posts have pyramid-shaped tops, which let rain and snow run off the post tops, thereby preventing rot and ice damage. To shape the top of a post, mark a cut line across all four faces 1¾ inches from the top. Tilt your circular saw to 45 degrees; position it on a marked line; and make your cut. Cut the three other sides in the same

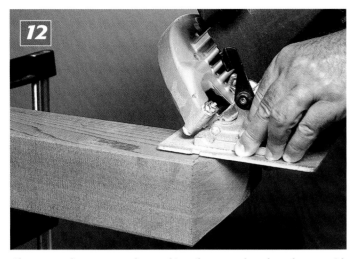

Shape each post top by making four 45-deg. bevel cuts with your circular saw, first clamping the post so that it doesn't move. Use care and both hands to guide the saw.

Lay out each bracket on its blank before actually cutting it. After drawing the arcs, draw the straight lines where the bracket will abut the post and the rail.

Cut the bracket arcs using a router and trammel. Make only shallow cuts on each pass, plunging a fraction of an inch deeper each time you swing through the arc.

Screw the latticework module to an end post with stainless-steel screws, first positioning the module by measuring from the post top and securing it with clamps.

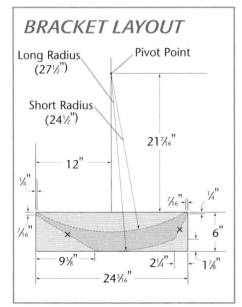

BRACKET LAYOUT

Long Radius (27½")
Pivot Point
Short Radius (24½")
21⅞"
12"
¼"
⅞"
¼"
⁷⁄₁₆"
6"
9⅜"
2¼"
1⅞"
24³⁄₁₆"

manner. **(Photo 12)** Repeat the process for the remaining two posts.

While the posts are on the bench and the measuring and marking tools are there, you might want to refer to the "Side Elevations" drawing, on page 108, and then mark the position lines of the module and trim, as can be seen in Photo 15.

Cut the Brackets

Each bracket is cut from a 6-inch-wide piece of 2x8 stock that is 24³⁄₁₆ inches long. Referring to the "Bracket Layout" drawing, lay out the shape of a bracket onto the wood before you cut it out. Use a simple pencil trammel to draw the arcs onto the wood for the bracket. **(Photo 13)**

To hold the wood for the bracket in position, clamp a piece of expendable plywood onto the workbench and use double-faced carpet tape to hold the wood, one piece at a time, to that. If the scrap wood is long enough, plan to tape the pivot block for the trammels to it; if not, tape the pivot block to another clamped piece of scrap, as shown in Photo 14.

To locate the two pivot points for the arcs, measure and mark a point 12 inches in from the end of the wood for the bracket. At this point, line up the corner of a framing square, and measure up 21⅞ inches to locate the pivot point for drawing and cutting the two arcs.

A basic plunge router, guided by a homemade trammel, works fine for cutting the arcs. For the longer radii, keep the bit outside the 27½-inch radius mark. For the shorter ones, keep the bit inside

Before mounting the second module *to the corner post, lay the assembly flat on the bench top. Then stand the second module in position; align it; clamp it; and drive the mounting screws.*

After mounting the bracket *to the top rail and attaching the rail to the module, drill a pilot hole and drive a 3-in. stainless-steel screw through the bracket into the post.*

the 24½-inch radius. **(Photo 14)**

Use a saber saw to cut the flats. Use a router and a ¼-inch-radius roundover bit to round out all the edges, except the face edges that must sit flat against the trellis post and top and rail (marked with an X in the "Bracket Layout" drawing).

Join Lattice Modules to the Posts

Lay one of the two end posts on your workbench or across a pair of sawhorses. Measure 5¼ inches down from its pointed top to mark the position of the frame top piece of the module. Stand the lattice module in place; center it on the post; and clamp it so that it doesn't shift.

Mark locations for four pairs of screws, locating four screws on each side of the module. Drill pilot holes, and then drive 1⅝-inch stainless-steel screws. **(Photo 15)** Exterior glue between the post and frame piece is optional. Secure the second module to the second end post in the same way.

Measure down 17¼ inches from the corner post's top point, and make marks on adjacent faces where the top frame piece of each module will line up. Align and clamp a module on the corner post; drill pilots; and drive assembly screws. Repeat for the other module. **(Photo 16)**

Add trim to the top of each post. *Cut the strips; then miter their ends. Set each piece in place, and mount each to the post using exterior glue and 1¼-in. stainless-steel brads.*

Install Rails and Brackets

Cut the bottom and top rails, first measuring from post to post to ensure a good fit. Then rip each to 3⅛ inches. Fit a bottom rail, centering it across the post; then clamp it in place. Working from the inside of the module's frame, drill pilot holes and drive four to six stainless-steel screws into the rail. Repeat for the second bottom rail.

Before mounting the top rails, fasten a bracket to each one. Set a rail on top of a latticework module; place the bracket; and scribe around the foot of the bracket onto the rail. Take these apart; align the bracket to the scribed line; and then glue and screw it to the rail, drilling pilot holes first. Join the second bracket to the other top rail in the same manner.

Fasten the top rails (with brackets

attached) in much the same way as you did the bottom rails. Position a top rail; drill pilot holes; and drive screws from inside the module frame into the rail. Secure the bracket to the corner post with one 3-inch stainless-steel screw. **(Photo 17)** Install the second rail and bracket the same way.

Trim the Post Tops

Add trim to the post tops, as shown in the "Side Elevations" and "Plan View" drawings, page 108. Rip the stock into 1½-inch-wide pieces, and round-over the face edges. Crosscut them to length, then miter the ends. Attach them to the posts using exterior glue and 1¼-inch stainless-steel brads. **(Photo 18)**

Install the Trellis Outdoors

Determine positions of the postholes by standing the trellis in place outdoors and pushing a stake into the ground by each post. Move the trellis aside and dig the three postholes. (See "Grape Arbor," pages 144–147.)

Include 3 to 6 inches of gravel in each hole for drainage. Place the trellis posts into their holes. To establish the correct height, either trim the bottom of the posts or adjust the gravel depth. Then use a level to plumb the posts, adjusting the level of gravel if necessary. Brace the posts, and finish setting them into the ground.

More Stand-Alone Trellis & Arbor Ideas

Stand-alone trellises and arbors *provide more options for placement than wall-mounted units. Set in the center of a garden, top, the trellis becomes a focal point. Be sure that the trellis you choose will look interesting when plants are dormant. Homemade bentwood trellises, right, support small vines.*

Form follows function *with these arbors. The gate arbor shown above provides a welcoming entry to the front yard. The vine-covered arbor, top right, is a popular choice for framing garden seating areas. Although open, the arbor still separates the area from the rest of the yard. The metal arbor at right leads people down this garden path.*

Tower trellises, *above, are available in a variety of shapes and sizes. The one shown here consists of four lattice panels joined together. The climbing vine seems to be growing inside of the tower and coming out the top. Arbors with benches, right, not only help mark a path in the garden, they also offer a spot to sit down and enjoy the view.*

Simple designs are often the best choice for showing off the plants that the trellises and arbors support. The tower trellis shown at left will blend into the background of this garden. Arbors set over a path are hard to miss, but when planted with a dense vine or climbing rose as shown below, the plants, not the structure, are what people will notice first.

MODULAR ARBOR

Here's a lovely arbor to install over a walkway. With climbing vines scaling its trellises and cresting overhead, this arbor provides an especially inviting passageway. Don't forget to surround the base of the structure with flowers.

EXPLODED VIEW

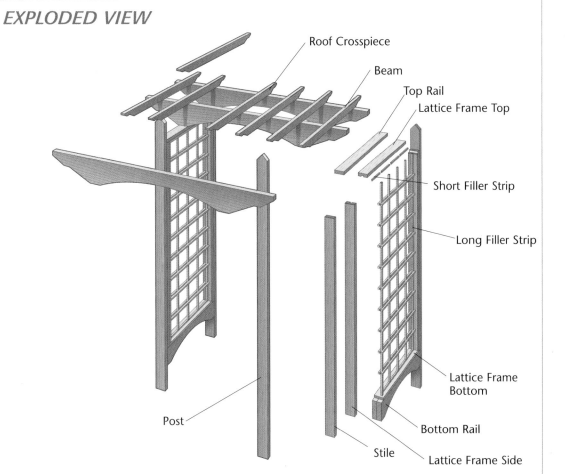

Roof Crosspiece

Beam

Top Rail

Lattice Frame Top

Short Filler Strip

Long Filler Strip

Lattice Frame Bottom

Bottom Rail

Stile

Lattice Frame Side

Post

SHOPPING LIST

- 5 pcs. 2×4 8" clear cedar
- 3 pcs. 2×8 8" clear cedar
- 4 pcs. 2×6 8' clear cedar
- 1 pc. ⁵⁄₄×4 12' clear cedar
- 5 pcs. 1×6 8' white oak
- 2 pcs. ½" × 36" hardwood dowel
- Box stainless-steel screws, #8 × 1⅝"
- Box stainless-steel screws, #8 × 2"
- Box stainless-steel screws, #10 × 3"
- Box 17 gauge, ⅞" stainless-steel brads
- Box 17 gauge, 1¼" stainless-steel brads

CUTTING LIST

Part	Quantity	Thickness	Width	Length	Stock
Posts	4	1½"	3½"	88⅜"	2×4 cedar
Bottom rails	4	1½"	5⅛"	29¾"	2×6 cedar
Top rails	2	1½"	3"	29¾"	2×4 cedar
Stiles	2	1"	3"	66¼"	⁵⁄₄-by cedar
Lattice frame tops and bottoms	4	¾"	2¼"	27¾"	white oak
Lattice frame sides	4	¾"	2¼"	65¼"	white oak
Vertical lattice strips	6	½"	½"	65½"	white oak
Horizontal lattice strips	36	½"	½"	26¼"	white oak
Long filler strips	4	½"	½"	65½"	white oak
Short filler strips	16	½"	½"	6"	white oak
Beams	3	1½"	7⅜"	76¼"	2×8 cedar
Roof crosspieces	7	1½"	2½"	45¾"	2×6 cedar

ELEVATIONS & PLAN VIEW

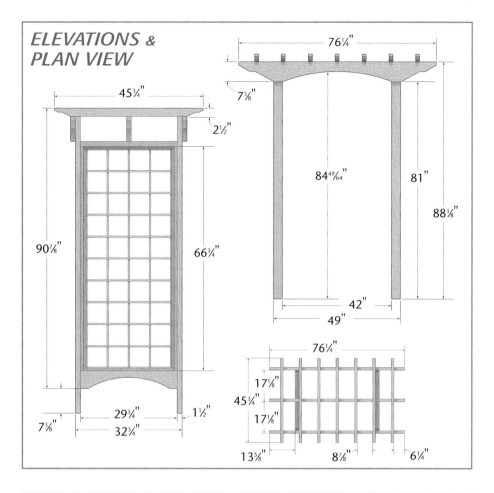

BUILDER'S NOTES

Building the modular arbor has much in common with the modular corner trellis (pages 106–113) in that both structures include framed lattice panels. I used the same types of wood for both projects, and the tools and techniques you find here closely match those used in the other project.

Materials

This arbor is made of western red cedar and white oak, both durable woods for outdoor projects. I used white oak for the framed lattice panels (modules) because of its strength. Other woods used for outdoor projects—such as cedar, redwood, and cypress—are too frail for the ½-inch-square lattice strips.

When shopping for oak, avoid buying the less durable red oak, which is commonly stocked at home centers.

For the other pieces of the arbor, you could also use redwood, cypress, and more exotic imported woods like ipé and teak.

Be sure to use stainless-steel (or aluminum) fasteners. If you mistakenly use iron fasteners, the tannins in both cedar and oak will react with the iron to produce black stains.

Because the beam template is more than 6 feet long, you need to buy a full sheet of MDF (medium-density fiberboard) for that template. Bear

in mind that a sheet of MDF is an inch wider and longer than 4x8 paneling. If that size presents a transportation problem, have it cut where you buy it.

Tools and Techniques

You'll need a table saw and a pusher to rip the stock for the lattice strips and the filler strips. You'll have to rip stock for the top rails, stiles, and roof crosspieces. You'll also need a router and a router edge guide.

Finish

I used a penetrating oil formulated for outdoor use. It is easy to apply and cleans up with water. (For more information on finishes, see "Tools, Techniques, and Materials," pages 48–57.)

STEP-BY-STEP

Cut the Framed Lattice Panels

The two lattice panels, or modules, are built the same way as those used for the modular corner trellis (pages 106–113), only the dimensions differ. An abbreviated description of that process is included.

Cut the lattice frame tops, bottoms, and side pieces to the dimensions specified in the cutting list. Then rout a ½-inch-wide by ⅛-inch-deep groove lengthwise along the center of the inside face of each piece.

Next, rip the stock to produce the lattice strips and the filler strips. To precisely dial in the saw's rip-fence setting, cut short test strips and test fit them into the groove. **(Photo 1)** When a test strip fits snugly, rip the boards to produce the ½-inch-square strips. Note: You will also need one ⅜-inch-thick strip as an assembly gauge strip. Mark it clearly. Crosscut the strips to the lengths given in the cutting list.

Finally, cut a half-sheet of ¼-inch hardboard into gauges to guide you in assembly—three that are 6 x 16 inches and a fourth that is 6 x 32 inches.

Assemble the Lattice

Place a frame side piece on edge, and clamp it to the bench top—its grooved side up. Lay out nine horizontal lattice strips with 6-inch-wide spacers between them. Butt the ends against the frame side, and clamp the end spacer and a few horizontal strips to immobilize all the parts.

Now lay the vertical lattice strips across the horizontals. The ⅜-inch spacer gauge goes against the side, followed by a long spacer gauge and then a vertical lattice strip. Apply glue where the vertical lattice strip makes contact with each horizontal strip. Then drill pilot holes, and drive a ⅛-inch stainless-steel brad through the vertical strip into each horizontal. **(Photo 2)**

Jump the long spacer over the just-fastened vertical strip, and use it to position the next one. Attach that vertical strip, and repeat the process.

To complete the lattice assembly, apply a second layer of horizontal lattice strips to the other side of the verticals. Glue, drill pilot holes, and then nail this second layer of horizontal strips to the verticals.

When you are done, unclamp the latticework from the frame side piece, and assemble the other side.

Cut and test-fit lattice strips *until you've dialed in the correct rip-fence setting. When a test lattice strip fits perfectly, rip all of them to that same square dimension.*

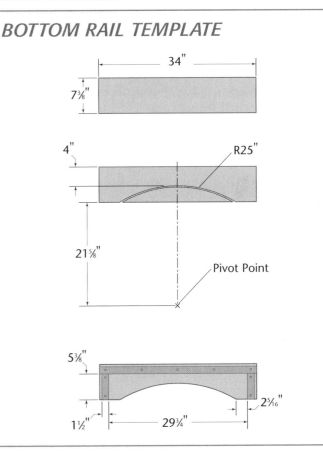

Position the lattice strips *to form the pattern, using spacers cut from hardboard. To drill pilot holes, use a brad as a bit. Then assemble the latticework.*

Install the second frame side *after seating the lattice vertical strips into the grooves in top and bottom pieces, the horizontals straddling the long filler strips of both side pieces.*

BOTTOM RAIL TEMPLATE

34"

7⅜"

4" R25"

21⅝" Pivot Point

5⅜"

1½" 29¾" 2⁵⁄₁₆"

Put the Lattice in the Frames

Glue a long filler strip into the groove in each frame side piece. Use glue and a couple of 2-inch stainless-steel screws to join the frame top and bottom pieces, their grooved sides facing in, to one of the side pieces, its filler-strip edge facing in. Slide the latticework into place. Be certain that the ends of its vertical strips are in the grooves in the frame top and bottom pieces and that the ends of the horizontal strips straddle the glued filler strip. Fit the second frame side piece between the top and bottom pieces of the frame. Sandwich its filler strip facing toward the latticework, between the horizontal strips. **(Photo 3)**

Secure the side piece to the top and bottom pieces using glue and screws, after making sure that the frame is square. Use stainless-steel brads to secure the horizontal strips to the long filler strips. Glue short filler strips into the top and bottom grooves between the vertical strips.

Set the lattice section aside, and frame the second one in the same manner.

Cut the Arbor Parts

Cut each of the four posts from a 2x4. Begin by trimming ½ to 1 inch from the ends of each post, thus squaring that end. Then measure off 88⅜ inches on one post. Set all four side by side, and after aligning the squared ends, crosscut the other ends to length. Finally, miter the tops as indicated in the "Exploded View" drawing, page 119, so that water won't collect there.

Cut the stiles to the same length as the height of the framed lattice panels. Then rip each to its 3-inch width.

Calculate the length of the top and bottom rails by adding the thickness of the two

Cut the bottom-rail template arc *with a router and homemade trammel. Attach the template blank and pivot support board to an expendable plywood base.*

Lay out the end cuts on the beam template. *Then cut to those lines using a saber saw. You can clamp a wood-strip gauge to guide the saw's fence.*

stiles to the width of the lattice modules. Using this dimension, crosscut two top rails from 2x4 stock and the four bottom rails from 2x6 stock. Then rip the top rails to 3 inches wide.

Cut the three beams from 2x8s, and the seven roof crosspieces from 2x6s.

Make the Bottom Rail Template

The rail at the bottom of each side of the arbor is composed of two identically cut pieces of 2x6. The bottom edge of each rail is curved, and the best way to make all four rails identical is to cut them all using the same template.

Make the template from medium-density fiberboard (MDF). Start by cutting a blank to the size given in the drawings in "Bottom Rail Template," page 121. It is larger than the rail so that you can attach MDF fences to trap the template on a rail blank.

Attach the template blank temporarily to an expendable, oversized piece (about 36 inches square) of plywood or MDF. Locate the blank flush with one edge of this base.

To trace the curve on the template, divide the template in half and extend the dividing line across the base. The pivot for the trammel you will use to cut the curve will be on this line. Determine roughly where the pivot point will be, and secure a scrap of template

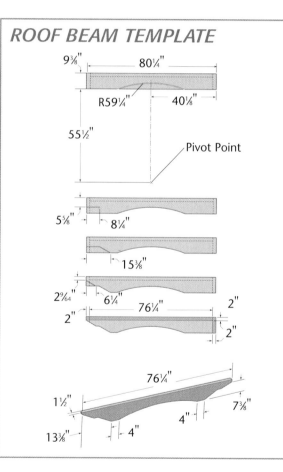

ROOF BEAM TEMPLATE

9⅜"   80¼"

R59¼"   40⅛"

55½"

Pivot Point

5⅝"   8¼"

15⅜"

2⁹⁄₆₄"   6¼"   76¼"   2"

2"   2"

76¼"

1½"   7⅜"

13⅜"   4"   4"

material to the base. This ensures that the pivot will be on the same level as the cutting surface. Locate the pivot point, and drill a pilot hole there.

Next, set up your router and make a trammel. Use a ½-inch bit. A strip of 14-inch-wide plywood will work well (if it's about 72 inches long it can be used for making the beam template as well). Attach

the router to one end of the trammel with carpet tape, pinching them together hard at each piece of tape. Turn on the router, and run the bit through the plywood. Using a measuring tape, measure from the bit (including the bit in the measurement) to locate the pivot point 25 inches away. Drill a pilot hole at the spot.

Drive a screw through the trammel and into the pivot hole. Check the swing, and then rout the arc through the template in a series of cuts, removing about ⅛ inch of material at a time. **(Photo 4)**

Free the template from the expendable plywood base. Screw fences to the template.

Make the Roof Beam Template

Using MDF, follow the drawings in "Beam Template," left. This template has a long-radius arc. Although the beams themselves have a series of straight and angled cuts in both ends, the template needs cuts in one end only because you can flip it over when cutting the opposite end of the beam.

Cut the template blank longer and wider than the beam (more than 6 feet itself), as indicated in the drawing. Secure the blank to the same plywood base you used to rout the bottom rail template. Center this template on the base, letting the ends overhang if necessary. Mark the

Screw fences cut from MDF to the roof crosspiece template so you can easily position it on the work. This will give you uniformly shaped parts.

Duplicate the template's arc on the bottom rail by means of a long pattern bit. To keep the router's outboard base from tipping away, carpet-tape it to wooden blocks.

centerline across the template, and extend a perpendicular line onto the plywood base so that you can position the pivot. Mark the pivot point, and drill a pilot hole. Locate the pivot for the radius on your trammel, and then screw it to the pivot base. Then rout the arc.

Free the template from the plywood so that you can shape the rafter end with a saber saw. You may want to clamp a fence to the template to guide the saw, though you don't need to if you have a steady hand. **(Photo 5)** Just lay out the shapes following the "Roof Beam Template" drawing, previous page, and make the cuts.

Finally, cut strips of MDF to serve as fences, and screw them to the template as shown in the drawing.

Make the Roof Crosspiece Template

This short template is for shaping the ends of crosspieces. After shaping one end of the roof crosspiece, simply turn the blank, end for end, and mark that face. Before marking, make sure you've marked a mirror image of the first cuts, not an upside-down cut. (See "Roof Crosspiece Template" drawing, page 124.)

Follow the sequence in the drawing. You'll find it easiest to first size the template blank on the table saw, and then make the end

Join the doubled bottom rail to a post. Position these parts, and clamp them to the bench so that they don't move. Then drill pilot holes and drive assembly screws. Install top rails in a similar way.

cuts with a saber saw. Attach the fence strips with screws. **(Photo 6)**

Shape the Bottom Rails

Use the template to draw the arc onto all four bottom-rail blanks. Using a saber saw, cut close to the drawn line. After sawing the arcs, you'll trim them flush to the template edge using a router with a pattern bit. **(Photo 7)** Place the template over a rail, making sure that the rail is seated against the three fences. Then clamp the assembly to the bench top.

Chuck the pattern bit into the router collet. Adjust the router so that the shank-mounted bearing will ride along the template edge without the bit's tip cutting into the bench top. Carefully rout the arc. Remove the template, and turn the rail

over. Switch to a flush-trimming bit, which has its pilot bearing on the tip, and trim away waste material.

Install Dowels in the Rails

Drive screws through the posts into the ends of the rails. Because screws do not hold as well in end grain as they do in long grain, install dowels in the rails to give the screws something to bite into.

About 1 inch from the rail's end, drill a ½-inch-diameter hole into the edge. Bore about 2½ inches into the top rails and about 5 inches into the bottom rails, but stop before boring all the way through. On the bottom rails, bore into the top edge, which will eventually be covered by the lattice module. On the top rails, bore into the edge that will be inside.

Cut lengths of ½-inch dowels. Apply gap-filling polyurethane glue. Drive a dowel into each hole. After the glue sets, trim the dowels, and sand them flush.

Assemble the Sides

To assemble the sides, cut six 3 x 5-inch shims from ¼-inch hardboard.

Now glue-laminate pairs of the bottom rails, using waterproof glue. Then screw a stile to the broad surface of the post. To join the posts and rails, clamp a post on edge to the workbench. **(Photo 8)** Position a doubled bottom rail against the post,

Tip the post onto its face, with bottom and top rails pointing up. Slide the lattice module into place; align it; and clamp it. Then drill screws through its frame into the stile, post, and rails.

Position the second post, with stile attached, onto the side assembly. Drive stainless-steel screws through the post into the rail ends.

with shims underneath it to raise it so that it aligns with the stile. Close the joint tight and square, clamping the rail to the bench top. Mark and drill four ⅜-inch-diameter counterbores in the post to receive the screws that will hold the side and rail together; a Forstner bit is best here. Switch bits, and then drill pilots in the center of the counterbores. Drive a 3-inch stainless-steel screw into each hole.

If your workbench isn't large enough, you may need to shift the position of the assembly in order to install the top rail. Next, lay down a couple of hardboard shims and position the top rail, oriented on its edge, on the shims. Pull the rail end against the post, and push it against the end of the stile. Then repeat the drilling and driving steps.

Now insert the lattice module. **(Photo 9)** For this, it's best to unclamp the side assembly, turn it so that the rails are jutting straight up, and then reclamp. Position the module, aligning it carefully, before attaching it to the post and rails with stainless-steel screws.

Finally, position the second post with attached stile. **(Photo 10)** Drill the counterbores and pilots, and drive the assembly screws through the post into the top and bottom rail ends. Also run screws through the lattice module into the stile.

Shape the Beams

Shape the beams in the same general way you shaped the bottom rails. That is, position the template over the blank for the beam, and draw the shape onto the

blank. To get the shape for the second end, you just flip the blank, set the template back in place, and draw the template's end shape there. Cut close to the lines with a saber saw.

Return the template to the blank, place them together on a scrap piece of plywood or MDF, and clamp them to the workbench. Using your router and pattern bit, rout the beam to match the template. After you've routed the arc and one end, flip the beam and rout the other end. **(Photo 11)** Remove the template completely, switch to the flush-trimming bit, and then complete the work. **(Photo 12)**

Join the Beams to the Sides

This is the time to decide whether to move the project outdoors to complete it. That is, before you decide to stay in the shop to join the sides with the beams, make sure that you can get the assembled arbor through your shop's doorway.

Set up a pair of sawhorses parallel with one

another and about 6 feet apart. Clamp a beam to each. One beam will become part of the top of the arbor and be the beam to which you attach the side assemblies. The beam on the second sawhorse temporarily

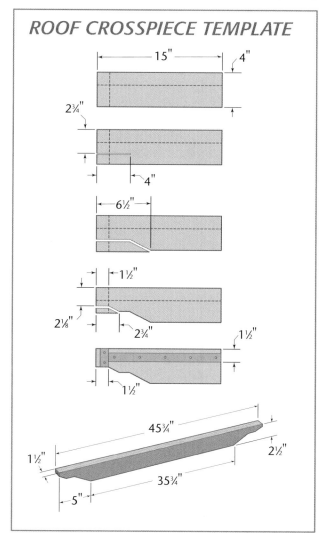

ROOF CROSSPIECE TEMPLATE

Shape the arc and one end of a beam with the template. Then flip the beam, end for end, and use the same template to shape the second end. Repeat for other two beams.

Rout along the beam template with a pattern bit to shape most of the beam's edge. Remove the template and turn the beam over. Trim the remaining ridge of waste using a flush-trimming bit.

Mount the first beam to the side assemblies while they are clamped across a pair of sawhorses. Use clamped-on braces to hold the sides until the arbor is set up.

Mount the roof crosspieces on the beams after the arbor is installed in its final location. Drive long screws through deep counterbores into the beams, and then plug the holes.

supports the sides. As you position the first side assembly, align its upper end on the appropriate beam, and square it. Use a framing square or the 3–4–5 method to check for square. (For details on employing the 3–4–5 method, see "Grape Arbor," pages 142–149.) Clamp the assembly to both beams. Then position the second side assembly on the beams, align it, and ensure that it is square to the beam, using a framing square or the 3-4-5 method. **(Photo 13)**

Lay out and drill holes for the mounting bolts. Use stainless-steel carriage bolts, with the heads oriented to the outside to secure the beam to the sides.

Lay a beam on top of the assembly. Line up the sides and this beam, and then clamp them. At the same time, attach tem-

porary braces at the foot end of the side assemblies to hold them in the desired relationship. Drill bolt holes, and bolt this beam to the posts.

Stand the arbor on its feet, and position the middle beam on the top rails midway between the posts of the side assemblies. Secure the beam by driving 3-inch screws at an angle through the beam and into the top rail.

Shape and Install the Roof Crosspieces

The roof crosspieces complete the arbor's construction. Though largely decorative, the roof crosspieces do provide some bracing for the arbor. You've already cut all to width and length.

Now it is time to shape their ends,

using the template you made earlier. Draw the outline of the template onto the ends of each roof crosspiece, and cut close to the lines with your saber saw. Then, one by one, rout the ends to their final contour.

If you haven't already done so, transport the arbor to its final location. Install the center roof crosspiece first. Mark its location 38⅛ inches from the end of the beams, and clamp it in place to two of the beams. Then drill deep counterbores and pilot holes through the top edge down into the beams. Drive mounting screws, and then plug the holes. **(Photo 14)** (For more on drilling deep counterbores and plugging their holes, see "Designer Trellis," pages 72–77.

GATEWAY ARBOR

This elegant, classic arbor is without peer as an up-scale entry to your yard or garden. It will speak volumes about your excellent taste in design, as well as your extraordinary woodworking skills.

EXPLODED VIEW

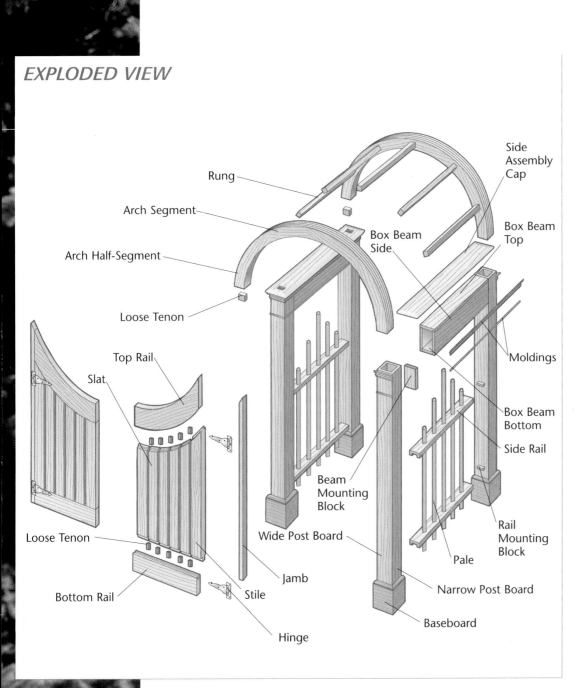

Rung

Arch Segment

Arch Half-Segment

Loose Tenon

Top Rail

Slat

Loose Tenon

Bottom Rail

Stile

Hinge

Jamb

Wide Post Board

Beam
Mounting
Block

Narrow Post Board

Baseboard

Side
Assembly
Cap

Box Beam
Side

Box Beam
Top

Moldings

Box Beam
Bottom

Side Rail

Rail
Mounting
Block

Pale

SHOPPING LIST

■ 7 pcs. ⁵⁄₄×8 10' #2 common eastern white pine (arch segments)

■ 1 pc. ⁵⁄₄×4 10' select eastern white pine (gate parts)

■ 2 pcs. ⁵⁄₄×4 12' select eastern white pine (gate parts)

■ 8 pcs. ⁵⁄₄×8 12' #2 common eastern white pine (posts)

■ 2 pcs. ⁵⁄₄×10 10' select eastern white pine (caps, gate parts)

■ 5 pcs. 1×8 8' select eastern white pine (rails and pales)

■ 1 pc. 1×8 10' select eastern white pine (cove moldings)

■ 4 pcs. 1×10 10' select white pine (box beams, moldings, baseboards)

■ 2 pcs. 4×4 8' treated southern yellow pine

■ 2 pr. strap-type decorative gate hinges

■ 2 gate handles/pulls

■ 1 gate latch/1 gate stake

■ 1 box each 1⅝" and 2" galvanized screws

■ 1 box 6d galvanized finish nails

■ 1 box 1¼" stainless-steel brads

CUTTING LIST

Part	Quantity	Thickness	Width	Length	Pine
Arches					
Arch segments	28	1"	7¼"	24½"	⁵⁄₄×8 10'
Arch half segments	8	1"	7¼"	12¼"	⁵⁄₄×8 10'
Rungs	5	2"	2"	39⅞"	laminate ⁵⁄₄×8 12'
Loose tenons	4	1"	2"	2⅜"	⁵⁄₄×8 12'

Cutting list continues on pages 133, 136, and 139.

FRONT AND SIDE ELEVATIONS

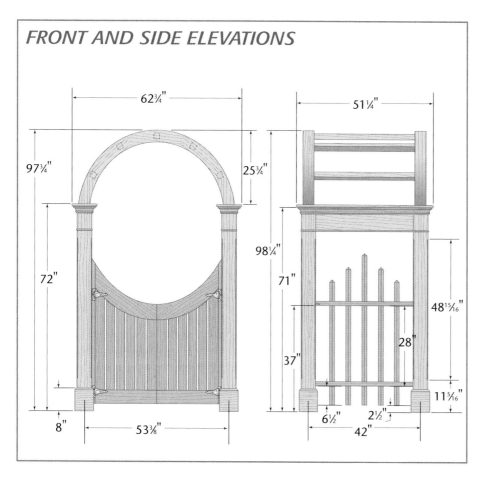

62¾" 97¾" 72" 8" 53⅜" 51¼" 25¾" 98¼" 71" 37" 48¹⁵⁄₁₆" 28" 11⁵⁄₁₆" 6½" 2½" 42"

BUILDER'S NOTES

Although this project involves some unusual techniques, it isn't especially difficult if you work methodically. Be sure to use high-quality, straight, flat, true stock. After you make the arch-and-rung assembly, posts, beams, and side assemblies, you dig postholes, set the arbor in place, and finish assembling it.

Materials
Because this project requires quite a bit of wood and top-grade outdoor woods can be pricey, I simply used white pine for almost all parts. For arches and rungs, posts, gates, and some of the trim, I used ¾-by stock, which ranges from 1 to 1⅛ inches thick. I used nominal one-by

stock (actually ¾" thick) for the box beams. For the side rails and pales, I glue-laminated one-by to create 1½-inch stock.

Tools and Techniques
You need a well-equipped shop, including a table saw, a good router (or two) with an assortment of bits, a couple of drill-drivers, a power miter saw, a saber saw, and sanders. Having a planer (and a jointer to complement it) will allow you to straighten your stock and produce parts of uniform thickness. To clamp the side assemblies and the arch assembly, you'll need bar or pipe clamps.

Constructing the two arches is the most time-consuming task

(several days) in this project. Each finished arch consists of four layers of arch segments. You start by forming four double-layer and glue-laminated arch blanks assembled from segments, cutting each to shape, and then layering and gluing pairs of them to form the two quadruple-layer arches. For the laminations, I used polyurethane glue, which dictates a clamping cycle of about four hours. I wound up using about 25 clamps at a time, of different varieties, including C-clamps, bar clamps, quick-action clamps, hand screws, and even short pipe clamps.

Finish
Paint is especially appropriate for this style of arbor.

STEP-BY-STEP

Cut the Arch Segments

Start with the 10-foot-long ¾x8 boards. Each one should give you five arch segments having ends with 67½-degree angles and measuring 24½ inches on the longest edge. (See the "Arch Segment Layout" drawing below.) In addition, you need eight half-segments, each angled on only one end and measuring 12¼ inches along the longest edge. Produce these by cutting full-size segments in half. These parts are easy to cut with a power miter saw and using a stop-block setup (as in Photo 1), so you don't need to measure and mark each segment for cutting—only the first one.

Turn the saw to 22½ degrees (90 degrees − 67½ = 22½). Because 22½ is half of 45, it is given a detent on most power miter saws. Lay the first board to be cut across the saw table, and cut off the end. This triangular scrap is the key part of the stop-block setup, which starts with scrap plywood as a base. To that, screw a stack of small scrap pieces that's flush with the miter saw's table. Screw the triangular scrap to the top.

Return to the long pine board. Turn it over. Measure from the mitered end 24½ inches on the long edge to mark the next cut. Line up the cut; carefully slide your stop against the mitered end of the board; and clamp the stop to the benchtop. Now make the cut. **(Photo 1)**

No additional measuring is necessary. Miter the end of each fresh board. Then turn the board over, slide it tight against the stop, and cut. Remove the cut segment, roll the board, and slide it against the stop. Repeat this process until you have cut 32 arch segments. Then cut four of them in half and you will have the required number of 28 full and 8 half segments. For best results, use only segments that are per-

ARCH SEGMENT LAYOUT

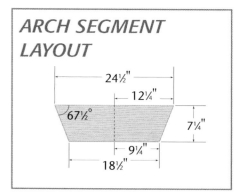

24½" 12¼" 67½° 7¼" 9¼" 18½"

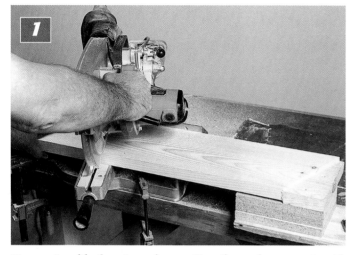

Use a stop-block setup when cutting the arch segments with your power miter saw. Its triangular top piece lets you cut the segments without further measuring and marking.

Each arch blank consists of two courses of segments. The ends of the top pieces meet at the center of the segment below them, their corners 1¹³⁄₁₆ in. up from the lower segment's edge.

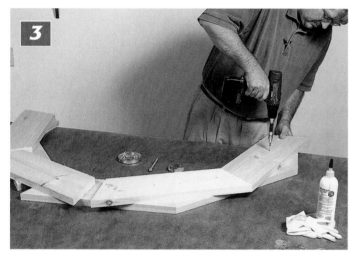

Assemble an entire two-layer arch blank, and then go back and drill pilot holes and drive temporary screws though each segment into the one below it.

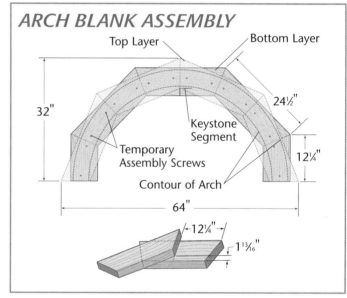

ARCH BLANK ASSEMBLY

Top Layer
Bottom Layer
32"
24½"
Keystone Segment
12¼"
Temporary Assembly Screws
Contour of Arch
64"
12¼"
1¹³⁄₁₆"

fectly flat. Don't even try to salvage twisted segments; instead, cut new ones. (If you have a thickness planer, you could run each segment through it, flattening both faces of each segment.)

Test-Fit the Arch Blanks

Set up a large assembly station to arrange four double-layer arch blanks from the segments, as shown in the "Arch Blank Assembly" drawing above. You may need to lay down a sheet of plywood or hardboard (preferred) and support it on saw horses. Begin at the crest of the arch, with two segments in the top layer meeting end-to-end over the centerline of the segment beneath. The inside corner formed by the top segments should be 1¹³⁄₁₆ inches up from the bottom segment's lower edge.

(Photo 2) With a pencil and square, draw the centerline and mark the intersection point.

A challenge during the glue-up (next step) is keeping the segments in place. To resolve this, I temporarily screwed the segments together. You'll still need to clamp the parts, but when you remove the clamps, you can also remove the screws. To prepare for the glue-up, lay out the segments without glue. When they are properly placed, tucked tightly end to end, drill pilot holes and drive screws, joining the two layers. Locate the screws within the curve of the arch. **(Photo 3)**

While the parts are joined, scribe a line along the top segments to mark the face of the underlayer. These marks will show you how far to spread glue (no sense wasting

it). Back out the screws just enough to dismantle the assembly.

Glue Up the Arch Blanks

For polyurethane glue, apply it to one of the mating segments. Wipe the other segment with a wet rag. Spread an even coat of glue over the face of the "keystone" segment, the one with the pencil centerline. Take up one of the overlay segments, and drive its partially driven screws so that their tips emerge on the underside. Wipe the bottom of this segment with a wet rag, and position it on the glue-slathered segment, catching the screw tips in its awaiting pilot holes. Drive the screws all the way, locking the segments together. Then apply glue to the butt end of the screwed-down segment. Then join the next

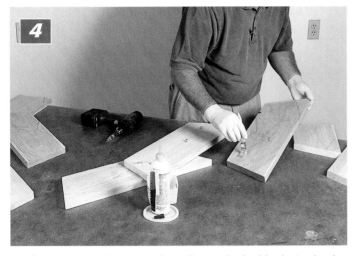

Back out screws *just enough to dismantle the blank. Apply glue to the pencil-marked segment, and reassemble. As you press each segment to its mate, align them by redriving the screws.*

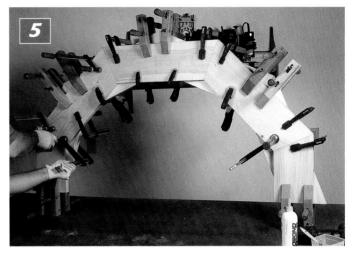

Clamp the two-layer arch blank. *Handscrews can serve as stabilizing feet. Distribute clamps evenly along both edges. You may need every clamp you own or can borrow.*

Draw the two arcs *on the arch template with a narrow trammel. Then step off the 29-in. radius from the top of the arc to begin marking positions of rung mortises.*

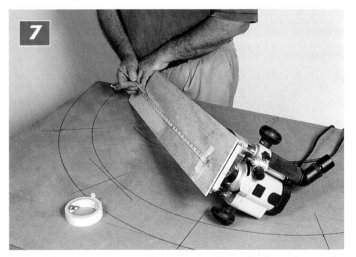

Set up the router trammel, *measuring from the bit to locate the pivot points. Masking tape can hold your measuring tape at the bit, freeing you to mark the pivot.*

segment in the same manner. **(Photo 4)**.

Continue in this way until you've joined all segments with glue and screws. Use the partially driven screws as alignment devices, catching them in the holes they made during the dry assembly.

Clamp the Arch Blanks

With the arch segments glued and fastened, apply clamps to the entire assembly, arraying them around the perimeter **(Photo 5)**. Set the assembled arch blank aside; let the glue cure. Repeat the process to make the remaining three arch blanks.

Lay Out the Arch Template

To cut the arches accurately, you'll use a router guided by a template that is cut to the exact size and shape of the arch (and

includes the placement for the rung mortises, as well). For cutting, use a plunge router, a ½-inch straight bit with cutting edges at least 2 inches long, and a ¾-inch outside diameter template guide. (You'll do the mortising with the same equipment, but with a shorter bit.) For the template, use ½- to ¾-inch plywood or MDF. To protect the benchtop when routing the template, lay the template blank on top of an expendable piece of plywood. Clamp both to the benchtop.

Referring to "Making the Arch Template," page 131, lay out the arch template. Locate the pivot point for the arcs; then draw the arcs. Make a trammel from a strip of wood: drill a hole for a marker in one end; then drill pivot holes for the radii needed. Draw the two full arcs. Lay out the bottom trim

lines. Lay out the radians that mark each rung mortise location. **(Photo 6)** Set up the drawing trammel for a 26⅞-inch radius (actual radius of 26¹⁵⁄₁₆ inches), and mark a line across each radian, which is the center of a rung mortise.

Cut the Template Arcs

Cut these with a plunge router and a trammel, using a strip of ¼-inch plywood as the trammel. Attach it to the plunge router. Measure along the trammel from the bit (unplug the router first) to locate the two pivot points for the inside and outside curves of the arch. **(Photo 7)** The bit's diameter is included in the 24¾-inch radius but is outside the 29-inch radius. (Thus, you hook the measuring tape over the bit when measuring the short radius and butt it

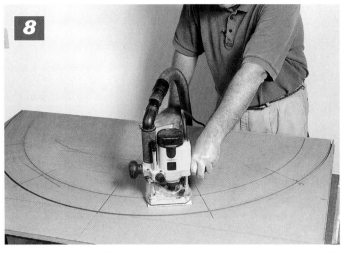

Swing the router through the arc, cutting a little deeper with each swing. Cut the longer arc first. Then shift the pivot screw to cut the shorter radius.

Use a mortising jig to cut mortises in the arch template, first lining up centerlines on each. If you use a fixed-base router, drill starting holes for the bit.

against the bit when measuring the long one.)

Rout the outside curve first. Run a screw through the appropriate pivot point in the trammel into the pivot point drilled in the template blank. Begin the cut at an edge, plunging the bit about ⅛ inch deep, then swinging the router through the arc to the opposite edge. Then plunge about ⅛ inch deeper, and swing the router back. Continue routing in this manner until you

have cut through the template material.

Rout the inside curve next. Using the same centerpoint on the template blank, move the screw to its pivot point in the trammel. Plunge-cut as for the previous arc. **(Photo 8)**

Cut the Mortise Openings

Make a rung-mortise jig to rout exact mortise openings into the arch template.

The jig is a 12-inch-square plywood base with four fences (strips of ¾- x 1-inch scrap) on top to limit the movement of the router. (See "Rung-Mortise Jig" drawing, page 132.)

Begin by making a setup gauge for locating the fences. The setup gauge represents the distance between the bit and the router's edge. To make the gauge, you must use the bit you are going to use for mortising. With carpet tape, stick a 4- or 5-inch-wide scrap of hardboard or plywood to your workbench edge. Clamp a straightedge tight against one edge of the scrap. Run your router along the straightedge, trimming the scrap.

Lay out the 1¾-inch-square mortise in the center of the jig's base, beginning with the mortise centerlines. Lay the setup gauge on one edge of the mortise layout; butt a ¾- x 1-inch fence strip against its other edge. Clamp it, and drive screws through both the base and fence. Trim away excess fence strip. Position and attach the other three fences in the same way. You will have to cut down the length of the setup gauge for locating the fourth and final fence. "Prove" the accuracy of the jig by routing through the base, just as if you were routing a mortise. Clamp the jig to a piece of scrap so that you don't damage the surface below.

To use the rung-mortise jig, align its mortise centerlines with one of those on the arch template, clamping the jig and template together. Rout each of the five openings in stages, increasing depth about ⅛ inch with each pass. **(Photo 9)**

MAKING THE ARCH TEMPLATE

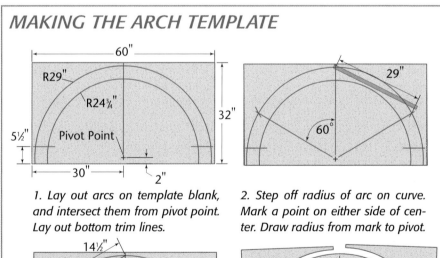

1. Lay out arcs on template blank, and intersect them from pivot point. Lay out bottom trim lines.

2. Step off radius of arc on curve. Mark a point on either side of center. Draw radius from mark to pivot.

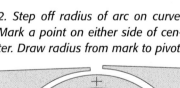

3. Connect marks; bisect line with a radian (the center of a mortise). Scribe short arcs bisecting mortises.

4. Use router and trammel to cut template from blank. Then trim off ends of template.

Rout out the arch, *guided by the template clamped to it. It requires many circuits around the template. Position clamps so that they won't block the router.*

Cut the rung mortises into the arch, *using the template. Temporarily screw the template in place to hold the layers together. Use the same router and guide but a shorter bit.*

Saw the rung tenons *on the table saw, cutting the shoulders first. Then stand a rung on end in a tenoning jig, and saw the cheeks, one at a time.*

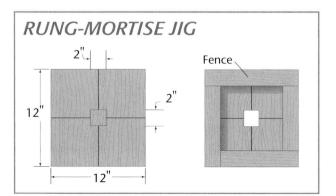

Assemble the arches and rungs without glue initially *to ensure that everything fits. Insert the rungs into the mortises in one arch before lifting the second arch atop the rungs.*

Cut Out the Arches

Position an arch blank on an expendable sheet of plywood so your benchtop will be protected. Place the arch template on top of the blank, centering the template over the keystone segment and aligning it with the ends of the blank. Then temporarily fasten the template to the blank with a few screws.

Before chucking the router bit, fit the ¾-inch template guide in place. Install the long ½-inch straight bit. (If the bit extends completely through the template guide's collar when the router's plunge is fully retracted, you should instead begin the cut with a short ½-inch bit. When you reach its maximum depth, switch to the long bit.)

Rout around the template, feeding counterclockwise. With the router resting on the template, the collar of the guide rides along the template's edge. Cut only ⅛ inch deep in each circuit. **(Photo 10)** Repeat the process for cutting the three remaining arch blanks into arch shapes.

Make the Two Arches

You now have four arches, each 2 inches thick, but for the arbor, you need two 4-inch-thick arches. To accomplish this, glue a pair of 2-inch-thick arches together, orienting their best faces out. Use the same glue you used for the laminating the arch blocks. Spread it evenly over the face of one arch (and dampen the face of the other arch, if using polyurethane glue). Position one arch on the other, rub the faces together to generate some tack, and then bring the edges into alignment. Apply clamps around the edges.

When the glue has set and you have

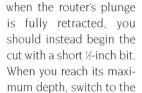

RUNG-MORTISE JIG

2"

Fence

12"

2"

12"

removed the clamps, designate one face of each as its inner face. Reapply the arch template to this face, and rout the rung mortises. Use your plunge router with the ¾-inch template guide and a ½-inch straight bit (not the long one). The mortises are only 1 inch deep. Each will be 1¾ inches square. **(Photo 11)**

Make the Rungs

Form blanks for each of the five rungs by glue-laminating pairs of strips of 5/4-by stock. Once the glue has cured, rip and crosscut each blank to final size. For accuracy in cutting uniform 1-inch-long tenons on the ends of the rungs, make a tenoning jig. Use scrap wood, and fasten the pieces with glue and 2-inch drywall screws, after drilling and countersinking pilot holes. Cut and join the sides first, as shown in the drawing "Tenoning Jig" at right. Add the brace to lock the sides at a perfect right angle. To guide the jig, add an outrigger that straddles the table saw's rip fence. This fit is important—you want the jig to slide along the fence, but without sideplay. Measure the width of your saw fence, and cut the outrigger to that width. Cut the outrigger guide and a pair of outrigger braces. Assemble all parts.

Saw the tenons on the table saw, using dimensions from the drawing "Rung Tenon Detail" below. Cut the shoulders with the saw blade raised ¼ inch and the rip fence set 1 inch from the outside of the blade. Guide the rung, sliding its end along the fence. Cut across each face at both ends of the rung. Use the tenoning jig to support the rungs as you cut the cheeks. Raise the blade to 1 inch. Set the jig over the rip fence, and adjust the fence to place the outside of the blade ¼ inch from the jig side. Cut all four cheeks. **(Photo 12)** Then round off tenon corners with a file so that they'll fit the routed mortises in the arches. Sand the arches and rungs. If you wish, you can use your router to round-over or chamfer the corners of the rungs (and arches).

RUNG TENON DETAIL

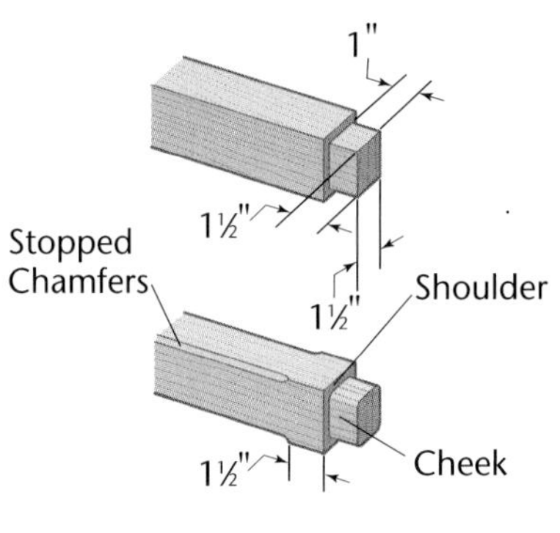

Assemble the Arches

Do a test-fit, without glue, to ensure that all parts fit. **(Photo 13)** Use this opportunity to set clamps and to tape cauls to the arches where the clamps will be applied so that the clamps don't dent the wood. When you are satisfied, glue the assembly together. Apply glue to the mortises in one arch and to the tenons on each rung. Jam a rung into each mortise in the first arch. Apply glue to the mortises in the second arch. Set the second arch atop the rungs, and align them so that the tenons fit into the mortises and the arch seats. Apply the clamps, and set the unit aside. Begin constructing the two side assemblies.

TENONING JIG

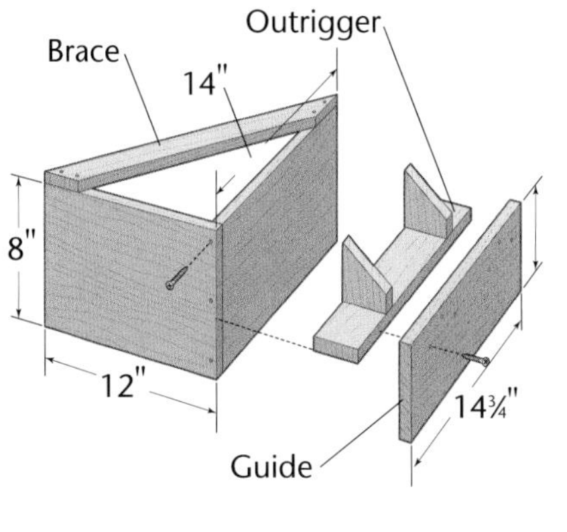

Cut Joinery in Post Boards

Rip and crosscut the boards for the posts to the dimensions in the Cutting List below. Make sure the boards are straight and have parallel edges. Then rout grooves in both edges of all eight wide post boards. (See the "Post Construction" drawings on page 135.) Set up your router with a ⅜-inch straight bit and an edge guide. Clamp the

SIDE ASSEMBLY CUTTING LIST

Part	Quantity	Thickness	Width	Length	Pine
Wide post boards	8	1"	5½"	71½"	5/4×8 12'
Narrow post boards	8	1"	4¼"	71½"	5/4×8 12'
Box beam sides	4	¾"	8¼"	36⅝"	1×10 10'
Box beam tops	2	¾"	5⅜"	36⅝"	1×10 10'
Box beam bottoms	2	¾"	4"	36⅝"	1×10 10'
Beam mounting blocks	4	1"	4"	6¾"	5/4×8 10'
Side rails	4	1½"	3½"	36⅝"	Laminate 1×8 8'
Center pales	2	1½"	1½"	54½"	Laminate 1×8 8'
Intermediate pales	4	1½"	1½"	51 1/16"	Laminate 1×8 8'
Outside pales	4	1½"	1½"	47 9/16"	Laminate 1×8 8'
Rail mounting blocks	8	¾"	2"	1"	1×8 8'
Side assembly caps	2	1"	9⅜"	51⅜"	5/4×10 10'
Baseboards	16	¾"	8"	7"	1×10 10'
Post extensions	4	3½"	3½"	48" min.	4×4 8' (treated)

Groove the wide post boards from end to end with a router and edge guide. Rout the ¼-in.-deep cut in two quick passes, rather than in a single labored pass.

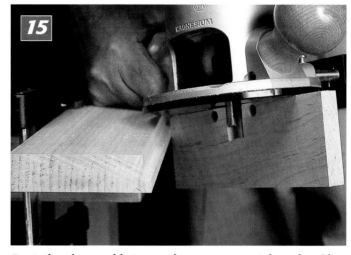

Rout the deep rabbets on the narrow post boards with a straight bit. An edge guide, here with a wide facing screwed to it, controls the width of the cut.

workpiece to the benchtop, and plow the groove from end to end. **(Photo 14)** Unclamp the board; turn it around; and plow a similar groove in the same face along the opposite edge.

Rabbet edges of the eight narrow boards next, using the same bit but adjusting the edge guide to produce a cut ¼ inch wide and the router to make the cut ⅜ inch deep. Rabbet a short scrap of the working stock, and fit it to a groove in one of the wide post boards. If the tongue fits properly, with the narrow board's face flush with the edge of the wide board, proceed with rabbeting both edges of each narrow post board. **(Photo 15)**

Assemble the Posts

Do a dry run of the assembly process, making sure the four boards of each post fit together completely and settle into a square section. Check square at several locations along the post using a try square. Dismantle the post. Apply glue to the grooves in the wide boards and to the rabbets in the narrow boards. Reassemble the post, and apply the clamps. Check again with the try square.

Cut the eight rail mounting blocks to the dimensions specified by the Cutting List, ensuring better glue bond by making their grain run parallel with the post's grain. (Refer to the drawing "Post Construction" on page 135 for the locations.) Glue the blocks to the post; then drill pilot holes and drive two 1⅝-inch screws through each block into the post.

Rip and crosscut the sides, tops, and bottoms to the dimensions specified in the Cutting List, page 133. Rout the grooves and

the rabbets. (Refer to the "Box Beam Construction" drawing, page 135.) Because the stock is only ¾ inch thick, use a ¼-inch bit to make the cuts. Each top board is grooved parallel with both edges. The sides are grooved parallel with the bottom edge. The top edge of each side is rabbeted to form a tongue to fit the groove in the top. The bottom boards are rabbeted along both edges. The grooves are ¼ inch wide and deep and are ½ inch from board edges. The rabbets are ¼ inch by ½ inch.

Before gluing the beams, do a test-fit. Ensure that the joints fit and that the beams are the same width as the posts. The sides of the beams must be flush with the sides of the posts. That done, glue and clamp the boards together.

Assemble the Posts and Beams

Measure the inside height and width of each end of both box beams, and cut four beam mounting blocks to these dimensions from ¾ stock. Make sure the grain of each block runs vertically, so it will parallel the grain in the post. Glue and screw the blocks to each post. (Refer to the "Post Construction" drawing, page 135.)

To join a beam to a post, you will apply glue to the edges of the mounting block, fit the beam over it, and then drive screws through the beam sides into edges of the block. To conceal the screws, first drill counterbores. Mark three or four points for pilots at both ends of each beam side, and drill the counterbores with a Forstner bit.

But first, test-fit the parts, and clamp them, just as if you had already spread the

glue. Make sure the assembly is square by measuring diagonally from the top of one post to the bottom of the other. Then measure the second diagonal. When the two diagonals are equal, the assembly is square. Drill a pilot hole in the center of each counterbore, penetrating the beam side into the mounting block.

Dismantle the assembly, and apply glue. Reassemble the posts and beam, and reclamp, checking the assembly for square before you drive the screws. **(Photo 16)**

Make the Rails and Pales

Glue-laminate stock for the rails and the pales, using two layers of one-by pine for each part. Rip and crosscut the elements, making them about ½ inch wider and an inch or so longer than the final width and length. Glue and clamp the elements face to face, orienting the best-looking face of each element out. After the clamps are off, re-rip the blanks, bringing them down to their final thickness and width. Crosscut the rails to final length. Chamfer the tops of the pales, forming a pyramidal contour. Then measure from the tip; mark them for length; crosscut their bottom ends. Sand all parts.

Make a jig for mortising the rails. See the drawing "Side-Rail Mortising Jig," page 135. This is similar to the jig used to make the rung-mortising openings in the arch template. The obvious differences are the dimensions of the opening in the template and the fact that the fences attached to guide the router are removed after you rout the opening.

Make a test mortise in scrap with the

Move the second post against the beam end. *Use long pipe clamps to pull posts and beam tight. Check for square. Drill pilots through counterbores, and screw the parts together.*

Cut mortises into the side rails *using a side-rail mortising jig. The jig has fences that align it on the rail. Simply slide it to the mark, clamp, and rout.*

newly made template. Do the full job, including squaring the mortise corners with a chisel or jigsaw. Check how a pale fits this mortise. If the mortise isn't right, determine how you need to alter the template—larger opening or smaller—and remake the template. Test again.

Rout the Pale Mortises

After you have a proven template, use it to rout the mortises for the pales in all four rails. The mortises are oriented on the diagonal; that is to say, opposite corners of the

mortise are aligned to the rail's centerline. To simplify further, align the template once and attach fences on its underside to capture the rail. Then you only have to align the template on the square layout lines that delineate mortise positions.

Rout the mortises with a plunge router with a ¾-inch template guide and a long ½-inch straight bit. (It has to extend as much as 2 inches beyond the router's base to make the through mortises.) Clamp the rail on top of an expendable piece of plywood (to protect your bench-

top). Slide the jig into alignment; clamp it; and rout the mortise. **(Photo 17)** Repeat the process for all of the remaining mortises.

Assemble and Mount the Rails and Pales

Make sure that the rails fit between the posts. Slide them into place, and mark the outline of the mounting blocks on the underside of the rails. Remove the rails, and rout a recess for the mounting block. To help guide the router, make a jig as shown in

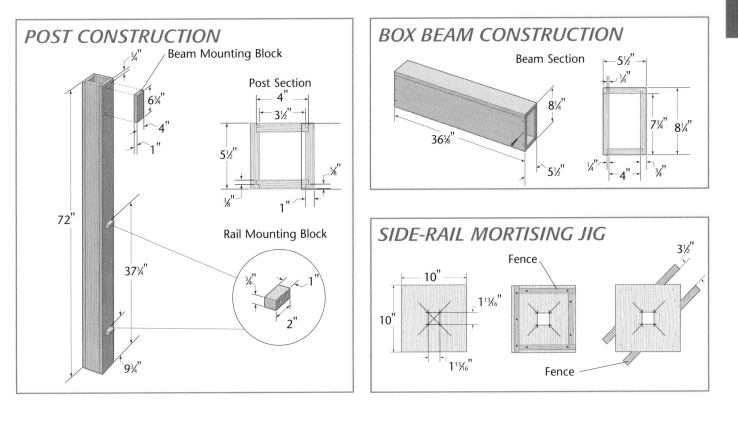

POST CONSTRUCTION

Beam Mounting Block
¾"
6¾"
4"
1"

Post Section
4"
3½"
5½"
⅝"
⅜"
1"

72"

Rail Mounting Block
¾"
1"
2"

37¾"

9¾"

BOX BEAM CONSTRUCTION

Beam Section
8¼"
36⅝"
5½"

5½"
¼"
7¾"
8¼"
¼"
4"
¾"

SIDE-RAIL MORTISING JIG

Fence
10"
10"
1¹³⁄₁₆"
1¹³⁄₁₆"

3½"

Fence

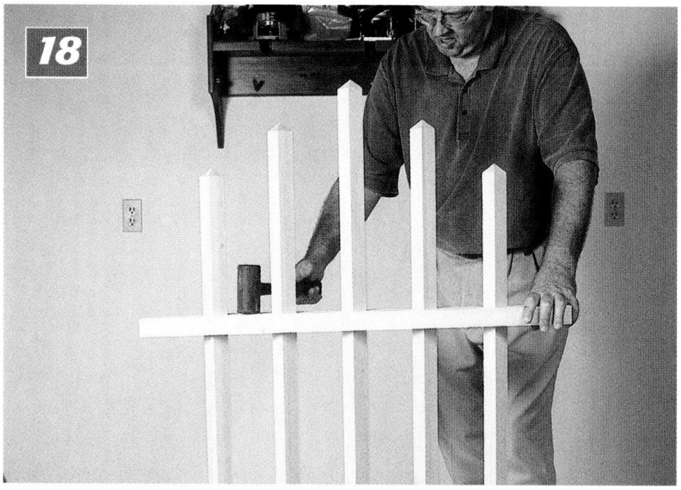

For a good tight fit of pale to mortise, *you must work the rail down onto the pales, tapping back and forth along the rail with a dead-blow mallet.*

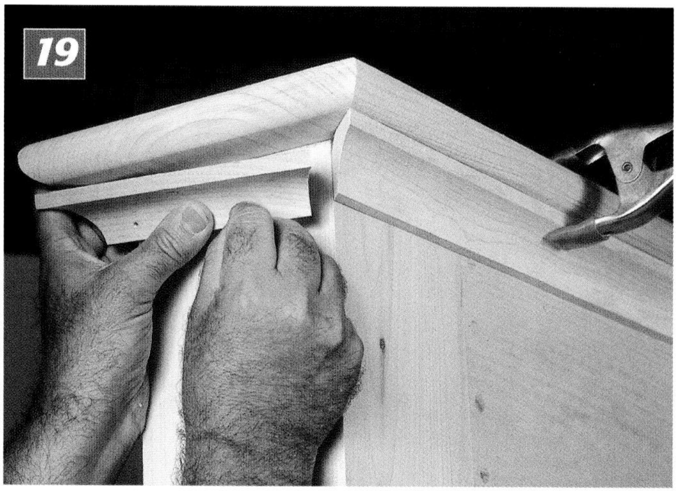

Install each piece of cove molding as you cut it. *This will ensure that you get good, tight miter joints. Fasten in place using glue and finishing nails.*

the drawing "Rail-Notching Jig," page 137.

Fit the rails to the side assemblies, seating them on the mounting blocks. Run a screw through the underside of the mounting block into the rail. Then remove the screws and the rails.

Use a chisel to square the corners of the mortises in the rails. Lay a side rail on the floor, and fit the bottoms of the pales into the mortises. Fit and drive the second rail down onto the pales. **(Photo 18)** Position the rails from the ground up. You want: 2½ inches of clearance from the bottom of the posts to the bottoms of the pales; 6½ inches from there to the underside of the lower rail; and 28 inches from there to the underside of the upper rail. With the upper rail positioned, drill counterbores and pilot holes through the one edge of the rail into the pales. Drive a 2-inch screw into each hole, pinning the pales. Lay the assembly on your workbench, and clamp the upper rail. Then drive the lower rail up into position. Check the assembly's fit to the post-and-beam unit; reposition as needed; then fasten the lower rail to the pales. Assemble the other unit the same way. Make wooden plugs; plug the counterbores in the rails; and sand them flush.

Make and Apply the Moldings

Dimensions for moldings applied around the tops of the side assemblies are shown in the drawing "Side Assembly Moldings," page 137. The largest piece of "molding" is the side assembly cap, which is really a board with molded edges that overlays the tops of the posts and the box beam. The cap edges are shaped with two different roundover bits: the top edge has a ⅜-inch-radius roundover; the bottom, a ⅝-inch-radius roundover. Cut these with your router. Because the pilot bearing of whichever bit you use second will have no square edge to reference, you'll need an edge guide for the second cut.

Once shaped, mount a cap onto each side assembly, gluing it to the top of the box beam. Fasten with finishing nails or with screws through the cap into the edges of the posts and the box beam. (If nails, countersink and putty over; if screws, counterbore and plug.)

Next, cut and attach the cove molding below the entire cap. Rout this with a special coving bit in a table-mounted router. (See the sequence in the "Making Cove Molding" drawings on page 137.) When you rout the cove and any other moldings, it is safest to work on a fairly wide strip of wood. You can rout the profile on both edges and then rip the molding from the workpiece. Make several extra strips of each molding, just in case.

Fasten the cove molding as soon as you cut it. Miter one end of a strip, and align it against the side, up against the post. Mark the square-cut end for mitering, and cut to the mark on your power miter saw. Mount the cove with glue and nails. Miter the next piece, and fit that end against the attached cove. Mark the square-cut end; miter it; and install that cove. Work your way around all sides, fitting and mounting. **(Photo 19)**

Completing this complex molding is a ½-inch-diameter half-round with a fillet, or step, below it. This is the "bead with fillet" in the drawing. Form the bead using a ¼-

MOLDING CUTTING LIST

Part	Quantity	Thickness	Width	Length	Pine
Cove moldings, long	4	1⅜"	1½"	52" *	1×8 10'
Cove moldings, short	4	1⅜"	1½"	10" *	1×8 10'
Beads with fillet, long	4	⅝"	⅞"	52" *	1×10 10'
Beads with fillet, short	4	⅝"	⅞"	10" *	1×10 10'
Beads, long	4	¼"	½"	52" *	1×10 10'
Beads, short	4	¼"	½"	10" *	1×10 10'

*Finished length. Cut a few inches longer, and trim to fit during assembly.

inch roundover bit in a table-mounted router. Install it tight under the bottom edge of the cove molding. Fit and mount it the same way you did the cove.

The final strip is a simple bead around the posts and along the edge of the beam. Rout the profile on the edge of a 2- to 3-inch-wide strip of ½-inch stock. Use a ¼-inch round-over bit in the table-mounted router. Rip the bead free of the stock. Rout a new profile on the workpiece, and rip it free. Repeat this process until you have enough bead for the arbor. Mount with glue and brads.

Lay Out and Dig the Postholes

Figure out exactly where you will install the arbor. Lay out posthole centers, as shown in the drawing "Setting Up the Arbor," page 139. Ensure they are at the corners of a rectangle, following the 3-4-5 squaring method, explained in detail in "Grape Arbor," pages 144–147. Check with local building officials about frost depth to ensure that your postholes will be dug below the frost line for your locality. To promote drainage, dump about 6 inches of gravel into the bottom of each hole.

Setup the Side Assemblies

Cut and install the post extensions. These are four lengths of 4x4 treated lumber that are long enough to reach 2 to 3 feet up inside the hollow arbor posts and extend to the gravel at the bottom of the postholes. Secure the upper portions to the posts with screws, drilling counterbores so that you can conceal the screwheads with wooden plugs. The portion extending to the bottom of the posthole will be set in concrete. If the 4x4s jam against dried glue runs as you insert them, try chamfering their corners.

Referring to the setup drawing, position one side assembly with its post extensions in their postholes. Adjust its elevation by adding gravel or removing it from the hole. Level and plumb the assembly, and brace it temporarily to stakes driven into the ground. Place concrete around the post extensions.

Erect the second side assembly in the same way, although you'll need to position the second one the correct distance away from and parallel with the first. Check for level from side to side by resting your level on a straight board long enough to span from unit to unit. Brace the second side temporarily to the first. Then place concrete around its post extensions, too.

Make the Mortising Template

The arch assembly joins the side assemblies with mortise and loose-tenon joints. For this, you cut mortises in both parts to be joined, and make a loose tenon to extend into each set of mortises. Make the mortises using a plunge router fitted with a ½-inch straight bit and a ⅝-inch template made from ½-inch plywood. (See "Arch-to-Post Mortising Template" drawing, page 138.) The mortises are 1⅛ inches wide and 2⅛ inches long. In the arches, the mortises should be 1½ inches deep. In the side assembly caps, they can be only ⅞ inch deep. (Depth is limited by the thickness of the cap stock.)

Lay out the mortise along with crossing centerlines to aid in positioning the template on the work. Make a spacer gauge to reflect the distance between the router base edge and the bit. Then use it to attach fences to the template in relation to the mortise window. Rout the window in the template. Then remove the fences.

Don't fret about specific dimensions of the mortises. Made using the template, they'll all be the same size. Later, just make the loose tenons to fit the mortises.

Mortise the Arches

Place the arch assembly upside down on the floor, arch bottoms up. Chock the arch with large wedges clamped on to keep the arch from rocking. Draw centerlines—both front-to-back and side-to-side—on each bottom. Align the mortising template on the first arch bottom, oriented side to side, lining up its centerlines with those on the arch. Drill pilot holes, and temporarily screw the template to the arch. Set up your plunge router with a ½-inch straight bit and a ⅝-inch tem-

RAIL-NOTCHING JIG

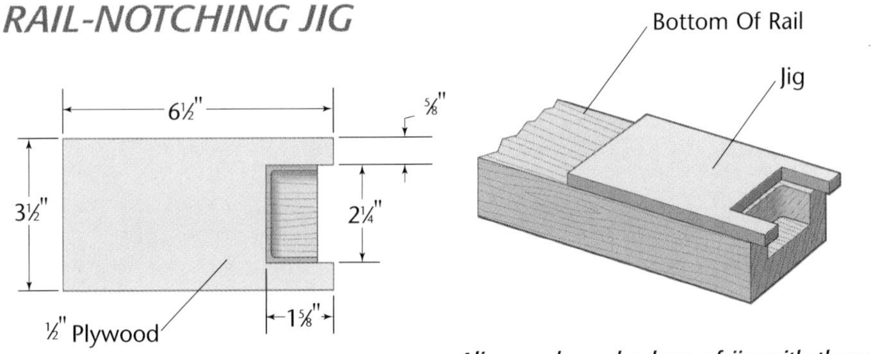
6½"
⅝"
3½"
2¼"
1⅝"
½" Plywood
Bottom Of Rail
Jig

Notch in rail is 2" wide by 1" long.

Align ends and edges of jig with those of workpiece. Extensions "carry" router clear of rail end.

SIDE ASSEMBLY MOLDINGS

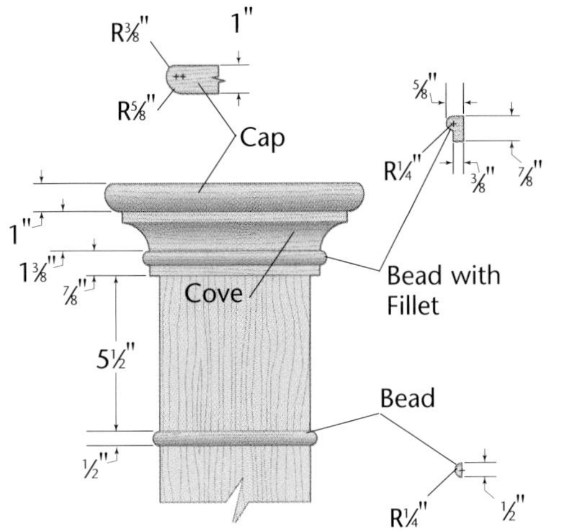
R⅜"
1"
R⅝"
Cap
⅝"
R¼"
⅜"
⅞"
1"
1⅜"
⅞"
Cove
Bead with Fillet
5½"
Bead
½"
R¼"
½"

MAKING COVE MOLDING

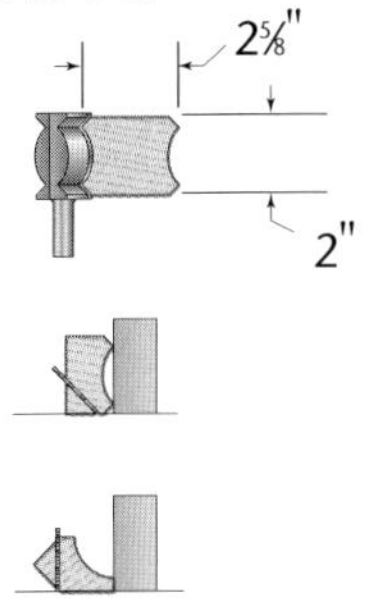
2⅝"
2"

Use cove bit to profile both edges of blank. Rip in half; bevel corner at 45°. Rip second facet to square back of molding.

Rout the mortises in the arch assembly, *using a plunge router guided by the arch-to-post mortising template screwed to the arch. Make each mortise 1½ in. deep.*

Transfer the location of the mortises *to the side assemblies by positioning the arch on top, inserting the loose tenons, and tracing around them on the side caps.*

Use the same template *for mortising the side caps that you used for the arches. Line it up with the traced outline. (The template opening is larger than the mortise itself.)*

With the pivot point of the arcs precisely set, *routing of curves for the top gate rail using the trammel is almost as easy as swinging on a gate.*

plate guide. Set the router in place, with the guide in the template window. Plunge the bit into the wood, and rout. Stop periodically to vacuum chips out of the mortise.

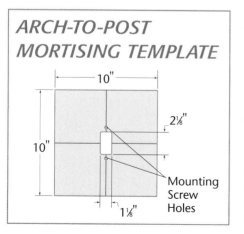

ARCH-TO-POST MORTISING TEMPLATE

10"

10"

2⅛"

1⅛"

Mounting Screw Holes

Plunge gradually deeper until the mortise is 1½ inches deep. **(Photo 20)** Move the template to the next arch bottom; screw it in place; and rout that mortise. Repeat the process on the other arch.

Make the Loose Tenons

The loose tenons are lengths of wood, no more than 2⅜ inches long, ripped to 1¼ inches by 2 inches. The edges must be rounded to match the rounded mortises. Because you need the tenons to mark positions of mortises in the side assemblies, make them now. Cut a foot-long scrap to the thickness and width of your mortises. Round-over the edges with a ¼-inch roundover bit in a table-mounted router. Fit the piece to the mortises routed into the arch assembly. The fit should be an easy slip fit. If it is too loose

and sloppy, try again on a new piece. If the fit is too tight, sand the appropriate faces. Then crosscut the lengths you need.

Mortise the Side Assemblies

To lay out the mortises on the tops of the side assemblies, lift the arch into position. (You'll need at least one helper, as well as stepladders.) Center the arch; square it up; and step back to study it. When it is positioned just right, fit the loose tenons into the mortises in the arch, and trace around them on the side caps. **(Photo 21)** Lift off the arch assembly, and set it aside.

Use the same template, router bit, and guide that you used to mortise the arches. Screw the template to the work after centering it over the layout, remembering that the window is slightly bigger than the mor-

SETTING UP THE ARBOR

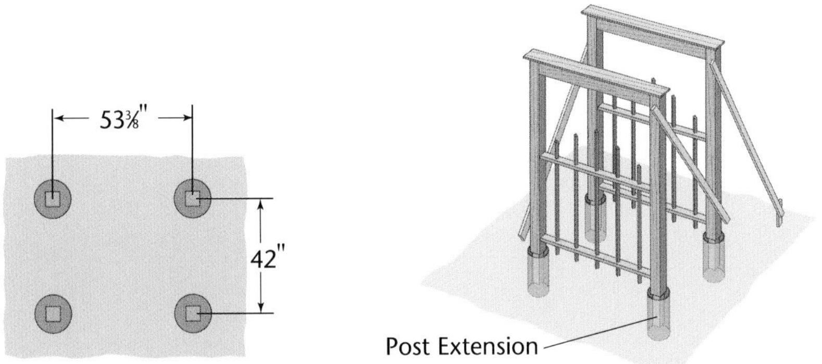
53⅜"
42"
Post Extension

tise. **(Photo 22)** Rout the mortise only about ⅞ inch deep. Otherwise you'll penetrate the cap. Repeat for the other mortises.

Finally, reposition the arch assembly, but this time with the loose tenons in place. If there's a chance that the arch could blow off in a heavy wind, drill pilot holes and drive a pair of 3-inch-long galvanized screws through the edges into the cap.

Cut the Gate Parts

Cut the stiles and slats, the top rail blanks, and the bottom rails to the dimensions specified in the Cutting List below. Use only flat boards. (If you have a planer and want to salvage some boards, do so, but you will have to plane all so that they are the same thickness.) For spacing stiles and slats when you rout the tenons, also cut and use seven waste strips, each of which are 1 inch wide, the same thickness as the gate stock, and as long as the longest stile.

Shape the Top Rail

Use a router and trammel to cut the two identical top rails for the two-part gate. The "Cutting Top Rails" drawing, this page, shows the setup. Use carpet tape to temporarily fasten a top rail blank to a piece of ¼-inch plywood; clamp the plywood to the bench. Attach a base for the trammel's pivot. (The arcs are made using the same pivot point.) For that, drill a pilot hole to receive a pivot screw on the trammel arm.

There's no need to mark the arcs themselves, but you should scribe a reference line across one end of each blank so that you will know where to cut after the gate is assembled. The extra length will help when you rout the groove for the stiles and slats and when assembling the gate.

Use a strip of ¼-inch plywood as your trammel. Mount a router to one end with carpet tape. Squeeze the router base and trammel together momentarily with a clamp at each patch of tape to strengthen the bond. Use any size straight bit for the cuts. The bit will bore its own hole through the trammel the first time you use it.

Measure from the bit along the trammel to locate the pivot points for the two radii. The bit is inside the short radius but outside the long one. Drill holes at the pivot points. Run a screw through one of the points on the trammel into the pivot point on the base. Rout that arc in several passes, cutting about ⅛ inch deeper each time. Then remove the screw and shift it to the other pivot point on the trammel, but drive it into the same pivot point in the base. Rout the second arc. **(Photo 23)** Establish the trim lines after the bottom arc has been cut. Remove the first rail blank, and mount the second one, routing the two arcs in it. Save the scraps for when you glue up the gates.

CUTTING TOP RAILS

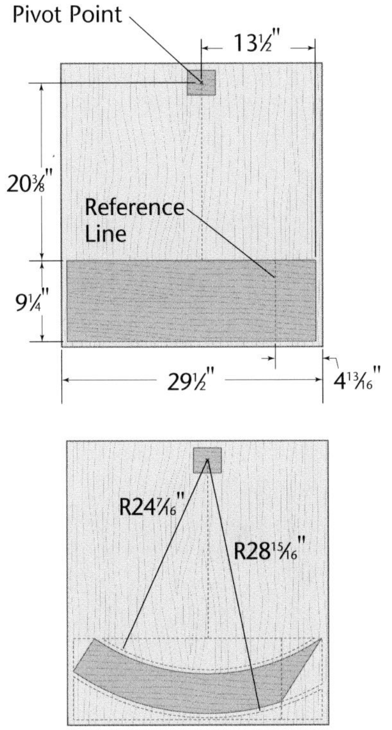
Pivot Point
13½"
20⅜"
Reference Line
9¼"
29½"
4 13/16"
R24 7/16"
R28 15/16"

GATE CUTTING LIST

Part	Quantity	Thickness	Width	Length	Pine
Bottom rails	2	1"	5½"	22½"	5/4×10 10'
Top rail blanks	2	1"	9¼"	29½"	5/4×10 10'
Stiles	2	1"	3½"	26¼" *	5/4×4 10'
Stiles	2	1"	3½"	37⅜" *	5/4×10 12'
Slats	8	1"	3"	32 13/16" *	5/4×4 10' & 12'
Jambs	2	1"	1½"	54¼"	5/4×10 10'

*Finished length. Cut a few inches longer, and trim to fit during assembly.

Make the Tenoning Template

While you have the router and trammel set up, cut a template to use in routing the tenons on the top ends of the slats and stiles. (See the "Gate Tenoning Template" drawing, page 141.) Use ¾-inch MDF or plywood for the template so that you can make a shallow cut. The template is large, allowing you to align it with the bottom edges of the stiles and slats. You must cut into both faces of these parts. Using the same template and the same alignment plane for both cuts ensures—as far as possible—that their shoulders will align.

Clamp the curved rail in your bench vise to allow an end-to-end cut. Orient the router knobs parallel with the cut to minimize risk of side-to-side wobble.

Clamp the stiles and slats, using scrap strips to produce even spacing. Align the template flush with the sides and bottom edges. Then rout along the curved top edges.

Guide a saber saw along the upper end of the tenons to cut off the waste. Do this while all of the parts remain clamped together.

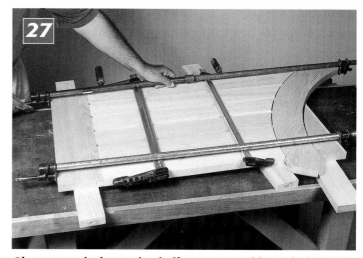

Glue up and clamp the half-gate assembly, including the curved top rail. Use the curved scraps left from cutting the top rail as clamping cauls; screw them to the rail for easier clamping.

The radius for the top edge of the template is 28$\frac{15}{16}$ inches, the same as the radius of the top rail's bottom arc. The difference is that for the rail, the bit is outside the radius. For the template, it is inside the radius. Attach the template material to the plywood substrate. Attach the pivot base to the plywood too. After setting up the trammel and router, cut the template.

Groove the Rails

Before cutting the tenons, use a fixed-base router to rout the groove in the rails so that you know how thick the tenons must be. Clamp two wood fences to the router base, using two small scraps of the gate stock as spacers. Center the ⅜-inch straight bit between them. This is difficult to do precisely, so you can be satisfied to get it as

close as you can to center. Use small C-clamps, with their threaded posts above the base, not hanging beneath it, where they could interfere with the router's movement.

Clamp the rail in the bench vise, catching the end of it between the fences on the router base. Switch on the router, and rout from end to end, forming a groove. **(Photo 24)** To center the groove, turn the router around and rerout. This will widen the groove slightly but will ensure that the shoulders of the cut are equal in width. Cut the 1-inch-deep grooves in stages, beginning with a depth of about ¼ inch, progressing in ¼-inch bites. Rout the grooves in the top and bottom rails.

You'll form the tenons on the ends of the stiles and slats using two cuts of a 1-inch-diameter mortising bit with a pilot

bearing on its shank. The bearing rides along the template, guiding the cut. The cut's depth must match the width of the shoulder of the grooves in the rails. The curved cut along the template top mirrors the top contour of stiles and slats.

Cut Tenons on Stiles and Slats

Collect the stiles and slats for a half-gate, each cut to rough length, along with seven spacers. Line these parts up, as shown in the "Tenoning Stiles and Slats" drawing, page 141. With spacers between, the stiles flank the four slats. Also position a spacer outside each stile. Carefully line up the bottoms. For now, top ends can extend randomly beyond the top arc. Because the template must be flat against the work, mount the clamps on the bottom. For this, line up the parts across

GATE TENONING TEMPLATE

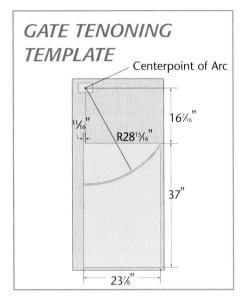

a pair of bar or pipe clamps. Shim up the parts so that the clamp jaws don't project above the top surface. Align the template, and clamp it and the work down on the workbench.

Test the cut depth. Clamp a piece of the template material on a scrap of the gate stock. Make a test cut. Turn the gate stock over, and make a second cut. Fit the resulting tenon into a rail groove. If it is too loose, decrease the cut depth; if too tight, increase the depth. Keep testing until the depth is set precisely.

Now rout the curved groove, guided by the template. **(Photo 25)** Shift the template to expose 1 inch of the gate parts across the bottom. Guided by the template, cut a rabbet across them.

Remove the template, and apply a pair of clamps across the surface of the gate parts. Carefully turn the work over, exposing the

clamps that had been under it. Remove them, and position the template on the surface. This alignment is critical in making the tenon's shoulders align. Clamp down the template, and rout the groove. Shift the template, and rout the rabbet.

With the parts still clamped together, cut the top contour of the tenons with a saber saw. **(Photo 26)** Save loose tenons trimmed from spacers. Repeat the tenoning process for the other half-gate.

Glue Up the Gate

Apply polyurethane glue to the grooves, and dampen the tenons and the loose tenons. Fit the parts together, inserting loose tenons between the stiles and slats to maintain consistent spacing within the grooves of the rails.

The challenge here is the clamping—not side-to-side but top-to-bottom. Because the curve of the top rail doesn't provide a purchase for clamp jaws, it makes top-to-bottom clamping difficult. This is where you need those arched scrap pieces from the trammel cuts. Cut them up, and screw them to the top rail, driving a long screw or two through the scrap's edge into the top edge of the rail. Position the scraps so that the clamp's jaws are parallel. Otherwise, the clamp will pull the assembly out of square. **(Photo 27)** To ensure that the gate is flat, apply top-to-bottom clamps across both faces. Check the assembly with a square to make sure it is square and flat.

Glue up both half-gates. When the glue has cured, remove the clamps and trim the rail ends. To cut first end, guide a saber saw along a straightedge clamped to the half-gate. Rip the parallel edge on a table saw.

Make the Jambs

The jambs are narrow strips of wood to which the doors are hinged. They are fastened to posts with glue and screws. Cut them to the dimensions specified in the Cutting List, page 139. Lay both gate halves and jambs on the workbench, aligning jamb bottoms 2½ inches below the bottoms of the gate halves. Extend the arc on the gate tops across the top ends of the jambs, and cut the arcs.

Outdoors, at the arbor, glue and screw the jambs to the posts. Jamb alignment on the posts is flexible. I located mine 4¼ inches from the front corner of the back posts. Drill pilot holes, and drive a half-dozen screws through the jamb edge into the post.

Hang the Gate

Mount the hinges to the face of each half-gate; align the hinge pins on a half-gate edge. Drill pilot holes, and screw the hinges into place. Hold each half-gate in place so that you can mark mounting screw locations on the jambs. Drill pilot holes, and mount both half-gates. Install the gate handles, gate stake, and latch mechanism, following package directions.

Install the Baseboards

Rip and crosscut one-by stock into pieces 8 inches wide by at least 36 inches long. You need about that much for each post. Rout a profile along the top edge of each piece. I used a cove-and-bead profile that I cut with a single bit. Miter one end of each piece. Then miter and fit the baseboards to the posts. Attach with screws or nails.

At posts with gate jambs you may find that the gate hinges interfere with the baseboard. If so, eliminate the piece in front of the jamb. Then cut the adjacent piece of baseboard ¾ inch short, and end it with a return, as shown in the drawing "Baseboard Detail," below.

TENONING STILES AND SLATS

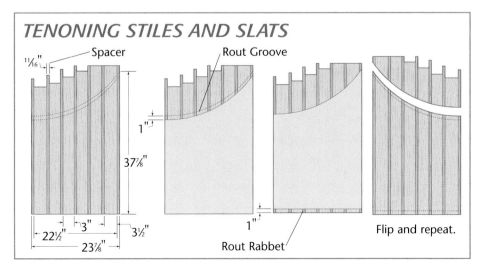

BASEBOARD DETAIL

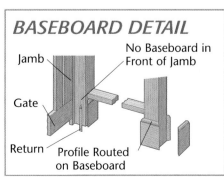

GRAPE ARBOR

L ike arbors that have graced gardens for centuries, this structure will support gorgeous, mature grape vines with bountiful harvests. It can also afford you a shady retreat. Building requires only basic skills and equipment, though you will need a helper to ensure precise alignment of all eight posts.

EXPLODED VIEW

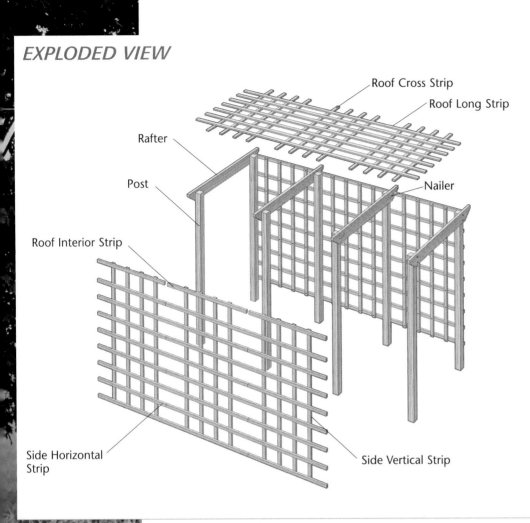

Roof Cross Strip

Roof Long Strip

Rafter

Post

Nailer

Roof Interior Strip

Side Horizontal Strip

Side Vertical Strip

CUTTING LIST

Part	Quantity	Thickness	Width	Length	SYP Stock
Posts	8	$3\frac{1}{2}$"	$3\frac{1}{2}$"	144"	4×4 12'
Rafters	4	$1\frac{1}{2}$"	$5\frac{1}{2}$"	67"	2×6 12'
Nailers	4	$\frac{3}{4}$"	$1\frac{1}{2}$"	4"	1×2 8'
Roof interior strips	6	$\frac{3}{4}$"	$1\frac{1}{2}$"	$42\frac{1}{2}$"*	1×2 8'
Roof cross strips	12	$\frac{3}{4}$"	$1\frac{1}{2}$"	55"*	1×2 8'
Roof long strips	7	$\frac{3}{4}$"	$1\frac{1}{2}$"	$59\frac{1}{8}$" **	1×2 8'
Roof long strips	7	$\frac{3}{4}$"	$1\frac{1}{2}$"	$85\frac{3}{8}$" **	1×2 8'
Side horizontal strips	16	$\frac{3}{4}$"	$1\frac{1}{2}$"	$47\frac{3}{8}$" **	1×2 8'
Side horizontal strips	16	$\frac{3}{4}$"	$1\frac{1}{2}$"	$93\frac{3}{4}$" **	1×2 8'
Side vertical strips	24	$\frac{3}{4}$"	$1\frac{1}{2}$"	77"*	1×2 8'

*Approximate finished lengths

**Approximate finished lengths. Sets of strips will be butted and then trimmed to produce strips to equal length of arbor.

FRONT AND SIDE ELEVATIONS

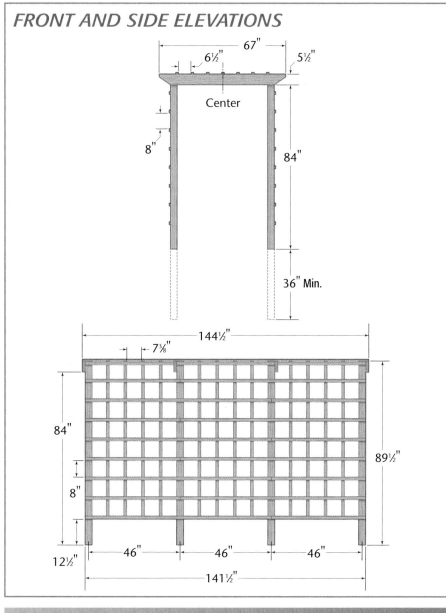

STEP-BY-STEP

Locate the Corner Posts

Set up eight batter boards as shown in the drawing, "Laying Out Postholes," page 145. A batter board consists of two 18-inch-long stakes and one crossbar to span the two stakes. Create the first batter board, placing it on the arbor's long axis a couple of feet beyond an approximate corner-post location. Drive the stakes into the ground; align the crossbar with a level; and screw it to the stakes. **(Photo 1)**

Erect a second batter board, opposite the first, using a measuring tape to position it about 16 to 18 feet away. Then run a string from the crossbar of the first batter board, pulling it taut and fastening it. Hang a line level on the string to establish the second crossbar's height. **(Photo 2)**

Erect a third and fourth batter board according to the positions shown in the drawing. The string stretched between should cross the first string at an approximate right angle. This is where the center of a corner post will be. Adjust two strings at a time to ensure that they cross at right angles by using the 3–4–5 method. It works this way. From the intersection, measure 3 feet along one string and affix a masking-tape flag to it. (You'll need a helper.) Go back to the same intersection, measure 4 feet along the other string, and flag that spot. Now measure diagonally from flag to flag. The diagonal distance will be exactly 5 feet if the strings are square to each other at their intersection. **(Photo 3)** If it isn't 5 feet, make it so by sliding one of the strings left or right on its crossbar, thereby squaring the strings.

Mark the locations of the strings on each crossbar, and label as the center line of a post. (Builders often kerf the crossbar at a mark to capture a knotted string.)

Set up two more pairs of batter boards (5, 6, 7, and 8 in drawing), measuring a little over 4 feet from one pair and about 12 feet from another pair (51½ and 138 inches in drawing). Run strings on them, exactly parallel with those strung on the first pairs of batter boards. Check these new strings for square. Mark the string positions on the new batter boards.

Establish Posthole Centers

Mark the centers of the four corner postholes first. Suspend a plumb bob from

BUILDER'S NOTES

Though large, this grape arbor is fairly simple to build. The trickiest part is setting the eight posts. Here, patient and methodical work pays off.

Materials

You can use any of a number of the woods that are durable outdoors. If you choose to use oak, cedar, or redwood, you need stainless-steel fasteners in order to avoid the black stains around every bolt and screw.

Tools and Techniques

A large part of this project involves layout and digging of holes for the eight posts. I used extra strips of the lattice material to construct batter boards, and then ran mason's string from one to another, thereby outlining the perimeter of the arbor.

When plumbing the posts, I found it helpful to use both an 18-inch and a 4-foot level to plumb the posts and the vertical lattice, and to level

the rafters and the horizontal lattice. When laying out the postholes, I used a tiny line level designed to be suspended on a horizontal string.

The primary power tools you need are a circular saw and one or two drill-drivers.

Finish

When built with treated lumber, the grape arbor will last many years without a finish. Stain, however, works better than paint on treated wood.

Install batter boards with care to avoid layout inaccuracies. After driving both support stakes, fasten one end of the crossbar to one stake and level it before fastening the other end.

Set the elevation of the second and subsequent crossbars using a string and line level. To obtain an accurate reading from the string, you need to stretch it tightly.

Use the 3–4–5 method to square the layout. Measure 3 ft. from the intersection along one string, 4 ft. along the other. Flag those spots with masking tape. Flag to flag needs to measure 5 ft.

Mark the corner-post center with a flagged stake driven where indicated by the plumb bob that is suspended from the string intersection. Then remove the strings.

the crossed strings, and mark the spot on the ground it points to with a stake, flagged with a length of colorful surveyor's tape. **(Photo 4)** After staking the corners, remove the strings to clear the work area, and then stake the intermediate postholes on each side of the arbor. Measure from corner post to corner post, and drive stakes to mark the centers of the two posts in that plane. Repeat to mark the two intermediate posts on the other side.

Dig the Postholes

For a sturdy structure, you need to sink the posts at least 3 feet into the ground even in frost-free regions. If you live where the ground normally freezes deeper than 3 feet, you will need to sink the posts deeper than the frost line so

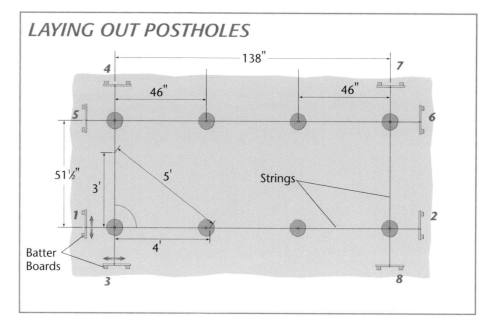

LAYING OUT POSTHOLES

Plumbing and bracing posts is a two-person job. One holds the post and monitors the spirit level. The other screws a brace to the post and drives an outlying stake before screwing the brace to it.

Position each intermediate post using a spacer (on the ground) to offset it 42½ in. from the corner post. Brace the post to a stake and to the nearest corner post.

Use a small trowel to smooth and slope the concrete surface away from the post, thereby conveying water away. After the concrete sets up, backfill with soil.

Mark the posts for trimming. Lay out the cutting line on a corner post, and extend it to the other posts in a level plane using a string and a line level.

that freezing water doesn't heave them. Follow the guidelines that are set by your local building department.

Dig a posthole at each of the marked points. When you've dug as deep as you can with a shovel, switch to a clamshell posthole digger. You may also need a digging bar to loosen the subsoil. Dig the hole deeper than required. Then backfill with 2 to 4 inches of gravel.

Set and Brace the Corner Posts

Align the outer faces of the four corner posts with four new strings outlining the arbor's perimeter. (See the "Setting Posts" drawing at right.) Offset these strings across the batter boards by 1¼ inches (one-half the thickness of the post) from the

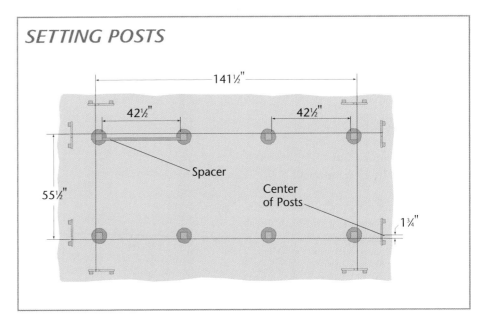

SETTING POSTS

141½"

42½"   42½"

55½"

Spacer

Center
of Posts

1¾"

Taper the ends of the rafters after cutting them to length. Lay out the cutting line with a pencil and framing square. Cut to the line with your circular saw.

Use a spade bit to make counterbores after boring the boltholes through the rafter and post. Counterbores allow you to recess washers and nuts. Note the prior clamping.

marks that located the centers of the posts.

Next drop a corner post into its hole against the two strings. Be careful not to deflect the strings as you plumb the post. Brace the post, using 8-foot furring strips. Bracing is best accomplished by two people. One uses a level to bring the post into plumb and into alignment with the new strings, while the other person screws a brace to the post, then drives a stake at an appropriate spot and screws the brace to it. **(Photo 5)** Be content to plumb one plane at a time. Begin by orienting the braces to the outside of the arbor so that they will be out of the way. Hold the level against one side of the post, bringing it into plumb and fastening the first brace. Then shift the level to an adjacent side, plumbing it perpendicular to the first, before the second brace is attached. Repeat for the other corner posts.

Set the Intermediate Posts

Next, set each of the four intermediate posts in relation to the string and its closest corner post. Crosscut a strip of scrap 42½ inches long, and lay this spacer on the ground with one end butted against a corner post. Set the intermediate post into its hole, and shift it against the other end of the spacer. Align the outer face of the post with the string while keeping the post butted to the spacer. Plumb the post on the side facing out of the arbor, maintaining the alignment with the string and the spacer. Brace the post to a stake outside of the arbor perimeter. Then plumb it side-to-side, and brace it to the corner

post. **(Photo 6)** Repeat this process to set the remaining three intermediate posts into their holes.

Anchor Posts in Concrete

Mix concrete according to package directions, and shovel it into one hole at a time, distributing it evenly around the post. While you don't need to fill the hole to grade, you'll get best support from it if you fill to within a few inches of grade. As you're adding concrete, work it with a stake to eliminate air pockets and settle it. Then use a small trowel to roughly slope the top of the concrete away from the post so that it will shed water. **(Photo 7)** Three or four hours after the pour, the concrete will have set enough to allow removal of the braces.

Trim Post Tops

This particular arbor presents a 7-foot-high passageway (but yours can be slightly lower or higher). Select one corner post as a reference point; measure up from the ground 89¼ inches; and make a mark. (This cutting line will position the post top ¼ inch below the top edge of the rafter.) Use a string and line level (or a water level) to extend level strings from the mark on the first post to all the others. **(Photo 8)** At the same time, measure up the post 84 inches to mark the

position of the rafter's bottom edge. Carry this mark from your reference post to the other posts with level string lines. Using a circular saw, cut each post on the cutting line, making a pass in each side.

Cut and Install the Rafters

Referring to the "Rafter Layout" drawing below, lay out each rafter, including the boltholes and tapers. **(Photo 9)** Then trim each to size.

Clamp each rafter across the two supporting posts, its top edge ¼ inch above the post tops. Drill the boltholes through the rafter and post, using a long ¼-inch-diameter twist drill. Use the galvanized carriage bolts to attach the rafters to the posts. To recess the washers and nuts, make ½-inch-deep counterbores with a ⅞-inch spade bit. **(Photo 10)**

Install Roof Cross Strips

Position the nailers and the interior strips one strip's thickness down from the rafter's top edge. Screw the nailers to the faces of the appropriate rafters. (Refer to the "Plan View" drawing on page 148.) Then screw the

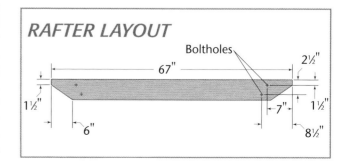

RAFTER LAYOUT

Mount the roof interior strips, *fastening them to a post or to one of the nailers that is screwed to the rafters. This starts the assembly of the roof latticework. Drill pilot holes for all lattice screws.*

Fasten the cross strips *to the roof interior strip with stainless-steel brads, first clamping a spacer to the interior strip and butting cross-strip edges to it.*

Install roof long strips, *after fastening cross strips. For this, clamp spacers to the rafters. Then drill a pilot and fasten the strip to the rafter (1⅝-in. deck screws) and then to the cross strips (1-in. screws).*

Use spacers to position side horizontal lattice strips. *Hold each new strip against the bottom of the spacers while you drill pilots and fasten the strip to the posts. Then move the spacers down.*

interior strips to the nailers. **(Photo 11)**

Install the 12 roof cross strips (in groups of four) to rest on the roof interior strips. To help position them, cut two spacers 7⅜ inches long. Begin by cutting the cross strips to a rough length, say 60 inches long. Then, one by one, you will scribe and cut them to fit.

Each grouping of four roof cross strips is aligned parallel with a post-to-post centerline (not post-to-rafter). To position each group of strips, first measure the post-to-post space and mark the center on the tops of the interior strips. Do this on both sides of the arbor.

Next, center a 7⅜-inch spacer over this centermark and clamp it. Do this on both sides of the arbor. Place cross strips across the interior strips, on both sides of the

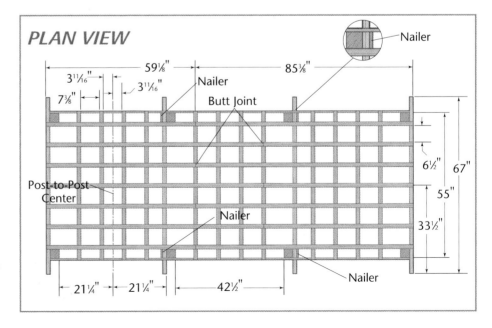

PLAN VIEW

Nailer

59⅛" 85⅜"

3¹¹⁄₁₆"

3¹¹⁄₁₆" Nailer

7⅜" Butt Joint

Nailer

6½" 67"

Post-to-Post
Center 55"

Nailer 33½"

Nailer

21¼" 21¼" 42½"

Align the side vertical lattice strips directly under the roof cross strips. Clamp each strip at the top and plumb it with a level before drilling pilots and driving mounting screws.

Screw each vertical strip to every horizontal strip, first plumbing and securing each strip at three or four joints. Then drill pilots at every joint; switch bits; and drive all screws.

spacers. Scribe along the outsides of the interior strips onto the cross strips, and trim the cross strips to fit. Attach them to the supporting interior strips with 1¼-inch-long stainless-steel brads. **(Photo 12)** (Use a brad as a bit to drill pilot holes in the cross-strip ends.) Screws installed later will strengthen these joints.

Next, jump the spacers over one of the strips; reclamp them; fit and attach the third strip; and so on for the fourth strip. Shift to the next post-to-post space, and install its cross strips in the same manner. Then install the third group.

Install Roof Long Strips

Mark the center across each rafter. Because the arbor is almost 12 feet long, you'll need to butt two pieces to create "each" long strip. Stagger these butt joints over cross strips as shown in the "Plan View" drawing at left. Determine the length of the arbor from the outside edges of its end rafters. Then mark and cut two roof long lattice strips to achieve that length and also butt in the center of a cross strip. Cut the strips, and then clamp them in position, starting with the center long roof strip. Where the strip goes over a rafter, drill a pilot hole for a 1⅝-inch deck screw and fasten. Where it goes over a cross strip, drill a pilot for a 1-inch screw and fasten.

Use four 6½-inch spacers to position a long strip to each side of the center one. Position a spacer on top of each rafter, butting and clamping the spacers against the center roof long strip. Measure and cut two new pieces of roof long strips so that

they will butt on a different cross strip than the previous long strip did. Repeat until you've installed the remaining roof long strips. **(Photo 13)**

Install Side Horizontal Strips

Here, you again need to butt two pieces to make up "each" horizontal lattice strip, one approximately 4 feet long, the other just under 8 feet long. Stagger the butt joint of each strip, centering it on an intermediate post. (See the "Side Elevation" drawing, page 144.)

Take the outside measurements of the span distance from corner post to corner post at three heights—the bottom, middle, and top. Determine the lengths of the two pieces needed for each horizontal strip. Then cut 16 shorter pieces and 16 longer pieces, cutting each a bit longer than is needed, and trim them to fit as they are installed across the actual span.

Begin installing the first horizontal strip at the top and work down. For this, clamp a 3- x 8-inch spacer to each post on one side, butting each against a roof interior strip. Attach two pieces of a horizontal strip to the posts, up against the spacers, after drilling pilots for 1⅝-inch screws. Remove the spacers. Check the strip for level. If it isn't level, back out the screws and adjust the strips as necessary.

Now position and clamp the spacers just below this first connected horizontal strip. Fasten another two pieces of horizontal lattice up against the spacers. **(Photo 14)** Continue until you have installed all eight horizontal strips. Repeat the process to

install the sets of horizontal strips to the other side of the arbor.

Install Side Vertical Strips

Add side vertical strips, installing them to the inside of the arbor, and extending from the roof cross strips to the bottom edge of the lowest horizontal strip. As with the roof lattice, you'll drill pilots and fasten them using 1-inch screws. Measure the locations here and there to establish the average length of the pieces that you need. Cut them to length.

Position each vertical strip directly under a roof cross strip and tightly up against a roof interior strip. (See "Vertical Lattice" drawing, below.) Spring-clamp it; then plumb it. **(Photo 15)** Drill a pilot hole, and drive a 1-inch screw through it into a roof interior strip. Replumb the vertical, and secure it the same way to one of the side horizontal strips. Secure several verticals this way; then go back and screw them to each side horizontal strip. **(Photo 16)** Install all 24 verticals in this way.

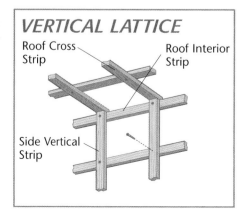

VERTICAL LATTICE

Roof Cross Strip

Roof Interior Strip

Side Vertical Strip

More Large Arbor Ideas

Details play a major part in even the largest arbor. The cutouts in the rafters above break up the straight lines of the structure. The patterns of the lattice, top middle, add interest to the arbor. Sunlight and shadow, right, are an important part of an arbor's design.

A large deck is the perfect setting for a shade arbor, top right. Its placement in the corner helps set off the area from the rest of the deck. Lining up arbors along a garden path, above, helps reinforce the shape and direction of the path. A simple arbor is completed by the addition of a movable bench, right.

Arbor seating is a popular choice for many homeowners. Using classical designs, such as the one shown above, is a good way to set the arbor off from the rest of the yard. A simple roof design turns a corner of a redwood deck into a comfortable seating area, top middle. The owners of the arbor at right took a different route. This arbor tucked away in the corner of the yard provides a place to get away and enjoy the garden.

Plants can hide *an arbor's structure or call attention to it. The climbing roses below do cover the side of the arbor, but set against the green of the garden they also point out the arbor's location. The classic pergola roof on the arbor shown below gets a different look. The rafters are left natural, and the beams are painted to match the posts.*

Resource Guide

The following list of manufacturers and associations is meant to be a general guide to additional industry and product-related sources. It is not intended as a listing of products and manufacturers represented by the photographs in this book.

ASSOCIATIONS AND TRADE GROUPS

California Redwood Association offers extensive information about redwood, including grade distinctions, structural applications, and finishing characteristics. Its Web site also has a section for customers' questions.
405 Enfrente Dr., Ste. 200
Novato, CA 94949
Phone: 888-225-7339
Fax: 415-382-8531
www.calredwood.org

Southern Pine Council is a joint promotional group supported by Southern Pine Lumber. The Web site offers construction details, building tips, and helpful brochures and books.
c/o SFPA
P.O. Box 641700
Kenner, LA 70064-1700
Phone: 504-443-4464
Fax: 504-443-6612
www.southernpine.com

Western Wood Products Association maintains quality levels for western lumber and conducts mill inspections. It also offers other services, such as training and certification programs for mill graders.
522 SW 5th Ave., Ste. 500
Portland, OR 97204-2122
Phone: 503-224-3930
Fax: 503-224-3934
www.wwpa.org

FURNISHINGS AND STRUCTURES

AvalonGarden.Com offers many home and garden products, including trellises and arbors.
200 Wildwood Rd.
Hendersonville, NC 28739
Phone: 800-854-0880
www.avalongarden.com

Elyria Fence Inc. provides custom fences, trellises, arbors, and decks all year round. Its Web site has a photo gallery of its many styles and designs.
230 Oberlin-Elyria Rd.
Elyria, OH 44035
Phone: 800-779-7581
www.elyriafence.com

Garden Artisans sells decorative backyard structures such as garden art, trellises, arbors, and planters. This includes a selection of copper and metal structures.
P.O. Box 4393
Crofton, MD 21114
Phone: 410-721-6185
Fax: 410-451-9535
www.gardenartisans.com

G.I. Designs is a manufacturer of wooden and metal garden structures such as trellises, arbors, and gazebos.
700 Colorado Blvd. #120
Denver, CO 80206
Phone: 877-442-6773
Fax: 303-377-5332
www.gidesigns.net

Homeproductsnmore is an online source of various products for the home, including garden furnishings and structures, such as arbors and trellises.
Phone: 800-690-0132
Fax: 515-967-0827
www.homeproductsnmore.com

Kinsman Company offers an extensive selection of outdoor accessories such as elegant trellises, obelisks, and plant supports.
Kinsman Company, M.O.
P.O. Box 428
Pipersville, PA 18947
Phone: 800-733-4129
Fax: 215-766-5624
www.kinsmangarden.com

Sycamore Creek specializes in copper garden furnishings such as arbors and trellises. Many designs are available in easy-to-assemble kits.
P.O. Box 16
Ancram, NY 12502
Phone: 518-398-6393
Fax: 518-398-7697
www.sycamorecreek.com

The Intimate Gardener carries garden furnishings and ornaments including trellises, arbors, and feeders.
4215 N. Sheridan Rd.
Chicago, IL 60613
Phone: 800-240-2771
Fax: 773-472-2043
www.theintimategardener.com

Trellis Structures, Inc., designs and manufactures western red cedar trellises and arbors, as well as other structures.
P.O. Box 380
60 River St., rear
Beverly, MA 01915
Phone: 888-285-4624
Fax: 978-232-1151
www.trellisstructures.com

PLANTS AND GARDEN SUPPLIES

Bloomers Junction sells a wide variety of flowers and plants, including rambler and climbing roses.
10027 N. Idaho Rd.
Post Falls, ID 83814
Phone: 208-773-3142
www.bloomersjunction.com

Completely Clematis Specialty Nursery carries over 200 unusual small- and large-flowered types of potted clematis.
217 Argilla Rd.
Ipswich, MA 01938-2617
Phone: 978-356-3197
www.clematisnursery.com

The Uncommon Rose carries a large selection of climbing roses that includes unusual, modern, and old garden rose types.
3333 SW Brooklane Dr.
Corvallis, OR 97333
Phone: 541-753-8871
Fax: 541-753-8640
www.uncommongarden.com

POWER TOOLS

Bosch Power Tools manufactures tools and accessories for a number of trades, such as woodworking and construction. Its products are widely available.
4300 W. Peterson Ave.
Chicago, IL 60646
Phone: 800-267-2499
www.boschtools.com

DeWalt Industrial Tools Company sells a wide selection of power tools, including drills, saws, sanders, and cordless tools, through licensed retailers.
Customer Service Division
626 Hanover Pike
Hampstead, MD 21074
Phone: 800-433-9258
www.dewalt.com

Hitachi Power Tools U.S.A. carries an extensive line of heavy-duty electric tools, including saws, drills, nailers, staplers, and more.
3950 Steve Reynolds Blvd.
Norcross, GA 30093
Phone: 800-829-4752
Fax: 770-279-4293
www.hitachi.com/powertools

Jepson Power Tools manufactures electric drills, saws, and other tools. Jepson is the distribution and marketing division of Ko-shin Electric and Machinery Company.
20333 S. Western Ave.
Torrance, CA 90501
Phone: 800-456-8665
Fax: 310-320-1318
www.jepsonpowertools.com

Milwaukee Electric Tool Corp. sells portable power tools and accessories through authorized distributors. It is a part of the Atlas Copco Group.
13135 W. Lisbon Rd.
Brookfield, WI 53005-2550
Phone: 262-781-3600
Fax: 262-783-8555
www.mil-electric-tool.com

Porter-Cable Corp. manufactures compressors, electric drills, and other professional power tools through national and international dealers.
4825 Hwy. 45 North
P.O. Box 2468
Jackson, TN 38302-2468
Phone: 888-848-5175
www.porter-cable.com

Ryobi Power Tools offers a wide selection of power tools, including cordless and benchtop tools.
1428 Pearman Dairy Rd.
Anderson, SC 29625
Phone: 800-525-2579
www.ryobi.com

Glossary

Actual dimensions. The exact measurements of a piece of lumber after it has been cut, surfaced, and dried. For example, the actual dimensions of a 2×4 are 1½ × 3½ inches.

Arbor. An open, overhead structure held up by posts and typically used to support climbing shrubs or vines and to provide shade.

Batter boards. Level boards attached to stakes and used to position strings that locate postholes and outline constructions supported by posts. The strings can be tied to nails driven in the batter boards or captured in saw kerfs.

Blank. The piece of lumber from which you plan to cut a certain part, as in "the template blank."

Carriage bolt. A bolt with a wide, rounded head, often used to create a finished appearance on the outer surface of joints.

Cauls. Small pieces of scrap lumber used as pads between the jaws of a clamp and the workpiece to prevent damage to the workpiece.

Chip-out. Wood fibers splitting off of the face of a board at the point where the router bit exits the wood. Because the bit is essentially cutting end grain as it exits the wood, the wood will chip out if not backed with another piece of wood.

Clear. A grade of lumber that is largely free of knots and other structural and cosmetic defects. Clear wood is generally recommended for applications where the wood is visible.

Collet. The chucklike device on the end of a router drive shaft that secures the router bits.

Counterbore. Enlarging the top or bottom part of a drilled hole so that a screw, bolt head, or nut will set below the wood's surface.

Crosscut. A cut across the grain of a piece of lumber at a 90-degree angle to the edge. For example, you shorten an 8-foot-long 2×4 to 6 feet by crosscutting it.

Dado. A groove cut across the face of a board. Dadoes are typically cut with a router or a table saw equipped with a special dado blade.

Frost line. Maximum depth to which the soil freezes in winter. Setting footers or posts below this depth prevents them from being heaved upward when the soil freezes. The depth of the *frost line* varies from region to region.

Half-lap. A joint between intersecting members formed by removing half of the thickness of each piece so that the two mate with the surfaces flush.

Heartwood. The harder, stronger, and usually more rot-resistant wood taken from the core of a tree.

Kerf. The space left behind by a saw blade as it cuts through a piece of wood. Several shallow kerfs, spaced closely, are often used to remove stock in a half-lap joint.

Knot. A dark spot on a board that is the base of a branch. The wood is very dense but often not connected to the wood around it.

Lap. A joint in which the full dimension of one member is set into a recess—the lap—cut in the other piece.

Lattice. A pattern formed by joining thin strips arranged in a crisscross pattern.

Nominal dimensions. The identifying dimensions of a piece of lumber (e.g. 2×4) that are larger than the actual dimensions (1½ × 3½ inches).

Miter. An angled cut across the end of a board. Some woodworkers insist that the term "miter" can only describe a 45-degree cut, but it is also commonly used for any angled cut.

Mortise. A hole cut into a frame member or another part to receive a tenon. One component of the mortise-and-tenon joint. See also Tenon.

Pilot bearing. A router bit's built-in steering mechanism. The bearing rides on the edge of the workpiece, limiting the cut and guiding the router.

Pilot hole. A hole drilled to receive a screw. It eases the entry of the screw and prevents it from splitting the wood.

Plumb. Vertically straight and perpendicular to a level reference line.

Plunge cut. A cut that doesn't begin at the edge of a board but is made by plunging the cutter into the face of the board. Sometimes referred to as a pocket cut.

Rabbet. A cut along the edge of a board that removes only part of the thickness of the board. Often made with a router, this cut leaves a small shelf that is useful in forming joints. Two shallow rabbet cuts on the top and bottom of an edge form a simple tenon.

Rip cut. A cut made with the grain to reduce the width of a board. This type of cut is easiest to make on a table saw, but it can be done with a handheld saw, as well.

Sapwood. The living wood near the outside of a tree trunk that carries sap. Sapwood is weaker and less stable than the heartwood.

Screw eye. Often called an eyescrew, this fastener has the top portion of its shank bent into a circle. It is often used with S-hooks or other hardware to support hanging swings.

Slat. A narrow strip of wood typically used in multiples to form a lattice.

Stop block. A scrap of wood that is attached to a tool's fence to limit the extent of the cut. For example, a stop block attached to the fence of a miter saw allows you to cut multiple parts to exactly the same length.

Stretcher. A horizontal member in a structure that extends from post to post.

Strut. A structural piece designed to resist pressure in the direction of its length.

Tear-out. Shavings lifted on a newly cut face but not trimmed off by the router bit. This is most likely to happen when you are routing with the grain, and the grain pattern twists and turns.

Template. A reusable pattern for shaping one or more parts.

Tenon. A tongue formed on the end of a board to fit into a mortise. See also Mortise.

Through-cut. A term describing the extent of a cut. A dado that goes all the way across the face of a board from one edge to the other is a through dado, while a dado that ends in the middle of a board is a stopped dado. A mortise that forms a hole through the board is a through mortise, while a mortise that ends inside the board is not.

Trammel. A beam-type compass system for guiding a router through curving, fixed-radius cuts. The router is attached to one end of the trammel beam, and the fixed pivot point is at the other end. By adjusting the distance between the router bit and the pivot point, you can cut arcs and circles of varying radii.

Trellis. A framework or garden structure of lattice used as a screen or as a support for climbing plants.

Wane. A defect in lumber in which either bark is present or wood is lacking on an edge or corner for any reason.

Credits

page 1: Charles Mann **page 3:** *all* John Parsekian **page 4:** *top to bottom* Trellis Structures; Jerry Howard/ Positive Images; Derek Fell; Walter Chandoha **page 6:** Brian Vanden Brink **page 7:** Jerry Pavia **pages 8–9:** *left* Walter Chandoha; *center* Richard Felber; *top right* Derek Fell; *bottom right* Jennifer Ramcke, garden by: Maggie & Frank Cefalu **page 10:** *top* Richard Felber; *bottom* Walter Chandoha **page 11:** *top* Brian Vanden Brink, architect: Ron Forest Fence; *bottom* Walter Chandoha **pages 12–13:** *top left* Walter Chandoha; *center* Brian Vanden Brink, architect: Dominic Mercadante; *top right* Jerry Pavia; *bottom right* Derek Fell; *bottom left* Positive Images, designer: Gay Bumgarner Design **pages 14–15:** *top left* courtesy of California Redwood Association; *top right* Brian Vanden Brink; *bottom right & bottom left* Walter Chandoha; *bottom center* Tony Giammarino; **page 16:** *top* Richard Felber; *center* Derek Fell; *bottom* Walter Chandoha **page 17:** *top* Charles Mann; *center* Walter Chandoha; *bottom* Jerry Pavia, Butchart Gardens **pages 18–19:** *top left* Brad Simmons; *center* Richard Felber; *top right* Philip Clayton-Thompson, garden by: Karen & Frank Capillupo; *bottom right* Brian Vanden Brink, designer: Weatherend Estate Furniture; *bottom left* Donna H. Chiarelli **pages 20–21:** *left* Donna H. Chiarelli; *center* Brian Vanden Brink; *right* Walter Chandoha; *bottom right* courtesy of California Redwood Association; *bottom left* Walter Chandoha; **pages 22–23:** *left* Tony Giammarino; *center* Richard Felber; *top right* Derek Fell; *bottom right* Jerry Pavia, garden by: Michael Engle *bottom center* Tony Giammarino **pages 24–25:** *left, center, & top right* Richard Felber; *bottom right* Jerry Pavia, garden by: Anna

Davis; *bottom left* Derek Fell **pages 26–27:** *top center* courtesy of Elyria Fence Inc.; *top right* courtesy of Trellis Structures; *bottom right* courtesy of Garden Artisans; *bottom center* courtesy of Elyria Fence Inc.; *bottom left* courtesy of Trellis Structures **page 28:** *top* courtesy of Elyria Fence Inc.; *bottom right* courtesy of www.gidesigns.net; *bottom left* courtesy of Trellis Structures **page 29:** *top left* courtesy of Elyria Fence Inc.; *top right* courtesy of www.gidesigns.net; *bottom right* courtesy of Garden Artisans **pages 30–31:** *both* Jerry Pavia **page 32:** *left* Jerry Pavia **page 33:** *top left* Anne Gordon Images **page 34:** *top right* Jerry Howard/ Positive Images; *bottom left* David Cavagnaro **page 35:** Jerry Pavia **page 36:** *top left* Photos Horticultural; *top right* John Glover *top right inset* Jerry Pavia; *bottom right* Derek Fell; *bottom left* John Bova/ Photo Researchers **page 37:** *top left* Walter Chandoha; *top right* Derek Fell; *bottom right* Alan & Linda Detrick; *bottom left* Anne Gordon Images **page 38:** *top left* Walter Chandoha; *inset & top center* Derek Fell; *top right* Jerry Pavia; *bottom right* Michael Gadomski/ Photo Researchers; *bottom center* Derek Fell **page 39:** *top left* Anne Gordon Images; *top right* Derek Fell; *bottom right* Michael Thompson; *bottom left* Jerry Pavia **page 40:** *top left* Walter Chandoha; *top center & top right* David Cavagnaro; *bottom left* Walter Chandoha; **page 41:** *top left* John Glover; *top center* Walter Chandoha; *top right* Neil Holmes/ Garden Picture Library; *bottom right* Jerry Pavia; *bottom left* David Cavagnaro **page 42:** *all* Derek Fell **page 43:** *top* Neil Soderstrom/ Michael Cady; *bottom* Derek Fell **page 44:** *top left* John Glover; *top right* Derek Fell; *bottom right* Jerry Pavia; *bottom left* Derek Fell **page 45:** *all* Derek Fell

page 46: *top left* Derek Fell; *top right* Jerry Pavia; *bottom right & bottom left* Michael Thompson **page 47:** *top left* Derek Fell; *top right* Jerry Pavia; *bottom right, bottom left, & left center* Derek Fell **page 78–79:** *top left* Philip Clayton-Thompson, garden by: Bev Cooney; *center & top right* Richard Felber; *bottom right* Tony Giammarino, designer: Martha Stobbs; *bottom left* Jerry Pavia, garden by: Maria Kiesow **pages 80–81:** *top left* Charles Mann; *center* Derek Fell; *top right* Richard Felber; *bottom right* Jerry Pavia; *bottom left* Jerry Howard/ Positive Images; **pages 114–115:** *left* Richard Felber; *center* Philip Clayton-Thompson, garden by: John & Sandi Oldenkamp-Sandercock; *top right* Jerry Pavia, garden by: Joann Romano; *bottom right* Liz Ball/ Positive Images; *bottom center* Tony Giammarino, Reggie Case **pages 116–117:** *left* Richard Felber; *center* Philip Clayton-Thompson, garden by: Carol & Dick Rees of Gilbert Inn; *top right* Alan & Linda Detrick, Morris Arboratum; *bottom right* Walter Chandoha **pages 150–151:** *far left* Donna H. Chiarelli, *center* Anne Gordon Images; *top right* Jerry Howard/ Positive Images, designer: Bernie Tatleis; *bottom right & bottom center right* Walter Chandoha; *bottom left* Brian Vanden Brink, architects: Payette & Associates **pages 152–153:** *top left* Brian Vanden Brink, architects: Horiuchi & Solien; *center* courtesy of California Redwood Association; *right* Derek Fell; *bottom right* Donna H. Chiarelli; *bottom left* Richard Felber **page 154–155:** *left* courtesy of Garden Artisans; *middle* courtesy of Elyria Fence Inc.; *right* courtesy of Trellis Structures

All illustrations by Frank Rohrbach except the following: **page 32, 34–35, 43:** Mavis Augustine Torke **page 33:** courtesy of USDA

Index

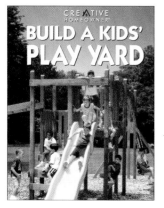

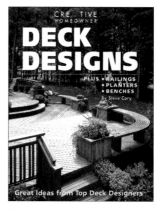
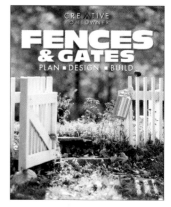
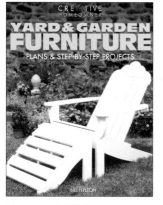
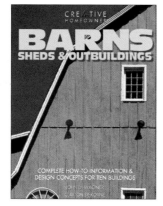
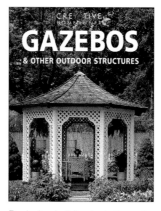
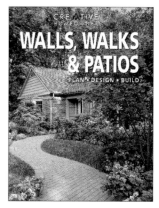
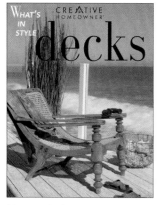